When History Returns

SUNY series, Transforming Subjects: Psychoanalysis,
Culture, and Studies in Education
───────────
Deborah P. Britzman, editor

When History Returns
Psychoanalytic Quests for Humane Learning

DEBORAH P. BRITZMAN

SUNY PRESS

Cover design by Jodi Nicholson, jodinicholson.com. Cover image, a red and blue vector composition, inspired by a Miro painting (Shutterstock)

Published by State University of New York Press, Albany

© 2024 State University of New York

All rights reserved

Printed in the United States of America

No part of this book may be used or reproduced in any manner whatsoever without written permission. No part of this book may be stored in a retrieval system or transmitted in any form or by any means including electronic, electrostatic, magnetic tape, mechanical, photocopying, recording, or otherwise without the prior permission in writing of the publisher.

For information, contact State University of New York Press, Albany, NY
www.sunypress.edu

Library of Congress Cataloging-in-Publication Data

Name: Britzman, Deborah P., author.
Title: When history returns : psychoanalytic quests for humane learning / Deborah P. Britzman.
Description: Albany : State University of New York Press, [2024] | Series: SUNY series, Transforming Subjects: Psychoanalysis, Culture, and Studies in Education | Includes bibliographical references and index.
Identifiers: ISBN 9781438497754 (hardcover : alk. paper) | ISBN 9781438497761 (ebook) | ISBN 9781438497747 (pbk. : alk. paper)
Further information is available at the Library of Congress.

10 9 8 7 6 5 4 3 2 1

Contents

Acknowledgments		vii
Prelude: A Special Reading and Writing Attitude		ix
1.	Reading Freud Today for the Destiny of Education	1
2.	Into the Middle of Things	13
3.	Turning to the Subject	29
4.	On the Pains of Symbolization	49
5.	Before and after Misogyny	63
6.	The Times of Friendship for Mrs. K. and Richard	77
7.	H. G. Adler and Themes of Uncertainty, Transformation, and Binding	97
8.	Once Again, but This Time with Feeling	119
Notes		135
References		143
Index		159

Acknowledgments

The work for this book has benefited from international invitations, participation in special topic conferences and, closer to home, university teaching, a three-year stint as director of academics for a three-year psychoanalytic psychotherapy training program in Toronto, and my clinical practice in psychoanalytic psychotherapy. I have the privilege of working with patients, with graduate, undergraduate, and postgraduate students, and with colleagues in universities and psychoanalytic institutes. Near the end of a long university career, between 2015 and 2021, I was awarded a York University Research Chair in Pedagogy and Psychosocial Transformation. The chair was the first recognition of theoretical studies of pedagogy with psychoanalysis, framed as a developing field of thought in consult with the exigencies of life and obstacles to their affiliation.

The COVID-19 pandemic occurred two years into the chair and the confinement of social isolation and closing of international borders partly explains my return to more writing, with time to revise and reconsider previous work written for international conferences, keynotes, and journals between 2014 and 2022. While composing some chapters, I had in mind problems of translation, transference, and reception, and although there is not one word in English that can convey their entanglements, I was aware that my writing would be communicated sense-to-sense with other languages and to unknown readers. Not knowing the fate of one's words, including why one speaks at all, also characterizes relations of pedagogy and psychotherapy. There, assumptions of meaning and expectations for communication can titter into illegibility, wrong-headed positions, confusion, and projective identifications. I welcome what theorists accept as the inevitable failures of translation.

A few of the revised essays were first written with the understanding that my work would go directly into translation in Portuguese, Japanese,

French, and Turkish. I would be excused from checking the galleys. In these translation efforts and for their friendship, I thank Professors Akira Geshi in Japan, Aziz Güzel and Alper Sahin in Turkey, Nilson Dinis in Brazil, and Hilbold Mej, Arnaud Dubois, and Rachel Colombe in France. I thank my research assistant, Catherine Mitro in Toronto, for her editing work on the manuscript. Thanks to my good friend and clinical partner, Dr. Oren Gozlan, for on-going discussions in psychoanalysis and to Dr. Michelle Flax for listening for the backstory of these essays. My writing also carries echoes of dinner talk with my partner, Dr. Alice Pitt. I love her wit, insight, and keen sense of language; her studied history of linguistics makes my writing better. I thank Dr. Rebecca Colesworthy, Senior Acquisitions Editor of the State University of New York Press.

Earlier versions of some of the chapters have been published elsewhere and revised for the current book. I am grateful for permission to reprint, in altered form, the following: Chapter 1 appeared as "Reading Freud Today for the Destiny of a Psychology of Education," *Knowledge/Cultures: An Interdisciplinary Journal* 3, no. 2 (2015): 82–97. Chapter 2 appeared as "In the Midst of Things: A Freudian Turn to Otherness for Educational Theory," *English E-Journal of the Philosophy of Education: International Yearbook of the Philosophy of Education Society of Japan* 6 (2021): 27–43. Chapter 3 appeared as "Thoughts on the Fragility of Peace," *LLineE journal* (Lifelong Learning in Europe) no. 2 (2014). Chapter 4 appeared as "Mrs Klein and Paulo Freire: Coda for the Pain of Symbolization in the Lifeworld of the Mind," *Educational Theory* 67, no. 1 (2017): 83–95. Chapter 5 appeared as "Before and After Misogyny: A Psychoanalytic Discussion," *Itineranius Reflectionis* 13, no. 2 (2017): 1–20, www.revistas.ufg.br. Chapter 6 appeared in Turkish as "Psikanalitik Durum Anlatıları: Bayan K. ile Richard'ın Dostluğu," *Psikanaliz Defterleri 3—Çocuk ve Ergen Çalışmaları: Öğrenme ve Bilinçdışı* (Istanbul: Yapı Kredi Yayınları, 2019), 27–45. Parts of Chapter 6 are revisions from "Narratives of the Psychoanalytic Situation," in Deborah P. Britzman, *Melanie Klein: Early Analysis, Play and the Question of Freedom*, 95–106 (London: Springer, 2016). Chapter 7 (2016) appeared as "An Imaginative Dialogue Between H. G. Adler and Psychoanalysis: Aesthetic Themes of Uncertainty, Transformation, and Binding," in *H. G. Adler: Life, Literature and Legacy*, ed. J. Creet, S. Horowitz, and A. Dan, 331–350. (Chicago: Northwestern University Press, 2016).

Deborah P. Britzman
Toronto

Prelude

A Special Reading and Writing Attitude

> It is hardly surprising that the problem opened by the *other* erupting into scientific process also appears in its object. Research no longer merely seeks successful comprehension. It returns to things that it cannot understand.
>
> —Michel de Certeau (1988), *The Writing of History* (39)

Across the span of thirty years, Sigmund Freud wrote eight prefaces to *The Interpretation of Dreams*, first published in 1900, although the backstory of both dreams and his writing to them began years earlier. The prefaces touch on a history of the book's reception and counted on passing time: one year later, eighteen years later, twenty years later, and then nine years after that. His last preface to the third English edition gave tribute to the value of psychoanalytic discovery as the fundamental situation of the dream and concluded, "Insight such as this falls to one's lot but once in a lifetime" (1900a, xxii). Freud (1917a, 1923b, 1925a) continued to publish subsidiary papers on the metapsychology of dreams, on their structural binds, and on their technical problems for dream interpretation. But it was his two volumes of *Interpretation* that introduced the novelty of dream-work, defined as the human capacity for dissimulating thought through the stirring psychical activities of condensation, displacement, reversal into opposite, consideration of likeness, and omissions of temporality. Dream thoughts, it turns out, are in search of lost causes, and do so without being encumbered by logical relations. They are in consult with emergent life and propose obstacles to learning. Freud (1900b) tried to clarify the complex procedures in dream construction and its myriad transformations: "Dream-work does not think, calculate or judge in any way at all; it restricts itself to giving things a new form" (507). "At bottom," Freud added in a 1925 footnote, "dreams are nothing other than a particular *form* of thinking, made possible by the conditions of sleep. It is the *dream-work* which creates that form, and it alone is the essence of dreaming" (506–507).

The trouble is that dream-work detaches ideation from reality while preserving the workings of affect. Then, the content of the dream plays fast and loose with latent history and consciousness of its time, sequence, space, and memories. Their distortions, however, are received as challenges to a waking sense of intentionality, including the propriety of wishes. All this conflict led Freud (1925a) to ask whether the dreamer was responsible for dreams that destroy or hurt others. His answer was unequivocal: the subject of dreams is the dreamer. Freud then looked to himself: "I shall perhaps learn that what I am disavowing not only 'is' in me but sometimes 'acts' from out of me as well" (133). His conclusion still astounds: "The ethical narcissism of humanity should rest content with the knowledge that the fact of distortion in dreams, as well as the existence of anxiety-dreams and punishment-dreams, afford just as clear evidence of his *moral* nature as dream-interpretation gives of the existence and strength of his *evil* nature" (emphasis original, 134).

Yet if dreams are the ushers of our worst and best selves and remind us there is no immunity from thoughts of ill will, revenge, sadistic wishes, and hopes that can never come true, they are safeguards to action. After all, sleep is an arrested state that permits dreams one would never have thought by thinking the thoughts one would never have. Dream thoughts perform this double negation and dream-work serves as a partial lifting of repression by taking away the *no*. Psychoanalytic interpretations give notice to the unsayable in waking life with dialogic interest in constructing significance from the urgencies of existence in confrontation with passing time. The reach of psychical reality is hard to accept and may explain why Freud, over the course of his work, continually introduced psychoanalysis to the public with its rules of free association, symbolic play, relationality, affectability, and affiliation. There comes the request to take personally both dreams and our history. We are invited to think within the difficulties that follow from claiming the outtakes of psychological life and the intakes of psychic reality as guide and blinder for perception, consciousness, and desire. The invitation is to our lot, beholden as it is to our wishes and to the worlds of others.

When History Returns regards the plays of psychical life and their cultural expressions in literature, social thought, fine letters, journalism, memoirs, and art with the antinomies of their reception in education. Returns are one way that current conceptions of pedagogy can awaken to the call of creating new social bonds and libidinal ties. But returns should also be acknowledged for their paradoxical qualities and the fate of their construction: We turn to history in times of facing the presence of crisis and crisis animates what is left unresolved, including how the conflicts of history can be acknowledged and worked through. We might consider the reception of history as an emotional situation, not as something passed down through the ages, but as more unstable in address and meaning. We might approach returns as creation, akin to the swirls of dream-work that ushers thinking into the tendrils of unconscious meanings. My interest is in the affecting work of relating to situations of past lives and events that may feel terribly familiar or strangely estranged from the present yet manage to carry news of today. In the broad strokes of education, the many contentions over identity, theory, sexuality, race, nation, development, gender, and social change, for instance—as forces of cultural lives and reanimated by history's return—led me to wonder more about theories for humane learning and the environmental provisions dedicated to "warm pedagogy." It may be well known that learning communicates our humanity. Not so known is that communication releases transferences, social conflicts, intimate sources of experience, language games, frustration, depression, and untold conditions of existence that follow from becoming a self with others. To explore these scenes as ripples of history and as our atmospheric study, I join psychoanalytic theories of temporality, deferral, and retroaction—such as found in the machinations of dream-work—to projects of presenting, remembering, and reassembling quests for humane learning. Freudian theory is particularly suited for developing learning's temporal anthropology since its methods are those of analyzing, with tact, the uneven ways the lifeworld is given, received, and altered when met with care for thinking and the questions that follow.

Of course, the returns of history are already overpopulated with our transference burdens created from psychodynamic mix-ups of time with place and person with situation, all in concert with the antinomies of education, family, and culture. While the brute material facts of history and its otherness do not change, the history of their receptions, our susceptibilities to their aftermath, and the uses and forces of their interpretations do. Paul Ricoeur (2004) has described these exigencies of life as philosophical quests to represent: "framed within a hermeneutics of the historical condition of the human beings that we are... [and] intent on exploring the modalities of temporality that together constitute the existential condition of historical knowledge; buried under the footprints of memory and history [that] then opens the empire of forgetting, an empire divided against itself" (xvi). Just as with dreams, the themes and methods that construct something called history carry forward the antinomies of the day's residues, their sources of thinking (affect, the body, and others), and the conditions of rearrangement that invite the designs for responsibility and care and the transference to personal history (Britzman 2003).

I came to think more with the flux and flummox of intersubjective life in my years as university professor, psychoanalyst, and researcher. These professions are theatres of care, education, and affiliation. They are all subject to the randomness of life, the diffusions of existential situations, the imaginative impulse, and the conflicts that spring from vulnerability, uncertainty, dependency, and desire with the world of others. They are professions that require choices to be made before any fate can be felt. They are the uncanny professions of strangers. They work between the fault lines of communication and the failures of translation. And they are transference professions. While I have not found much discussion on preparing for these ephemeral signs of life, with these matters come speculations on the significance of the other and those rustles of human transitions needed for a self to develop, communicate, and desire. One has been there before.

In short, the primary condition for both the birth of psychic functioning and curiosity toward the fate of that history begins with maternal care: the one who responds to the infant's profound helplessness by accepting its inchoate screams, incontinence, hunger, and urgencies of life as harbingers of meaning and calls for love. Psychoanalytic history is predicated on the exigencies of life's beginning, and as Freud (1895) observed, as always met by "a fellow human being" (*Nebenmensch*), someone nearby, who responds and "furnishes the perception and [who] resembles the subject" (331). While psychoanalytic theories may differently highlight the designs, differences, and imperatives of first objects—such as the breast, the voice, the hands, the smell, the breath, and the mother—their likeness, as the grounds of recognition, still serves as enigmatic humanity (Van Haute and Geyskens 2004). Indeed, we are never free from the figurations of cry and care, the resemblances and messages of transference, and the panorama of maternal holding that binds psychical life to its otherness and to searching for likeness in the external world. D. W. Winnicott ([1960] 1990) is perhaps most known for his frame of likeness and care with "the good enough mother" as primary relationship and environmental provision for the self to come about. Winnicott described these environmental conditions as a particular kind of holding and containment that creates "elbow room for the experience of concern, which is the basis for everything constructive" (87). Without the second chance of putting thoughts together, and without what Raluca Soreanu (2018) argues as "the pleasure of analogy" that joins past scenes in relation to present hopes (25), life would only be subject to schizoid qualities of destruction, blame, persecutory anxiety, melancholic despair, denial, misogyny, fragmentation, and attraction to bad dreams.

Faith and attention to these originating and tenuous psychological drives of self with other serve as the backdrop for my research into the conflicts of the return of history in pedagogical exchange, public dialogue, archival research, and aesthetic work. These are the materials of pedagogy as much as they are the harbingers of breakdown and repair. I use the frame of "difficult knowledge" both as an address to encountering past losses, disregard, and the sad weight of their recognitions and as a condition for studies that attempt to create poignant positions for the emotional situations of learning (Britzman 1998). The humane quest is to think from the residues of history one has and has not lived but that, nonetheless, conveys what each of us carries without names such as the daily residues of love, fear, and choice, and is born from the ambles of experience, inexperience, and misrecognition. One can neither project what will have been experienced nor predict what will have been said of experience. These inscriptions of experience provoke an epistemological paradox that belongs to the nature of thinking and its acts, repetitions, entrenchments, and, at times, un-representability (Levine 2013, 2023). Over the years I came to the view that missing in discussions of education dedicated to agency, creativity, and transformation is an epistemological paradox of subject formation: One may know something of the past but be without care for the contingencies of vulnerability and dependency that tie the presence of current breakdowns of civic life and means for affiliation to what has already happened. Missing is a humane theory of learning and a warm pedagogy to accommodate the quests and wonder for thinking that only emerge from tolerating frustration, anxiety, uncertainty, and the sway between otherness and likeness such as found in scenes of every day in life. Eve Kosofsky Sedgwick (2011) considers these exchanges of affect as possibilities for "the middle ranges of agency" and as features of discovery instead of splitting into good and bad that lend havoc to the violent and omnipotent demand of *all-or-nothing* (130). Comparable to what D. W. Winnicott (1988) termed "good-enough," these middle ranges of agency, Sedgwick advises, can be a tonic to anxiety: "This all-or-nothing understanding of agency is toxic enough that it is a relief and relaxation for the child eventually to discover a different reality. That sense that power is a form of relationality that deals in, for example, negotiations... the exchange of affect, and other small differentials, the middle ranges of agency... is a great migration, although it is also a fragile achievement that requires to be discovered over and over" (130). Indeed, in slowing down affect, middle ranges of agency are a relief for both the child and adult who may be attracted to the thralldom of panic and temper tantrums. Quests for humane learning reside in these middle ranges of agency and introduce what is already there, namely fellow humans of likeness, the *Nebenmensch*, responding with warmth to the fragilities of learning to live with others.

Learning to live with others belongs with the question *What now?* found not only in survivor testimonies of life after humanly induced destruction. The question is also an animation for therapeutic action, for memory, and for the thinking given over to the unknown tomorrow. And yet, memory of what has not happened or cannot happen become like a holding pen for anxiety, phantasy, and repetition. Such thoughts are the stonewall of affect. My formulation follows from the work of André Green (2000), who proposed the ideas and situations of history and passing time as dissonance because psychical reality attracts and refracts more than one's manifest development and logical inheritance. There are, within the reception of history, latent qualities and deferrals that catch the subject within several interlocking phantasies and defenses that include what has happened, what has not happened, what has happened to others but not to me, what has not happened at all, and what I would never have thought to have happened (Green 2000, 2–3). There are anxieties that kill time: what always happens, what never changes, and what cannot stop happening. To take history personally and consider its intersubjective pathways and subterrain movements, then, is the condition for memory's revision, the capacity to tell time, the quest for likeness, and the choice of what to face now. If one replaces Green's difficult concept of history with the unconscious force of "learning," a similar mash-up of phantasies occurs. Learning is difficult for the psyche because something happens, something has already happened without me, something cannot happen for me, something must be given up, something should have happened to others, nothing has happened, and then, something I would never have imagined happens if only left to me.

Then and now, how difficult it is to accept the conflicts rooted in situations of ill-preparedness, dependency, helplessness, and vulnerability that also give rise to the question, *What now?* Ilse Grubrich-Simitis (1997), one of the elegant scholars of the early and late Freud, suggests that objections to Freud have their origin in the conflicts that gave rise to his theories: "On the one hand, there seems to be a widespread and uncontrollably powerful need to get rid once and for all of the disagreeable and uncanny insights about ourselves which Freud and psychoanalysis have imposed on us. On the other hand, the ubiquity and stubborn persistence of the attacks must surely be regarded as a sign of the still unbroken vitality of Freudian thought" (2).

Introductions—and the exemplary model is birth—herald the difficulties of response and, perhaps, the strangeness of their enigmatic vitality. A comparable challenge for readers can only be met with a humane acceptance of imagination, care, and passing time. Grubrich-Simitis (1997) recommends the courage of tact: "The attitude commended to the reader can perhaps best be likened to that of 'evenly suspended attention,' which we assume in relation to the analysand's communication in the course of our analytic work.... a special reading attitude.... of not obtruding on the text so as to allow it the free space it needs" (5). Freud, too, may have wished for the mental freedom needed to write for "a special reading attitude."

Indeed, before completing *The Interpretation of Dreams*, in a letter to his colleague and one time friend, Wilhelm Fliess, Freud discussed his writing stratagem (Freud 1954). It was, however, the relationality of writing letters that ushered in what we may now describe as virtual conversation and what became, for Freud, the container for the sotto voce of transference. With her analysis of Freud's voluminous correspondence written with Fliess between the years 1887 and 1902, Hannah Zeavin (2021) relates the history of teletherapy to our contemporary reliance on technological scaffolds of virtual communication. Zeavin planted the roots of distance therapy in Freud's creation of the therapeutic practices of writing as psychoanalysis. She argued that Freud's letters with Fliess involved more than working out his theories of psychical development. Letters took history personally and served as a playground for complaints, disappointments, dead ends, second thoughts, travel plans, birthdays, births of children, losses, and breakthroughs. Just as in psychoanalytic treatment, Freud's letters followed from the drifts of life. He wrote of weather reports, confessed both fatigue and depression, and accepted that he, too, lived in and was affected by the concepts he created. Indeed, letter writing was akin to a subvocalized psychical working through; while not quite writing in one's sleep, free association opened the day's residues with new words that could carry forward forgotten traces of history, Freud's own and of his time. Zeavin (2021) termed the purpose and effect of this writing as the first "distance cure," a framing apropos to the contemporary conduct and experiences of virtual therapies that transform the cure by words into "cure by communication" (58). Or perhaps this distance writing could serve as a personalization of absence.

As for the exchange of letters, one might also venture the writing cure as an experience of one's emotional development that Winnicott ([1958] 1996) described through the paradox of the capacity to be alone in the presence of others. Freud and Fliess knew that passing mental life through the thickets of sexuality, fantasy, mythology, hysteria, neurotica, Oedipal longing, and dreams would be subject to double jeopardy—erotic and obscure, and mythical and hard to believe. They both understood that psychical life and its delegates of dreams and drives were in search of objects and concepts without a name. Like the dream, both experience and meaning of psychical life would have to sail against the wind and be that battered, fragmented, and flailing thing. And so too would efforts in interpreting the deferrals and omissions of its expression. Something would remain unsayable.

Well into the correspondence, and in his report on work in progress, Freud imagined two kinds of readers. There was the scientific community of his time, who he knew would find fault with the book. There were also the dreamers, a general readership of interest. The first chapter of *Interpretation*, Freud thought, would address the scientific readers, and so had to be boring:

> But there is not much to be done about it, except to put a note in the preface, which we shall write last of all. You did not want me to deal with the literature in the body of the book, and you are right, and you do not want it at the beginning, and you are right again. You feel about it as I do; the secret must be that we do not want it at all. But, if we do not want

to put a weapon into the hands of the 'learned,' we must put up with it somewhere. The whole thing is planned on the model of an imaginary walk. First comes the dark wood of the authorities (who cannot see the trees), where there is no clear view, and it is very easy to go astray. Then there is the cavernous defile through which I lead my readers—my specimens with its peculiarities, its details, its indiscretions, and its bad jokes—and then, all at once, the high ground and the prospect, and the question: "Which way do you want to go?"
(Freud 1954, 289–290: Letter 114, August 8, 1899)

I imagine Freud's portrait of late writing contained dual purposes. One was an archaeology of his own education in the form of self-analysis with Fliess (Zeavin 2021). By writing, Freud began to take history personally; that it must be constructed with others and from the ruins of experience, and that the dream of theory implicates the theorist who dreams. The other purpose concerns a wish for the reader's affiliation and transference. And this required an animated, affected address. Freud wrote as if to grab the reader by the shoulders and ask, *What kind of reader do you want to become?* From a literature review that might put readers to sleep and from introductions that have no end, Freud had to create something like a wakeup call and perhaps send a writing lesson to the future. Dreaming, interpretation, reading, thinking, relating, and learning from uncanny history could be just like an imaginary walk. The reader's reverie is their pace. The drifting mind would be used as its own specimen and as the basis for free association. Later, Freud (1913a) would give such reading advice to his patients: "Act as though, for instance, you were a traveller sitting next to the window of a railway carriage and describing to someone inside the carriage the changing views which you see outside" (135). To accept the fundamental rule of free association, to accept an affiliation with one's untold history and their changing inside and outside views, the analyst/reader would have to listen with free floating attention and without preconceptions. For communication to have a second chance, readers and writers would have to wait for meaning's evolvements.

Near the close of the twentieth century, Grubrich-Simitis (1997) reflected on why she kept returning to Freud when bringing her reading attention to her contemporary world, and perhaps, asking again why introductions are always needed when speaking of psychoanalysis. Just as Freud did, Grubrich-Simitis reviewed a history of dismissals of psychoanalysis with renewed attention to the primary one that Freud identified in his letter to Einstein dated March 29, 1929: "All our attention is directed to the outside, whence dangers threaten and satisfactions beckon. From the inside, we only want to be left in peace. So, if someone tries to turn our awareness inward . . . then our whole organization resists" (cited in Grubrich-Simitis, 2). Is this why the learner can feel left out? The quest for humane learning comes from the inside out and invites interest in the phenomena, sources, and adventures of psychical life. Grubrich-Simitis took the side of advocacy for internal consideration, needed, she argued, because so much of our attention is diminished without a thought as to what is being evaded and why. She then asked, "Might insistence on the link with one's private unconscious *internal* reality—a connection that can be maintained only by the expenditure of much effort—prove to be an effective antidote to losing oneself in the new *virtual* reality, to the progressive enfeeblement of one's capacity for responsible intercourse with the threatening and threatened *external* reality?" (emphasis original, 3).

While the current essays that compose *When History Returns* travel a long way from Freud's prefaces, they take into heart psychoanalytic conditions that approach the difficulties and obstacles to knowing as if they are yours and mine. I take a page from his backstory and write and read as if on an imaginary walk, now through the thickets of internal education made from the wakes of history's disturbances and its uncanny returns as encountered in pedagogical conflicts, in expressions of them, and in their aching transformations. The method is associative, finding my way into new reading attitudes and new sites of friendship and belonging, all for the sake of learning from the receptions of early and late education. For those interested in an education beyond what we have learned to expect and fear, let us return to a question that helped Freud arrange his newly discovered method. Dear reader, *Which way do you want to go?*

Returns

Even with a new method of action, our choices remain affected, and for this reason, it is useful to imagine returns. Psychoanalytic views of life are oriented by human susceptibility to the other, to the transference, and to the enigma of the otherness that follows. When psychoanalytic dialogue is used to study relations of education, our proclivities for learning would have to include breakdowns in meaning, adventures in misreading, conflicts of pleasure and pain, and then both shared attempts at repair and toleration of the frustration involved in not knowing the fate of understanding and not understanding. Our study would have to include curiosity toward what cannot be seen but can be felt. Theories of and attitudes toward learning would need to exceed the one-dimensionality of mastery and be subject to the myriad problems given by the urgencies of existence. One would have to enter the world of unbelievable beliefs. Melanie Klein's work with children and adults resides in this unconscious anxiety, stretched to extremes. Klein's theories opened the quagmires of learning with a child's phantasies of pleasure and pain, sadism and masochism, separation and belonging, and love and hate (Frank 2022). She proposed learning as an emotional situation and rooted deeply in the forgotten relations and logistics of infantile life made urgent again with a nameless catastrophic anxiety of losing everything. Our earliest education is the one we do not know, an affectability to the other that returns as if it might be a fleeting impression of missed or stolen experience. The temporality of this private education, then, carries the logic of dreams into the conflicts of desire (Britzman 2016). History, not yet symbolized because it has not happened, emerges for Klein (1957) from the revenants of prehistory, fragments of a time before time, that she termed as "memories in feelings" (180). Through the dream-work of displacements, condensations, reversals, and their projective identifications, these early memories without words return as anxiety in the guise of phantasy.

Klein supposed upbringing and formal education to be a two-edged sword. The other's help can lead to inhibitions in reading as much as it can invite free thinking. But who can tell? When faced with the object of learning or simply a situation that calls upon thinking from what is unknown, Klein linked the bodily decision of whether to take something inside or spit it out as turning on an infantile history of orality, our earliest partial drive. She followed along the lines of Freud's (1905) theory of infantile sexuality and the epistemophilia, or urge for mastery, that characterizes the little sex researcher's quest for their origin. Both Freud and Klein argued that very young children devised their origin theories with libidinal wishes to be their own cause and created phantasies of history before their time that could never become history. Klein (1923) speculated on this urge to be the source of one's origin when she introduced their fantastic dilemmas with the case of "Lisa," a seventeen-year-old girl who hated history class and somehow found a way to symbolically collapse the task of learning history with parental intercourse. "In Lisa's analysis

I learnt that in studying history one had to transplant oneself into 'what people did in earlier times.' For her it was the study of the relations of the parents to one another and to the child, wherein of course the infantile phantasies of battles, slaughters, etc., also played an important part, according to the sadistic conception of coitus" (71–72). Lisa's emotional logic, or rather, her tragic interpretation of what the teacher wanted in the study of history was felt as if it should be an invitation to scopophilia, where pleasure and pain are made from forbidden looking and aggression. The confusion leaves Lisa with a lonely inhibition and a hatred of something that returns prehistory, confirmed by the phantom violence of a militaristic destruction that Klein named, without any irony, "the sadistic conception of coitus." Studying history was symbolically equated with having sex with one's parents and watching a phantasy of sexual gymnastics with the anxiety and hope that someone is being hurt. For the adolescent that Lisa was, sexuality appeared as fantastical, violent, mesmerizing, ridiculous, inconceivable, and beyond any model of information. If, then, history signifies one's own birthday, time must also reference what happened before birth. Thinking of history, it turns out, is not a cognitive problem. Encounters with history have to do with both what happened without us and encountering the pains of association and reparation impervious to transplanting oneself into "what people did." And while Klein's case of Lisa may appear fantastical, one might just as well admit that so too is psychical reality, subject as it is to the dissipations of sexuality.

So, what is it? As farfetched as Klein's case of Lisa may appear to readers today, phantasies of what knowledge brings and what one does with it are not so different from the ways contemporary conflicts in representations of history are handled by prohibitions on free thinking, governmental censorship, and trappings of identity with the language of the absurd. For psychoanalysis, the return of history is far more unruly because history occupies that odd category of a borderline concept, somewhere between presence and absence and with links to life and death, memory and forgetting, envy and gratitude, repair and unity, and separation and affiliation. These are the tenders of human variations in time through combination and contradiction, through binding and unbinding, and through repeating and working through. The return of history is subject to the conditions of erasure, conviction, ideology, aphasia, new generations, symbolic collapse, and the limits of knowledge. Psychoanalysis could not occur without all this struggle, and neither could the human be human without the force of time. There are different names for what transpires in the wake of history: trauma as shattered time, development as growing up, gestation as potential space of culture, the unconscious as timeless and driven, and loss as the work of mourning and melancholia. Dominique Scarfone (2015) considers these intimate conflicts with the claim that psychoanalysis has, as its purpose, the reordering of time: "one of its most important goals is the production of the past" (2). One important goal is to learn to tell time. And herein begin the dilemmas presented to life.

Temporality is always already a feature of the dynamics of history. History's transformational enigmas and interpretational dynamics are described by the German word *Nachträglichkeit*, a term that contains the registration, deferral, and retroactive impressions of experiences. Freud's word anticipates and carries forward the delay and return of meanings such as are found in the associative pathways where words and things serve as the transcriptions of memory. The delay of significance or deferral indicates a temporal mistiming or gap between the force of event, its fallout, a coincidental happening, and then through the dispersals of meaning, a new understanding. It is difficult to say whether the term signifies a function of psychical life or its constitution. The shared complication is that the registration of time is a measure of its oppositions: now and never, here and gone, then and there, too early and too late, and before and after. Such affecting commotion and consternation over mistiming shapes the ways history is encountered and the conditions for its return to be narrated and revised. In the view of Giuseppe Civitarese (2013), "*Nachträglichkeit* . . . not only expresses a sophisticated concept of psychical causality but also reflects how meaning in general is structured—at the same time as reflecting how its own meaning is structured on the basis of a variety of translations" (179). From the work of anthropologist Stefania Pandolfo (2018), "*Nachträglichkeit* [signifies] the fact that events happen in the space of delay and retrospection, where future and past are intwined, where contingency is the other side of repetition" (4). Pandolfo pointed to the necessities of alterity "that aim at addressing the predicament of feeling and thinking in a context of social, political, and spiritual crisis, and do so through the confrontation with human vulnerability and unreason, through a concrete ethical engagement in the world, and through the task of critique" (137). Indeed, temporal happenstance, sources of discontentment and thinking, and the tasks and fate of critique describe the creation and now predicaments of academic traditions, the politics of curriculum, and the representations of history. This twilight also casts a shadow on the temporality of introductions, written after the events have occurred.

Nachträglichkeit is sometimes described as deferred action, retroaction, the unpast, afterwardness, après coup, belatedness, and disjuncture that moves the forces of experience, translation, and thinking (Laplanche 2017; Scarfone 2015, 2016). Its temporal procedures are considered retroactively as a function of primal dependency and fear of madness (Abram 2022; Winnicott [1963?] 1992). Within models of development, sexuality, and trauma, Green (2002) proposed the following diphasic sequence: "The moment when it happens is not the moment when it acquires meaning, implying that for psychoanalytic thought, meaning is not so much linked to immediate experience as to a retrospective interpretation of it" (32). These hovering constructions are subject to disruption, hesitation, reversal, substitution, displacement, and wish, and affected by derivations of time, difference, accident, and otherness. The twilight zone of *Nachträglichkeit* signals meaning's deferral along with our ways to study the intertwining of absence with presence. While the dynamic qualities of temporality provide a way to conceive of representation, there remains the problem of affiliation. Where and with whom do we cast our lot, if time is a strange loop?

From the view of psychoanalytic field theory, our lot is already cast in the fissures of intersubjective exchange, in the primary experience with an object, and in affiliation with the unknown, such as expressed in dreamlife (Bion 1995; Levine 2022; Ferro and Civitarese 2015; Civitarese and Ferro 2020). Antonio Ferro and Giuseppe Civitarese's (2015) survey of psychoanalytic field theory proposes three laws that characterize and at times undo affiliation: that unconscious communication cannot be controlled, that dream thoughts are active in sleep and waking life, and that the stronger emotional involvement becomes, the greater is the passion (163). These laws of intersubjectivity are also working assumptions for considering the field theory for learning, where the reception of communication cannot be controlled, where daydreams and reveries actively transform perception and reception, and where emotional involvement creates passion, at times in the form of certainty, at other times as object investment, and, still at other times, as split-off object relations. So, what is it to write with an introductory awareness of the history of emotional life and transfer this interest into a study of history's return? And what kind of reading and writing attitudes are involved?

Curriculum Vitae

John Forrester's (2016) *Thinking in Cases* proposed writing as curriculum vitae, thought here as both affiliation and its history, where personal experience is to be read, discussed, argued with, wished for, and even admired, and where an education is being written. Forrester suggests that a case cannot be whole. Authorial commentary leaves out a great deal, seemly due to necessary discretion. Yet disguise is only a symptom of representation, since the case involves the writer with their subjectivity and with it the difficulties, confusions, and disorders that resist their knowing. Readers may sense these gaps when they attempt to imagine how they might have interpreted and reported what should or should not happen and even feel they could have done better. But readers, after all, were not there and cannot give the writer instruction. Julie Walsh (2020) identified a conflict shared by readers and writers: "namely to find a form of expression that both attends to the particularity of the subjective experience and answers to a general interpretive frame of reference" (18). In a most peculiar way, the genre of case study invites the reader's transference through the arts and crafts of interpretation and, at times, their envy, or identification with the patient, analyst, or illness. Klein (1923) pointed to some of this transference neurosis in her case of "Lisa," where identification could only mean erotic death. Forrester's description of case studies ups the ante. The studies, Forrester (2016) agues, are wagers and rest on the idea that "analysis of them reveals that the process of their writing obeys the same laws of transference and countertransference as the analytic situation itself" (65). But that also means that without knowing why, readers and writers are affected.

Yes, it is expected that the author of case studies protects actual identities and does so using linguistical devices of the dream-work: disguise, substitution, reversals, condensation, omissions, and consideration of likeness. Except for the author, the anonymity of subjects also means that any reader can imagine they are being diagnosed. Perhaps this involvement cannot be otherwise since a working case communicates affective experience of both the case and writing. Material is treated through affectations of literary devises: unfolding drama, the rising and falling action, the buildup and breakdowns of emotional situations, the conflicts and ruptures in events, and denouement. If cases then resemble short stories, it is likely that the necessary distortions and rearrangements of material reality, along with the inkling transference between subjects, preserve what the writing buries. Returning to Walsh's (2020) observation, readers are left to think more of the fragile ties that serve to relate their singular situation of reading to the general claims of theory. Both writer and reader are challenged to judge whether the study contains enough verisimilitude to create renewed interest in the work of constructing a view of unfolding life that has already happened and yet invites a new register of experience.

Case studies, then, are exemplars for the difficulties of affiliation with their theoretical expressions of four dimensions of "reality"—material, psychical, cultural, and historical. Each joust of reality seems to vie for one's attention and each scene of the actual, the phantasmal, the ritual, and constructional raises new questions for writing within human practices. Where to turn and who to believe when the story behind the case disappears and leaves to readers what Freud (1925d) often noted as no more than "a torso," or fragmented, incomplete experience. The paradox is that the more of himself Freud revealed, the less we contemporary readers know of him. Forrester (2016) identified the enigma: "All Freud scholars have the sense that for every act of disclosure there is something passed over in silence. The act of building a theory out of a well-examined life only makes more evident the deafening silence that constitutes that life's secret truths" (11). Who better than Freud would know that if we cannot tell the whole story, it is only because there is no whole self to tell it?

What is passed over in silence returns as feelings of loss. Wilfred Bion (2005) suggested an epistemological problem of having no words that does more than gesture toward the insufficiency of our vocabulary in the face of turbulence and uncertainty. A feeling is being written and no words may be unbearable:

> When we are at a loss we invent something to fill the gap of our ignorance—this vast area of ignorance, of non-knowledge, in which we have to move. The more frightening the gap, the more terrifying it is to realize how utterly ignorant we are of even the most elementary and simplest requirements for survival, the more we are pressed from outside and inside to fill the gap. You have to ask yourself what you do individually in a situation where you feel completely lost; you are thankful to clutch hold of any system, anything whatever that is available on which to build a kind of structure. . . . Since we don't know what is there, we invent these theories and build this glorious

structure that has no foundation in fact—or, the only fact in which it has any foundation is our complete ignorance, our lack of capacity. (2)

I think this transference anxiety of losing words may be the analyst and educator's plight; loss and absence also begin quests for humane learning.

∼

I can now outline the key themes, sources, methods, and conditions for thinking with questions of otherness, temporality, crisis, and creativity and that are described as quests for humane learning. I am treating the concept of history as qualities, method, situation, and frame and as returning in ordinary places that open actuality. History returns in the psychoanalytic session, in dreams, in literature, music, painting, film, and art, in education, in the bodies of children, adolescents, and adults, in the words we mishear and forget, in the languages one cannot speak, and in becoming a person with other people. It is the events and anniversaries one leans on to justify feelings but also the situations one forgets. When history returns through our dreams, it takes the shape of distortions in the day's residue or those barely noticed perceptions and vague impressions that quickly seem to be overturned when new preoccupations crowd attention. When history returns, it can be taken personally, as if it happened to me (Bollas 2015; 2018; Steinberg 2022), even as one can argue that history has never left and that, even when buried, its force shapes the intricate affairs of memory and becoming. In these ways, the return of history shares the qualities of dream-work and its call for interpretation, engagement, imagination, and the capacity for concern.

In the chapters that follow, the return of history is taken personally and the conditions for thinking of education and rewriting its imperatives for a warm pedagogy are presented through transitional scenes of inheriting a past one could not make, experiencing a present affected by what came before, and facing a future one can neither know nor predict. The on-going challenge of the present is to somehow find a way to symbolize what has happened to others and now for the self. To give a sense of this affinity beyond the call to witness crises, each chapter presents a case of education in the making that follows from imaginative dialogue, missed encounters, emotional situations, new vocabulary, friendships that come and go, and the turn to life expressions as reflected in the activities of creative writers, teachers, philosophers, historians, dreamers, and psychoanalysts. My writing approach mirrors many of the dilemmas of transference affecting the construction and reading of case studies, and with an additional move from the strictures of so-called realism to the evocative gestures of expressionism and surrealism. I treat representations as invitations to reconsider the sways of identity—voluntary, coincidental, and accidental—through to their innumerable emotional situations where selves are lost and found. In this sense, the coming of identity vies with the leftovers of experience and the attractions to unresolved arguments carried forward. This delicacy of encounter has influenced my style of writing, choice of topics, juxtapositions of agency and historical actors, and the frame for problems found and created. Writing becomes a means to resist the doldrums of circumstance. My hope is that readers think more about their situations and experience the wonders of reading into things.

Chapter 1 winds its way into one of the great paradoxes of contemporary education: The more education we have, the less we can explain why and how learning occurs. The chapter sets aside arguments over the right method and content and instead considers learning configurations of education as affected by the shifting conflicts made from changing minds and changing theories. To make this case, I present a brief history of Freud's reordering of education. I find instructions for our own time in Freud's attempt to consider the idea of education with a vocabulary of relational change. He manages to address tensions between the designs of knowledge and the activities of encounter with the history of reception. The progression involves education for enlightenment, education for insight, education for development, wild education, and education for free association.

Chapter 2 turns to the vexations of representing situations of learning with the tensions of otherness and in response to the urgencies of existence and the randomness of life. Scenes of otherness are presented as overturning attractions to and defenses of certainty, regimentation, omnipotence, and compliance. The chapter then pictures learning as human vulnerability created from the contingencies of getting to know imperceptible yet deeply influential impresses of self and other experiences. Whereas Freud considered a vocabulary for education from the vantage of the teacher's hopes and fears, chapter 2 sketches the outlines of learning as situations of relationships and from its difficulties, failures, and receptivity presented through four psychoanalytic entanglements: (1) the emotional situation; (2) the anthropological situation; (3) the transference situation; and (4) the ethical situation or the human turn. Each situation proposes scenes of otherness as natality, inherited histories, the limits of language, and primal unspoken wishes for love and fear of breakdown. Each vexing situation carries forward Freud's discovery of the unconscious as the open heart of intersubjectivity. The chapter then extends a Freudian anthropology of learning to characterize the *Umwelt* of education affected by a random world that can be neither controlled nor known yet can, nonetheless, be the most important threshold of existence.

Chapters 3, 4, and 5 return to the revenants that both big and little history leave as an address to education. While many analysts and educators have lamented the loss of attention to interiority, these three chapters posit a borderline between inside and outside worlds. The cases at hand symbolize the lateness of history's reception, arguing for a warm pedagogy to counter the coldness of destruction and apathy. I explore why we talk of peace from the ravages of war, why the challenges of integrating the trade of oppression and depression matter to social thought and care of the other, and how psychoanalysis and education may discuss the difficulties of representing hatred and its fallout of misogyny to open the clinics of education and psychoanalysis to working through their unresolved history. Chapter 3 returns to Theodor Adorno's thoughts on post–World War II Germany with his writing of education as coldness and warmth. Chapter 4 sets in dialogue Melanie Klein's theories of depression with Paulo Freire's meditation on oppression. Here, the boundaries between the internal and the external world are fluid and subject to the defense of symbolic collapse. Chapter 5 considers why fluidity is a conflicted space. While the psychoanalytic field agrees that maternal care inaugurates psychical life, there is little agreement on addressing the universe of misogyny. Chapter 5 considers the making and breaking of maternal order and how the focus on symbolizing worded loss affects psychoanalytic discussion on misogyny today.

Chapters 6 and 7 are studies in resemblances and affiliations and the conflicts entailed in reflections on coming to terms with historical crises. They are studies of the *Nebenmensch*, nearby others of likeness who, in one way or another, bring character to thinking. Chapter 6 returns to one of the longest psychoanalytic case studies, of a child analysis that occurred during World War II but that was written from notes twenty years later. Again, the quest for humane learning emerges from a special friendship only available in child psychoanalysis. Chapter 7 is framed as an imaginative dialogue in the spirit of affiliations with history's return. I read across a group of writers and analysts of who survived the European genocide toward Jewish life during World War II and came to write later of their destroyed worlds with their humane quest for survival, reparation, and restoration of the self and society. Both chapters perform a new way of writing case studies by questioning how writers, educators, analysts, and readers take the affinities of representation personally and create their afterlife of love and loss. Whereas in chapter 6 I read Mrs. Klein's last case rewriting of Richard's analysis as giving new form to psychoanalytic friendship, in chapter 7 I bring together people who have never met but did share a history of despair and revelation. In chapter 7 the work of the author H. G. Adler and the lives of psychoanalysts and writers are brought to debate the new problem of *What now?*

Chapter 8 replies to the question "What comes after profound loss of love and life?" with the simple response, "What comes after is likeness and more life." The writers discussed have never met and leave me to ponder their thoughts and lives with my own. Some may see this work as a turn toward an empathic history and a sentimental education. It may be both, and yet to greet history's return carries on the attempt to reorganize the self with warm expressions of resemblances and affiliations as needed elements of personhood. This last chapter, then, performs the reading and writing cure, in contact with the work of mourning, reparation, and reconciliation. I treat this chapter like a dream.

Bion's advice after listening to an analytic case presentation is pertinent to thinking quests for humane learning. During a particularly thorny case report given by an analyst, Bion was asked, "What should the presenter do?" The question is common and comes with its untold commotions. I hear it in my clinical work, in my pedagogical supervisions, and in classroom disputes. It is echoed in my dreams and falls through the cracks of my day's residues. Regardless of contexts, the question is raised in times of deep frustration, as a response to the paradoxes of belonging, when there is a glimmer that things could have been otherwise, or when one is simply stuck nowhere and still, must find a way to go on. Rather than answer pleas of what to do, for who can really tell since the experience has already happened and since the future is unknown, Bion (2013) stayed with the sources of the plea. He told the presenting analyst, "The only point of importance in any session is the unknown. . . . Progress will be measured by the increased variety of moods, ideas, and attitudes seen in any given session" (136–137). I believe the same holds true in any learning when we take to heart history's return. Look for a point of potential importance. Then ask, *What now?*

Chapter 1

Reading Freud Today for the Destiny of Education

While no one can predict the future of education, touches of its presence in our hopes and fears can be just as difficult to grasp, since education is subject to mistiming. Education, after all, is a concept, a problem, the means to address itself, a measure of its own success and failure, a preparation, a transference neurosis, and, for each generation, an archive of ambitions, disappointments, and conflicted learning. As cultural imperative, education is also the playground for practices of and attitudes toward humane involvement, its study, and its transformation. Freud's (1925c) often quoted formulation of education and psychoanalysis as two of the impossible maddening professions (the third is that of law) gave a nod to their vulnerabilities, subject as they are, to asymmetrical relations, dependency, and the emotional world of others. Anyone who has tried to present these fields of human inquiry and practice as more than a technical function of instilling authority and specifying directives to be followed, and anyone who is interested in the professional formation of the impossible professions, is likely to question more than just how and what kind of learning can or cannot occur. These professions are also subject to the transference, to the emotional situations of communication, and to contingencies of their history. They bring their own questions as to how they affect their own imaginary. If these human professions require thinking, they are situations where the mind can be lost, dropped, misunderstood, and even denied. And how difficult it is to picture these professions as flowering from the earliest situations of infantile and group life.

Freud's on-going project of specifying why we have education at all was slow to evolve and is found in his interest in constructing a metapsychology of learning that, he argued, was needed to better relate to the human problem of suffering, repetition, and pleasure and to instruct the future of psychoanalysis. Freud wished to create a more capacious presentation situating education in a psychoanalytic field but in so doing, the idea of education as our epistemological paradox may have fallen away from the Freudian project. We can still ask, what is it about the working through of education that captured Freud's imagination? And what happens to the psychoanalytic field when the problem of education is seen through the prisms of psychical life? (Britzman 2011).

When I discussed these questions with colleagues in the fields of education, psychology, and psychoanalysis, some were surprised that Freud had anything at all to say about education. While many knew that Freud rooted the destiny of sexuality in the affairs and imagination of the asymmetries made from relations between adults and children, their thoughts of education remained affixed to a strange combination of the needs of early life, the imagined children, their own childhood reminiscences, and the protective functions of compulsory institutions. Many forgot that when Freud's (1914a) essay "On Narcissism: An Introduction" called the baby "His Majesty the Baby," he gave a sly nod to the early influences of family narcissism as our first education (91). But in doing that, he fused education with narcissism, narcissism with omnipotence, and learning with the other. When I tried to work out some of these surprising outcomes with my colleagues, many could not consider psychoanalysis as a theory of education beyond institutional control and subject to the transference and what follows, namely expressions of uncertainty, vulnerability, love and hate, and dependency in intersubjective life. While most of Freud's technical concepts emerge from scenes of affected life and its functions such as transference, working through, and even free association, these psychical procedures seemed too far removed from education as both environmental provision that has to do with relationality and as bounded by prohibitions against touching. I was left to wonder how it has come to be that thoughts of education feel so far away from the developments of internal life and from imagination. Would it be the case that a stark censorship that limits where education and psychoanalysis meet is symptomatic of superego anxiety (the cruelest education) and the imperative of having to suffer and learn without knowing why? And if so, was this one reason why Freud's depth psychology had to propose the invisible hand of education as one of the impossible professions?

Throughout Freud's writing, education takes on increasing significance and pressure, not only for the child who requires education but also for the adult who bears the psychical weight of presenting authority, love, knowledge, and desire, along with communicating their cultural frustrations, hatreds, and misprisions. Even in these situations, there is something unruly or self-theorizing about the human's quest to interpret their world, usually with little to go on and against all odds. Such was the case of Freud's (1905) "little sex theorist," where the child joined their wishes to the instinct to know. With this little group psychology, themes of happiness and unhappiness and love and hate became the holdouts of psychical life. Freud proposed we study the fate of affect in our trials and tribulations with the hope of translation and thinking needed for opening minds. Here is where education becomes our problem: learning depends on taking in the world with an interest in knowledge of the world of others, and those attempts to find out what the world is really like with others who have their own minds. But learning also depends on our fantasies of learning and our theories of where knowledge and people come from. Conflicts are inevitable and even needed. In these relational gestations, education presents as unfinished, incomplete, and subject to resistance, forgetting, denial, and heartbreak. The epistemological paradox is that while we have all been through an education as our childhood, we have hardly come to terms with its afterwardness in our capacity to both know and not know the self. How difficult it is to consider impressions of education never thought to be education.

Freudian theory has also provided the tactical gambit for contemporary writers to critique current psychological theories of learning that rely upon the diagnosis of deficits and preoccupations with affect regulation and anxiety disorders. For example, responding to the growing industry of the many editions of the American Psychological Association's *Diagnostic and Statistical Manual of Mental Disorders* and its creep into schools, universities, hospitals, clinics, insurance agencies, popular self-diagnosis discussions of websites, social media platforms, and campaigns for mental health, Paul Verhaeghe (2004) has proposed "the impotence of epistemology" that flounders on the error of the categories of the normal and the pathological. Much earlier, Georges Canguilhem (1991) refused to split off these terms from the stream of life: "there is not in itself an *a priori* ontological difference between a successful living form and an unsuccessful form" (31). Darian Leader's (2011) response to the history of madness in psychiatry puts the contemporary dilemma this way: "However valid we might believe such conceptions of illness and health to be, we must surely take seriously the inner life and beliefs of each person and avoid imposing our worldview on them" (7). A case in point is Barbara Taylor's (2014) memoir on madness. She examined the social abandonment of humane treatment that she argues must depend upon the environmental provision of safe space and holding. Each of these critiques has a foothold in psychoanalysis with education. There is the education of a profession and then the primary education where childhood finds its own diagnosis in success and failure, and feeling smart or dumb, good, or bad, normal or freakish, and loved or hated. There is the education that cares for us, the education we flee, and the one we create.

My working assumption is that Freud's unfinished correspondence with the education of psychoanalysis, and this includes his own learning, provides a frame in which to work through our educational and psychological malaise that often comes in the form of a failure of imagination, depression, fear of indeterminacy, and an attraction to quick solutions. It is a dilemma that founds one's sense of education and often felt as alienation and as déjà vu. Feelings of repetition have their roots in how each profession is affected by a psychology of education crafted while growing up and in compliance, opposition, or revolt with one's parents and teachers (Britzman 2003; 2011; 2012). While Freud leaves us with the idea that novel practices of education might usher in an important future for psychoanalysis beyond the clinic, he also proposed on-going psychical contradictions created from trying to imagine the future of education as more than a repetition of the past lessons. The playground of education begins with Freud's capacious formulation of incomplete psychology as ushered in by the primacy of the other, the *Nebenmensch*, someone nearby who helps. The educator's dilemma belongs to meeting the representations of human drives while having to lean on them. And today, if the response is "too bad, no one wants the drives anymore," we may ask, *But why?*

From Insight to Construction

There were urgent reasons why education mattered to Freud, some of which were tied to the problem of treatment while others involved problems of transmitting psychoanalysis and its views on sexuality, upbringing, mental life, professional training, and cultural unhappiness. Throughout his writing Freud experimented with variations of three formal models of formative and destructive education that tried to bridge the gulf between psychical reality and material reality: the Kantian Enlightenment of *Aufklärung* (or the disillusionment of superstition through dogmatic means); the romantic *Bildung* (or the bringing up of culture and life through the creation of a self with genetic means); and the adult treatment, *Nacherziehung* (or the analytic position of novel education, translated as after-education and, at times, as re-education). The model for after-education belongs to the technique of handling the transference, both negative and positive. These fields of theory and their scenes of affiliation and construction in analytic work have created new conditions for expressing the sources of intersubjective education along with critiques on the proprietary limits of consciousness.

While Freud's orientations to education tended to focus the movements from affect to intellect and then from insight to conviction, the idea of self-knowledge in our time has shifted from the mastery of expertise to a capacity to tolerate the pain of incompletion or frustration that involves us all in the contemporary work of historical reparation and learning to live. The new models oriented by Freudian relationality and pedagogical transitions are occasions to rethink objects of affiliation and scenes of politics, and, with deconstruction, turn toward internal critiques of what psychoanalytic education can do for those undergoing its training (Parker 2019). There is also a great interest in the study of contradictions as affecting the object of knowledge, the framing of the problem, and the knower's generational point of view (Smith 2023). Instead of enlightenment, the current interest is with disaffecting education and the consideration of a ruthless education, mainly led through protest and movements for social change that also now have the responsibility to critique their own assumptions so as to affect internal and external conditions for transformation (Swartz 2019). Instead of a discovery model of things unseen but there all along, one finds novel interest in the urgencies of existence and the field of dreams, sexuality, and translations of psychical reality (Levine 2022; Scarfone 2018a; Soreanu 2018). And where psychoanalysis was initially dedicated to making the unconscious conscious, attention has turned to emotional situations of trying to affect the course of education by simply asking, *What now?*

It is, however, with Freud's first model of education that one finds psychical activity through its entangled relations to family romance, civic life, and cultural discontentment. The eighteenth-century European

Enlightenment proposed a revolution in knowledge, authority, reason, and publicity with the introduction of a speaking subject who, with proper education, may step into the wider stages of politics, think for the self, tell the truth, and obey the law (Schmidt 1996). With Immanuel Kant's *Critique of Pure Reason*, Freud placed philosophical education into the human condition with the argument that humans are the only species that need education. Extending Kant's moral philosophy of education into the folds of psychical reality, Freud then joined natality to the problem of enlightenment with the idea that the child's helplessness and dependency on others and its need for care quickly transforms the utility of need into the desire for love, being, and the drive to know, all jubilant libidinal urges that impress sexual curiosity and the wish for how the other must meet these demands (Freud 1905). The special knowledge that reasons without much cause and that gives the self a foothold into language and thinking, Freud argued, belongs to phantasies of sexuality, to the self as other, and then, to curiosity toward what other people are like. From these radical premises that link the desire for knowledge to love and the authority of the other, Freud's first model of education developed from the studied ethical pressures of *Aufklärung*, or Enlightenment. By the mid-twentieth century, Hannah Arendt (1993) proposed the crisis of education as the problem of knowledge that involved both an ethical quest and psychological tie to the adult's responsibility to tell the truth about what life is like. Inevitably, psychology was pulled into the fray and new obstacles were made from this demand for truth. Michel Foucault's (1998) exemplary historicity treated psychology as "a cultural form ... in which there emerged such things as confession, casuistry, dialogue, discourses, and argumentations" (249) that incite the triad of knowledge/power/pleasure. Foucault then added a new set of constraints: "Every psychology is a pedagogy, all decipherment is a therapeutics; you cannot know something without transforming" (255). At stake in enlightenment is the limit of knowledge and what transformation or learning may and may not signify. What could not be accounted for in the civic model of education was human aggression and the additional factor of human desire. How does one prepare for what is already there?

Yet the science of subjectivity, as it played out in the clinic, also meant that psychological knowledge was not transcendent. The flux of psychology involves figuring out the qualities of encounter and the challenge of understanding the understandings of others. Freud's method was also a function of learning where pathways of association were animated by the transference. Here is where the civic model takes an interpersonal turn, such as the one described by Harry Stack Sullivan's life history interview, where the patient takes the lead and serves as the bridge between the clinic and the world and speaks of "records of encounter" (Wake 2011, 14). What could not be accounted for in the enlightenment model of knowledge was precisely a record of encounter, or how a story of anyone becomes a self.

Freud's second model of education turned to the formation of libido and otherness. To grasp the destiny of childhood love and its infantile theories of sexuality, Freud drew from the romance of *Bildung* as educational formation made from the aesthetic conflicts of love, knowledge, beauty, and authority in the bringing up of culture and life. Here knowledge as reason emerges from its psychical impressions—the affects, representations, and drives—and carries a challenge to perception and symbolization. He placed into this intersubjective mix the contingencies of object relations, conflicts in the family romance, the return of infantile theories of sexuality and anxiety, the question of belief, certainty, and ideality, and the destruction of the Oedipal complex. *Bildung* involves an adolescent revolt in inner life and narratives of the belatedness between ignorance and self-knowledge with the difficult conflation of knowledge with guilt (Strachey 1941). The aesthetics of *Bildung* is expressed through its literary representation of the *Bildungsroman*, or the novelistic bringing up of the adolescent's suffering from the thickets of love, culture, and life to the fleeting consolations of self-knowledge as limit (Bloom 1979; Kristeva 1990, 2010; Neubauer 1992). Here we find that education is no longer a progressive march amassing the building blocks of knowledge but instead a crumbling edifice of knowledge that provokes a destructive or negative element constituted through retroaction and deferral. The subjective aspect of internalizing knowledge leaves in its wake the feeling that learning comes too late. Such regret or "if only I knew..." is associated with anxiety and the pathos of lost time, broken hearts, and awareness of the body's limitations. Essentially, the *Bildungsroman*, or novel education, proceeds error-by-error and Freud's literary model may have drawn from Jonathan Wolfgang van Goethe's tragic novella of adolescent love as revolt, *The Sufferings of Young Werther*.

With his interest in building a psychoanalytic movement and creating what had never existed before, Freud's third model of education linked the fate of clinicians to the public and the psychoanalytic clinic to the publication of psychoanalytic knowledge. *Nacherziehung*, or after-education, was made to distinguish the education of children from that of the adult looking back on a childhood's education of desire. After-education became a treatment of language and thought and so a cure by narrative. The problem of reason then gave way to the desire for free association needed for the designs of rendering meaning capacious and with conviction. It is here that memory is under construction, threaded with the transference, and proceeds by way of remembering, repeating, and working through (Freud 1914b). His third model, however, contains elements of both Enlightenment—now as knowledge dedicated to free association, honesty, and truth—and of *Bildung*—transformed into a narrative that relates authority and suffering to desire. Only in his third model, however, did Freud add the question of pedagogical style that he supposed was instructed by a psychology of transference-love and resistance. The sticky concept of resistance, however, is perhaps the most misunderstood idea in psychoanalysis, for the question is, *What is resisted?* Resistance comes in many forms: transference, ego, love, and resistance to resistance. But it was only the third model of after-education that allowed Freud to open pedagogy to the experiences of free association, meant to loosen the defense mechanisms of repression, resistance, and splitting and permit the wondering mind its capacity to bind affect and idea into significance.

Freud's turn to education also involved imagination as the heart of the psychoanalytic situation and, in this way, leaned on his second relational model of *Bildung*. Much of what Freud had to say is unimaginable: linking education to sexual curiosity, forces of repression, and forgetting and negation; finding in education its group psychology, the erotic transference, and the aftermath of the Oedipal complex; and asking educators to confront or at least imagine the precarious problem of the reality principle as a poor substitute for the pleasure principle. In his late lectures Freud (1933) argued that the situation of education, if it is to be felt as more than a repetition of what has already happened to teachers and parents, must somehow find an approach between non-interference and frustration. "Unless this problem is entirely insoluble," Freud wrote, "an optimum must be discovered which will enable education to achieve the most and damage the least" (149). As a signifier for the clinic of human relations, the education Freud constructed cannot be extricated from the human condition of neurosis considered as an unsolvable problem of love and anxieties over its loss. Indeed, education does make us nervous. And in this sense, Freud changed the imaginary of learning from the accrual of knowledge found in his first two models to the subject's capacity for tolerating the uncertainties of life, loss, separation, and working through.

Late Pedagogy

In one of his last, incomplete papers written in his exile in London, which carried the English title "Some Elementary Lessons in Psycho-Analysis" (1940b), Freud had in mind the difficulties with presenting psychoanalysis to "an uninstructed public" (281). But we should be wary as to whether we are ever uninstructed. Freud is most concerned with transmission as tied to reception, and this short paper thinks out loud with a note on the problem of pedagogical style, now linked to a psychology of education. Much of what he has to say mirrors his earlier series of papers on beginning psychoanalytic technique. If the topic is so unpopular, if there is resistance to resistance, how might the limits of pedagogy be recognized? Freud debates whether it is best to begin introducing psychoanalysis with what is self-evident but underappreciated, then gradually add new ideas, and finally invite the audience to contribute their understanding. We should recognize a basic pedagogy here. Freud calls this style "the genetic approach" and finds it unconvincing; learning by experience is akin to the problem of self-cure and *Bildung*, his second model. He named his other pedagogical method "dogmatic," but knew its dangers. A dogmatic pedagogy suffers from critics, since dogma demands unconditional acceptance and ignores the nagging conflicts agonizing the weaves of learning. Elements of both pedagogical styles lean on a combination of Freud's early models of enlightenment and *Bildung*: the genetic approach constitutes student-centered learning, whereas the dogmatic approach may be found in critical pedagogy. Yet the problem resides with the subject of psychoanalysis and Freud tells us what any pedagogy must gamble with: "Psycho-analysis has little prospect of becoming liked or popular. It is not merely that much of what it has to say offends people's feelings. Almost as much difficulty is created by the fact that our science involves a number of hypotheses... which are bound to seem strange to ordinary modes of thought and which fundamentally contradict current views. But there is no help for it" (1940b, 282).

Education does gamble with "ordinary modes of thought" and these conventions do foreclose the question of why both teachers and students carry forward the old wishes for immediate gratification with wishes that learning be devoid of conflict, paradox, and contradictions. It is within the nexus of wishes and defenses that Freud treats education as a psychical entity subject to the pleasure and reality principles. He passed this other education through to its narcissistic blows, felt in the work of parenting, in the schooling of children, in university teaching, in the psychoanalytic clinic, and in the formation of the impossible professions. Quite a bit interferes, including the asymmetrical situations that involve not following instructions. Frustration is its atmosphere since education resides in the slips of unaccountable meaning, the gap between experience and knowledge, and libidinal conflicts of group psychology. The psychological paradox is that if there is no happy education, it must still lean upon happiness and pleasure. And Freud wondered if the unconscious lifeworld (*Lebenswelt*) of education as a psychological address to pedagogy could be remembered and worked through (Laplanche 1999a, 1999b; Leader 2000). Indeed, this approach may constitute a pedagogy for otherness.

Freud's (1919) earlier discussion on psychoanalysis and the university mentions his hopes for the future of psychoanalytic education, and today, one might stretch this essay into a psychoanalytic approach to both teaching and learning beyond the clinic and the work of psychoanalyzing education. While his discussion focused on a psychoanalytic curriculum for medical schools, one might extend his comments to general education and to a general theory of learning from emotional situations made from being with others. Freud gave a key distinction as to the order of psychoanalytic learning and, in setting aside the split between genetic and dogmatic pedagogy, created a third space of culture. One may learn *about* psychoanalysis, and one may learn *from* it. The abiding learning—where conviction takes hold—belongs to the speech theatre of the psychoanalytic couple. And yet for those outside the clinic, there is still psychical reality. It may be apprehended and felt with literature, mythology, history and art, and passions for what exists and does not exist. In any event, psychical reality brings knowledge of self and other into tension with illusions, breakdowns, and cultural fictions. In this third space of culture, pedagogy and psychology become "a literary genre" (Felman 1987, 91), to be read as a case affected by the rearrangements of its own fictions. We may see here the bare elements of *Bildung* and its privileging of affect, along with aesthetic conflicts over the nature of beauty, knowledge, relationality, and truth.

Umwelt Education

At the heart of Freud's psychoanalysis is a recommendation that we analyze our psychology of education from the vantage of what is forgotten in childhood and treat its history both as a piece of current psychology and as our psychological situation. Not only does education have psychical consequences, education is itself a psychological effect of the human's need for education. And because this need for socialization confronts epistemophilia, or the drive to know and master, any education is affected by the combine of love and authority and anxieties over their loss. How difficult it can be to distinguish the structures, techniques, and imaginary of education from the affects, desires, phantasies, and wishes of those involved. But this merging of the inner and outer world may also be precisely what makes education so difficult to know and to find.

There is an emotional logic at stake in Freud's radical claim for "depth education" and it has to do with the elaborate dispersal of chains of associations and their broken links. Dispersed scenes of education animate a forgotten history of learning that has a second chance in transference via the channels of success and failure, punishments and rewards, and certainty and resistance to knowledge that generally fall between the lines of frustration and gratification. It is probably no mistake that when Freud (1914b) described "the playground of transference" he borrowed his metaphor from the schoolyard, where what does rule are games of let's pretend, role switches, accidents, cries for help, fights with enemies, hiding from others, worries over friendships, jealousy, pride, and rough-and-tumble play (154). Freud (1914c) observed these antics that occur behind the teacher's back as his schoolboy psychology. A year earlier, in "The Claims of Psycho-Analysis to Scientific Interest" (1913b), a hopeful Freud left the future of this education to educators: "Whatever we can expect in the way of prophylaxis against neurosis in the individual lies in the hands of a psychoanalytically enlightened education" (190).

Freud's early work, founded in the values of education as enlightenment, was optimistic about the relation between knowledge and understanding and teaching and learning. It may have been his most cognitive approach. His theories of the drives as border between psyche and soma, however, pressed education to its breaking point. With a measure of ambivalence, Freud's (1933) "New Introductory Lectures on Psycho-Analysis" proposed that the greatest challenge to the psychology of education emerges from what is already functioning, namely "the power of an insubordinate instinctual constitution" (149). He was referring to the mythology of the drives of Eros and Thanatos. In acknowledging the conflict between unity and destruction and the thin line between them, Freud pressed the purpose of education beyond our nature, when he wrote, "[education] must be given another and higher aim, liberated from the prevailing demands of society" (150). This "higher aim" of freedom is also embroiled in the conflict between the immediacies of the drives in their search satisfaction and objects, and the capacity for delay from acting made from thinking, sublimation, imagination, and free association. Freud leaves us to grapple with this great unsolvable problem: that education should have a higher aim because our original aim misses the mark.

So too with the world at war where Freud penned his most stringent critiques of education. Near the end of *Civilization and its Discontents* (1930), Freud asked again about the future of care, learning, and suffering by providing an answer: "As regards the therapeutic application of our knowledge, what would be the use of the most correct analysis of social neuroses, since no one possesses authority to impose such a therapy upon the group?" (144).

The psychoanalytic models we inherit and revise for a psychology of education belong to the intimacies of the clinic, the ethic of free association, the destiny of the drives, the enigma of the unconscious, and now our unfinished return of history that will indeed challenge what any theory of learning can mean today. These humane situations may only be met with respect for the challenges of intersubjectivity, the depths of intrapsychic life, and the uncertainties of communication. As for the soft ground for ethics, if education is to become more than a repetition of what has already happened to us, we would have to ask, *Where is education now?*

Chapter 2

Into the Middle of Things

While reading across psychoanalytic discussions, I have been struck by the diverse use of the term "situation." To name just a few that may also borrow from the gradations of existential urgencies, analysts work within a psychoanalytic situation, a transference situation, an anthropological situation, an emotional situation, an anxiety situation, and an ethical situation. These are scenes of interaction, frame, concept, techniques, reception, susceptibility, and encounter. They lean on Freud's discovery of otherness—dreams, sexuality, and the unconscious—as the heart of the human condition. As contingency, otherness issues from a psychoanalytic insistence that consciousness is the exception to mental life, that not knowing is an active state, and that the human activities of transference are ever present yet evasive. Otherness is smack in the middle of things. It presents when least expected, veers from dreams to the dailiness of loss of attention, and is inexplicable in tendencies, variabilities, and entanglements. I understand these situations as creating a perpetual *Umwelt* of education whereby untold and unknowable experience is a feature of atmospheric life and antagonistic with consciousness of this life (Jacobson 1964). I also understand that to approach education from the vantage of its situations is a move away from the qualities of knowledge and into enigmatic qualities of learning. How may all of this be accepted and studied if what is studied is barely perceivable and without a residence?

I picture the contingencies of otherness as a quality of subjectivity and as an intersubjective situation founded through four psychoanalytic entanglements that propose learning *in medias res* and where one finds oneself with others. These entanglements are (1) Wilfred Bion's use of the emotional situation; (2) Jean Laplanche's anthropological situation; (3) Melanie Klein's transference situation; and (4) Koichi Togashi's ethical situation. These are treated as enigmatic features of learning and as its phenomenon. Each proposes scenes of existence as natality, as inherited histories, as the limits of language, and as primal unspoken wishes for love and fear of breakdown. All are affected by the Kantian thing (*das Ding*) that can be neither controlled nor known yet can, nonetheless, serve as the most important threshold of existence. Togashi's (2020) Eastern perspective, when considering a decolonization of the therapeutic dialogue, has named a process of surrender as "the psychoanalytic zero." Without assumptions, without stories, and without diagnosis, the psychoanalytic zero is "a moment without context" (ix) and situation without name. As leftovers of experience, each of these scenes of otherness plays between the lines of human incompleteness, dependency, and uncertainty.

A Special Charge

Psychoanalytic theory admits into its practices the enigmas of otherness as an unknowable quality of human psychology and as a response or even protest to the force and persuasions of an external world. Otherness is also a philosophical concept but here is treated as its own method needed to dissolve the façade of certainty and fixations to timelessness. Freud's (1900a; 1900b) sudden and disruptive discovery of his own otherness occurs amid his dreams. There and nowhere, meaning is inexhaustible, inadmissible, objectionable, and inexplicable. For these dimensions of thinking, there are no objective measures to depict, predict, or stabilize the causes of either subject or object. Due to a constitutive uncertainty brought to understanding, reasons too are affected and can become mired in tautologies, anxiety, defenses, and language games. And while all of this affects psychoanalysis, it may also be felt as alienating manifest education.

As difficult as it may be to admit, a failure of translation is a quality of psychoanalytic work, the source of its otherness, and a condition of its education. Failure is ever present in clinical discussions, although not from any measure of success or best practices. Instead, the flux of life and obstacles to knowing are the work. Analytic advice on offer is counterintuitive to the idealizations of professionalization. Freud (1915a) urged modesty in practice and even advised analysts to expect to be wrong, while Jacques Lacan (2006) suggested the analyst's position as dummy. Winnicott ([1962] 1996) expected to be mainly off the mark in his interpretations to the patient and gave interpretations to prove to the patient that he was not sleeping. Joyce McDougall (2005) recalled a comment of Winnicott's, "We must admit that it is always fatiguing to be a bad breast.... [he] went on to explain that it was very important that the bad breast analyst survived the attacks of the enraged infant within" (35). Bion (2000) warned that whenever two people meet, there would be bad jobs and emotional storms. Kohut (1982) argued that empathy can only occur when analysts accept the relativity of their knowledge as also affecting their views on human development. Indeed, empathic response has to do with experiences of being changed by the other. McDougall (1992) too urged analysts to be affected by the limits of their practices. Admissions of failures of translation are deepened by the fact that there is no objective reality to reach, and that failure is a contingency of the human condition.

What is left is the charge of psychoanalytic vocabulary as both mirror and refractor to unconscious life. The vocabulary is itself an enactment of situations made from those barely remembered features of learning that emanate from susceptibility to unknown life. These psychoanalytic ideas lend a special challenge to philosophy's turn to emotional experience, since so much of our lifeworld is out of our sight and proceeds without memory, consent, or control. When psychoanalysis quests for how the world is registered, felt, and perceived as communication, and when the field takes interest in the sources of its thinking, philosophic inquiry opens onto the suppleness of inner life as issuing from a place it must also comment on while being affected by it.

Responsiveness to the unknown, however, brings with it the weight of reflections on our practices, limits, resistances, repetitions, and failures to learn. And these transitions in the psychoanalytic field of thought preoccupy such varied contemporary analysts as Lewis Kirshner (2017), Donna Orange (2020), Koichi Togashi (2020), Julia Kristeva (1991), Michel Émile de M'Uzan (2019), and Gohar Homayounpour (2012, 2023). Each has taken an ethical turn in their consideration of why the power of uncertainty and vulnerability in the lifeworld of the mind is related to an acceptance of otherness and the capacity to stand experience. They draw from philosophical debates, compelling myths, and literary fiction, and from analysis of the cost of humanness, political divisions, trauma, and psychosomatic incompatibilities. Their ethics stem from the priority of the other and all propose the desire to think and be receptive to scenes of both suffering and pleasure. They urge us to read, write, think, and live.

"If One Only Knew..."

Receptivity to the unknown gives birth to a new sense of temporality, where time is always passing and must also include its retrospective accounts of experience. Scarfone (2015), for example, considers the antinomy between presence, absence, and meaning. He observed that gap made from event, situation, and remembering, where "a matter of time" becomes a dilemma for knowledge and a problem of belief. Freud (1914c) identified disjuncture as a perpetual *Umwelt* of mental life when he drew his analysis of infancy, childhood, and family into the conundrums of love and hate and, when looking back on his schoolboy years, had to treat his own education as a disturbance of memory.

Here then is the birth of an affected science, touched by the procedures it names. Its knowledge of subjective life would be described by Michel de Certeau (1993) as "jeopardized and wounded by its otherness (the affect, etc.)" (27). It cannot be otherwise, since the object of psychoanalysis is a subject that forces, invents, deceives, loves, worries, interprets, repeats, sleeps, cries, laughs, desires, eats, dreams, and retreats. This subject of otherness serves as a specimen of knowledge while becoming the source of its own inquiry. Laplanche's (1999a) *Essays on Otherness* offers psychoanalytic geometrics as "a method of free association polarized by the transference" (162). Through this entanglement of speech, desire, and the other, psychoanalytic theory is not only confronted with an object but also remains a method instructed by its psychical mobilities: "There where there was id, there will be always and already the other" (83).

When commenting on unreachable reality while feeling its pull, Kant's approach to antinomy in thinking is often cited by the fields of psychoanalysis and critical theory. Kant's many arguments in *The Critique of Pure Reason* pictured human knowledge from two irreducible sources: objects given to perception and thoughts about them. Kant wrote, "Without sensibility no object would be given to us, and without understanding, no object would be thought. Thoughts without content are empty and intuitions without concepts are blind" (93). What situation can exist between a thought and reality? Freud might reply, anxiety. The psychoanalyst and philosopher Donna Orange (2020) might reply, radical ethics are made from the situations of learning to hear.

For psychoanalysts the difficulty for existence emerges from accepting the difference between perception and the object and between the source of its representation and its fate. Laurence Kahn (2018) traces this aporia to Freud's exasperated exclamation, "If one only knew what exists!" made after he asked Charcot to discuss the source of hysteria, to which Charcot famously replied, "Theory is good, but it doesn't keep things from existing" (122). It is not only that theory comes too late. It is also that theory cannot stop reality. Freud (1900a) acknowledged this otherness in his work on dream interpretation when he admitted that no interpretation can reach the navel of the dream and when he argued for two realities that occupy the same space: psychical reality and material reality. In Kahn's (2018) wise view, while no one can know reality as such, one can, at least, try to understand its consequences (146). And trying to understand what has happened constitutes our educational situation.

Bion (1993) has written extensively on the problem of experience with his focus on the consequences of learning and having psychical reality while trying to know the object of perception. He can be read as working from the proposition, "well, if one only knew what exists with a thought!" His answer is surprising. Bion linked the otherness of thoughts and intuition to estranging situations that he called "thoughts without a thinker" and "empty thoughts" (91). Thoughts are prior to their thinking, and the sources of thinking come from the other. Bion imagined the beginning of the psychical apparatus when he proposed thinking through three embellishments of experiences. The mother's embellishment provides containment for the infant's chaotic thoughts, screams, and bodily urges. Her reverie is the second embellishment where the infant's chaos is translated and returned to the infant in a manageable way and as a thinking breast. It is as if the mother's reverie said, "You exist and you can relax, for meaning is coming." The infant can then use that wish to develop an apparatus of thinking, needed to contain the mind as a thinker of its own thoughts. A third *embellishment as experience* involves the situation of digesting or chewing over the emotional situations of love, hate, and knowledge. In Bion's view, a thinker handles the frustration of experience by tolerating the uncertainties of not knowing.

Critical theory would take a different tack by focusing on obstacles to the ethics of representation as opposed to confusion within perceptions and appearance of objects. Theodor Adorno's (2001) lectures on Kant introduced his students to the challenge of abandoning their idealization of the self-enclosed subject described as the "'I think' that accompanies all of my representations" (176). The self is not an isolate of enclosed meaning but in the middle of unknowable things. Adorno proposed this fundamental dilemma as "the Kantian Block" that he eulogized as "a kind of metaphysical mourning, a kind of memory of what is best, of something we must not forget, but that we are nevertheless compelled to forget" (178). It is difficult to decide whether Adorno is referencing the infantile past or the need to create an unknown future. From whatever vantage, we know there is something more, but we cannot reach it. Or, if there is something more, it can only be an empty space that will not exist if entered (Britzman 2009).

The Lateness of Early Situations

Melanie Klein's (1959) theory of the adult world and its roots in infancy provides some clues as to the entangled destiny of subjectivity, intersubjectivity, and history. Hers is a theory of an adult affected by very early and unknown things, perhaps what Bion would simply call "thoughts without a thinker." Klein's early theories are visceral and her speculation that the mind is an emotional situation, as opposed to only having to encounter the emotions of others, can come as a shock. Perhaps just as shocking is her claim that the contingencies and destiny of early anxiety situations and their constellations of phantasies and defenses have a second life in transferences found in the fields of education, law, politics, medicine, parenting, and group psychology and that these major edifices of libido and authority contain kernels of infantile reality, the most dominant of which involves omnipotent thoughts, identifications, and magical thinking. What do we really know about the infant's psychical life and the fate of the ego that emerges from the profundity of helplessness, dependency, care, love, vulnerabilities, and the phantasies that follow from and lead our situations with others? How can one get in touch with that other Kantian Block described by Klein (1930) early on with the *Umwelt* of anxiety as our attraction to "unreal reality" (221)? Klein placed into the midst of things early anxiety situations over loss of love, then defenses against loss made by retaliatory and paranoid phantasy, and from this distress, the urge for reparation and the giving of gratitude. It is a sequence that eerily forecasts the difficulties of uneven development that involve having to learn before one can understand and feeling the force of experience before one has learned.

Klein (1952) considered mental life as the original transference, an assemblage of emotional situations of homemade crowds of others, part objects, and object relations that would serve as the center of life: "I hold that transference originates in the same processes in which the earliest stages determine object relations. Therefore, we must go back again and again in analysis to the fluctuations between objects, loved and hated, external and internal, which dominate early infancy" (53). The emotional world then would be a tiny inchoate theatre of otherness starring a series of introjected part objects as figurations of split-off worried object relations. There would be the stranger, the foreigner, the uninvited, the lover, and the disturber. I take these figurations as affects, situations, and memories of learning, and as phantasy for the raw material for symbolization, analysis, and creativity. They are also the delegates of anxiety and defense. In Freud's (1924) terms, such imagoes are reflections of identifications with the world of others: "To the imagos they leave behind there are then linked the influences of teachers and authorities, self-chosen models and publicly recognized heroes, whose figures need no longer be introjected by an ego which has become more resistant. The last figure in the series that began with the parents is the dark power of Destiny which only the fewest of us are able to look upon as impersonal" (168). Parents, infants, teachers, heroes, cultural objects, lost objects, and knowledge seem like helpers until there come disruptions, accidents, starkness, mistakes, coincidences, illness, and disasters. Even then, when all seems lost, we are never finished with elaborating our beginnings with others and do so each time we love, learn, hate, turn away, and reach for more.

The Emotional Situation

There are plenty of variabilities within emotional situations, although the dominant tendency involves nameless dread and catastrophic anxiety. Bion's (1994) insight was to join knowledge with the problem of trying to know emotional experience and the pain of its evasion. He argued that difficulties in learning are intimately tied to one's theory of knowledge and preconceptions that seem to dictate how knowledge should be acquired, transmitted, felt, received, recognized, and transferred. Imagine a teacher who can do without these preconceptions and implicit how-to instructions. Being instructed and having to instruct have a long history: they are ready-at-hand in the child's game of "let's play school" where the omnipotent child teacher dominates those other bad children due to a theory of knowledge as possession and a will to punish. The "child teacher" is a dictator who yells and hits misbehaving others. The phantasy is that only one person can be in charge and others must obey. The child who plays teacher may not have been humiliated but was once a witness to the humiliations of others.

A situation, then, is emotional when it is felt as if it can forecast destruction. Bion (1993) argued that every encounter with unknown ideas or what one has not expected carries threats of catastrophic change because new knowledge may destroy the valence of deeply held beliefs and shake one's foundational myths to the core. His conception of knowledge, or what he termed as "K," simply means getting to know the emotional experience of frustration. The constellation of "K" contains elements of Freud's (1905) confrontation with the figure of the child as sexual researcher who links phantasy with theory and theory with belief. "K" also leans on Klein's (1928) notion of states of being as our most radical relationality constituted through phantasies and the early sadistic epistemic instinct for curiosity. When Antonio Ferro (2017) surveyed the psychoanalytic field with Bion in mind, he pointed out that the emotional situations of trying to know constituted "the development of psychoanalysis, where every change could be experienced as turbulence to be avoided, even though we cannot evolve without disturbing what we know" (177). To be subject to the tenders of its own theoretical disturbances is, perhaps, the only means by which receptivity to unknown life can even be considered. And this admission of the otherness of self-knowledge preoccupied Freud.

Freud's (1937) most difficult claim for psychoanalysis appeared near the end of his life. With some irony the problem he presented may also be a mirror to the anxieties of education as they involve the length of treatment and running out of time. And yet while it is common for people to dismiss psychoanalysis as too long, the same worry is not given over to the inordinate time spent being educated. Freud had to acknowledge, almost forty years into his psychoanalytic theory, that more was unknown than known, that it was a matter not of time but of its contingencies, and that even the work of trying to know—thought of as interpretations, wishes, dreams, and transferences—was subject to the defenses of ideality, omnipotence, and magical thinking. A matrix of miscommunication is also a part of the analytic relationship, since communication is disrupted by desire and the associative pathways of the signifier. But there is another problem that Freud's (1937) late essay "Analysis Terminable and Interminable" had to admit. A gain in knowledge does not necessarily translate into affective change. One can seem to know a great deal of knowledge and still not know what has happened to the self. One can hold a great deal of knowledge and still repeat the child's game "let's play teacher."

What counts as knowing has always been a tricky matter. Freud's (1917c) "A Difficulty in the Path of Psycho-Analysis" emphasized the defense of resistance that he understood as an emotional situation rather than as an indication of lack of knowledge:

> I will say at once that it is not an intellectual difficulty I am thinking of, not anything that makes psychoanalysis hard for the hearer or reader to understand, but an affective one—something that alienates the feelings of those who come into contact with it, so that they become less inclined to believe in it or take an interest in it . . . the two kinds of difficulties amount to the same thing in the end. Where sympathy is lacking, understanding will not come very easily. (137)

It is a grand irony that interest in emotional life is felt as a suspicious activity since emotions are already suspicions. Indeed, where suspicion is, there will be an emotional situation unclaimed. And yet, psychoanalysis must be an emotional situation that invites reading into the difficulties that follow from affected life. Freud understood that psychoanalytic views hurt people's feelings and that did not stop him from an emotional truth when he described our nervous conditions as in the middle of things, objects, others, and affects. Our nervous condition includes upbringing, separation, culture and unhappiness, ego ideals and superego guilt, sexuality and unconscious life, and egotistic fear of loss of love. Freud's (1917c) discussion is memorable for its unrelenting description of a universal psychological blow to the illusions that consciousness is the sum of mentality and that sexual drives are unimportant: "But these two discoveries—that the life of our sexual instincts cannot be wholly tamed, and that mental processes are in themselves unconscious and only reach the ego and come under its control through incomplete and untrustworthy perceptions— these two discoveries amount to a statement that *the ego is not master in its own house*" (emphasis original,143).

The Anthropological Situation

The ego is not master of its own house because others are already living there. Laplanche (2017) presented the problematics of the experience of life as an anthropology: "a body of thought about the essential foundations of the human being. One of these foundations, perhaps the most important one, is the fact of the little human's entry into the world of adults.... It is a 'universal' for human beings ... the fundamental anthropological situation" (19–20). As a body of thought, the situation is to be interpreted as well as to serve the sources of latency in theory. The anthropological situation begins when someone is born and when the infant is confronted with the world of adult desire it can know nothing of. These imperatives of relationality constitute our original asymmetry. What is unconsciously conveyed between the infant and adult is this radical gap. Laplanche has theorized this situation of care with the primacy of the other who transmits enigmatic messages, or scenes of unconscious seduction, that implants sexuality for the infant. These enigmatic messages cannot be translated yet carry the gift of life to the bodily mind. In one fell swoop, and due to the human's self-theorizing, the anthropological situation frees sexuality from the anchors of biology and tosses its enigmatic qualities into the middle of intersubjective life.

Scarfone (2018b) painted the anthropological situation with broad brushstrokes. The situation is one of "compromised messages to which each of us is exposed, from birth by way of the infant's unpreparedness with regard to the sexually saturated adult universe" (89). And yet, everyone is ill-prepared for the human condition, and no one can predict what becomes of the fate of the anthropological situation. There cannot be a complete translation of desire because no completeness exists. Instead, our earliest relationships leave erotic traces, impressions, yearning, and a desire to translate, however wrongheaded. Communication carries this affective disturbance or excitement and a failure of translation. The anthropological situation is one of ill-preparedness for culture, birth, sexuality, education, and otherness. It is also the soft ground for transmissions and transferences into learning.

The Transference Situation

Transference is another term for the enigmas of desire that communication carries. Klein (1952) coined the term "transference situation" to point out that even when her patients say the most banal things and even when they complained they had nothing to say, these seemingly empty utterances carried on persuasive forces of love, hate, and ambivalence into phantasies of reception, destruction, and reparation. Through her focus on anxiety and defense as the stirrings of mental life Klein listened to what could not be said but could be acted out between her and the patient as conflict, demand, compliance, hatred, sorrow, regret, envy, and wish. She thought the self's paranoid perception of the other and the depressive worry over destroying the other characterized the make-up of the mind's oscillations and affected the ways the self could deny or get to know the pain of incompleteness and sources of otherness. Klein found clues to these psychic events in interpretating the transference. The patient transferred to the analyst an imagined and real history of learning in the form of object relating that blurs the lines between inside and outside, perception and object, and present and past.

Betty Joseph (1996) described transference as both a means to understand and a quest for and disrupter of relationality. Her focus was on the contrary transmissions of unconscious attempts at influence:

> Much of our understanding of the transference comes through our understanding of how our patients act on us to feel things for many varied reasons; how they try to draw us into their defensive systems; how they unconsciously act out with us in the transference, trying to get us to act out with them, how they convey aspects of their inner world built up from infancy—elaborated in childhood and adulthood, experiences often beyond the use of words, which we can only capture through the feelings aroused in us. (62)

Transference situations signify not so much why we feel anything at all. Rather, as situation, transference carries the additional element of affect, that acts as attractors to the feelings of the other. The teacher's affects are a complex of matters, beholden to frustration, competing investments, and projections of the introjected accumulation of educational biography and imagoes. The force of all this history is projected each time a teacher acts, each time a teacher worries over the loss of knowledge, and each time the teacher listens before they can understand. The transference situation then may contain the *Umwelt* of education and so, for example, the teacher's sinking feeling of something not right may well be in contact with the silent student who feels wronged. Transference situations are our means of relationality but also of resistance to that connection.

The Ethical Situation

Togashi (2020) has made the claim that psychoanalysis consists of several turns: structural, linguistic, subjective, intersubjective, relational, and the ethical that he attributed to the late work of Heinz Kohut. Kohut (1982) was interested in the development of selfhood and all that stands in the way of finding meaning. He arrived at the understanding that there is no objective reality to perceive, but only "the unknowability, in principle, of reality" (400). Our incapacity to dominate reality and even the ways one can insist on how reality should then be perceived, Kohut and now Togashi have argued, are a challenge to static knowledge. They both understand stasis as trauma and a call for a new version of empathic thinking. What needs to change, Kohut advised, are our theories of development, since unknowability has, as its principle, a psychological subject always involved in and acting from its own development and growth. The ethical turn, as Togashi understands, is an empathic one that has more to do with accepting the relativity of knowing and the relativity of perception than it does with any intuitive understanding of the other.

Togashi (2020) names his ethical turn as a decolonizing Eastern perspective, with efforts in overcoming the dominance of Western views of the self-enclosed individual and the dichotomy between one's humanity and professionalism (29). *Decolonization* here refers to a radical transformation without concepts and an emptying out of experience in self/other relations. In this sense, the area of concern is emotional and forgiving, and the basic encounter is between two vulnerable humans who meet as strangers. Togashi works within Eastern values dedicated to openness, variability, and a surrender to the unknown. For Togashi (2020) "there are many patients we cannot describe" and so he asks, "How shall we understand our work and our patient's sufferings?" (109). Togashi's perspective emerges from his clinical work in Japan with people who have survived trauma as humanly induced and trauma as randomness. He views the analysis of one's work as beginning from a vanishing point of "being thrown into a world without informed consent" (59). So, the ethical turn is one not of goodness but of humanity that involves acknowledging the cruelty of the world as our human contingency. From this situation, Togashi writes, "the analyst [must] decolonialize from Western paternalism" (xiii). For Donna Orange (2020), radical ethics is grounded in encounters with history as a therapeutic project. She draws from the historian and psychotherapist Thomas Kohut (2020), son of Heinz Kohut, and his advocacy for an empathic relation to the work of writing history, by which he means understanding from the other's perspective. The emotional work is harrowing as Kohut explores the murderous minds of National Socialists dedicated to genocide, and so one may question what we mean by understanding if what is understood is horrific. Orange (2020) comments on this historical inquiry as reparative of the return of history: "What [Thomas] Kohut calls 'authority' of historical experience means that we cannot escape our history" (111). Precisely because the worst has happened, we are obligated to understand and recognize its revenants.

The decolonization of practices of social engagement has also reoriented the affecting psychoanalytic method of interpreting countertransference. Sally Swartz's (2019) Winnicottian analysis of political protest movements in South Africa and Donna Orange's (2020) engagement with the radical ethics of listening are challenges to psychoanalytic orthodoxies, cultural overreach, and entrenched intolerance. Their interest is with the priority of the other as avenue for self and social dialogue. Ethics come in the middle of things, a situation made with the autonomy of the patient and the analyst's willingness to reflect on her own affectations.

Togashi's (2020) question, however, exceeds technical and material orientations when he asks, "Can we be open to our patient's accounts without formulating stories about it?" (8). His quest is for a stunning alteration and challenge to the history of psychoanalysis and its transference desire for speaking subjects who narrate their stories. Of course we wish for expression and of course we wish for the analysand's desire to speak, to construct, to revise, and even to forget. And yet, many experiences born of unspeakable pain and horror, specifically those of social violence, natural catastrophes, accidents, war, trauma, and profound loss of life—many humanly induced catastrophes and untold loss—cannot become a story. From this awareness and respect for suffering, Togashi formulates "the psychoanalytic zero," as emptiness that expresses a fundamental void without consent or will: "The psychoanalytic zero requires us to be in this vulnerable position when we see our patients who are themselves afraid to be vulnerable" (110). All this humanity is prior to assuming the roles of patient and analyst. He describes the ethical situation as the meeting of two humans that occurs before the frame is explained, before the presenting problem is placed between the analyst and analysand, and before there is any knowledge of either party. The psychoanalytic zero belongs to no one, and is there, in the here and now, without consent. It is our radical humanity.

Togashi asks analysts to attend to the ways patients are encountered. It is advice well suited for educators since, after all, what they do is receive groups of students they do not really know. Yet typically, educators hardly begin their greetings by presenting themselves as vulnerable people meeting their students who are afraid to be vulnerable in their presence. And the approach of accepting fallibility, vulnerability, and unknowability is quite other to Western discussions that urge the analyst to focus on the patient's presentations and the teacher to focus on what they think students need before the student speaks. The psychoanalytic zero is a refusal of categories and identification. One of Togashi's patients, for example, survived severe facial disfiguration in a home fire and while he attempted to feel what the patient felt, he had to conclude "that it was impossible for me to sense her pain at all; I had to accept the radical incommensurability between us—through which, ironically, we could become equally human" (37).

What is striking for me is Togashi's (2020) emphasis on human beings as "prior to an analyst's and a patient's awareness of their identities, their sense of self, and their professional, therapeutic, social and cultural roles" (17). It is almost as if we can be returned to a community of infants given over to the enigmatic qualities of our anthropological situations. Whereas Freud suggested complete honesty with his method of free association, Togashi considers an ethic of sincerity, not knowing, and acceptance of what cannot be chosen or given as consent: "The randomness of the world creates human vulnerability and loneliness" (37). He is moving to the edge of representing an empty void, that is, an unspeakable situation of otherness without grounding. For Togashi, the ethical turn is acceptance of the analyst's vulnerability, "to surrender herself to the moment without any distinctions including right and wrong" (116). It is a turn to face vulnerability, needed to forget preoccupations and accept the limits of understanding as the ground for listening to human otherness. The ethical turn begins with the question of "how can we help ourselves to live with a sense of uncertainty?" (107). The question has no predictive frame. The ethical turn, for Togashi, is "where we find ourselves in a state of radical vulnerability" (109).

In Medias Res

Jacques André (2013) suggested why early contact with the other matters: "There is no such thing as human nature from a psychoanalytic point of view. Not that nothing is innate, but there is nothing human that is not subjected to the vicissitudes of early intersubjective relationships" (190). Even if our birth is inescapable, involuntary, and largely forgotten, it matters that we are born into a world of others. André provides a rough sketch of infancy as destiny rather than as nature. Nothing belongs to the subject yet there are no blank slates. The intersubjective field begins with birth, a situation the neonate cannot consent to and for which we are ill-prepared to receive and be received. Laplanche (2017) named this homemade cultural investment as the fundamental anthropological situation, an introduction to life where otherness and reception are nearly inseparable.

So it is that the field of education inherits and is itself an inheritance of unconscious experience that orients emotional expressions, wishes, anxieties, and attitudes toward the mental lives of self and other. These are our educational situations that broadcast human incompleteness, dependency, and unknowable life. But because we are also affected by randomness, the ethical situation calls on our vulnerability as acceptance of humanity (Togashi 2020). Ethics in the making presents the fragile means to tolerate the frustrations of emotional experience that are readily expelled through preconceptions, rigid knowledge, and exhaustion. Lack of toleration can only lead to breakdowns and harsh defenses. These situations—emotional, transferential, anthropological, and ethical—as our daily contingencies challenge education to stop treating itself as if curriculum, modes of authority, theories of knowledge, and social arrangements took instruction from reality, as if reality was knowable, and as if there was no value to the situation of not knowing. What would it be like to take instruction from our vulnerability? And yet, what stands before education is myriad otherness. Its institutions are always beholden to life's uncertainties, to the randomness of life and death, to the histories inherited and denied, and to our anthropological situation of ill-preparedness. The dilemma for trying to symbolize all this anxiety through the care of language is that words amid otherness may feel as if they are delegates of abstract expressionism. There are so many brushstrokes, erasures, over-painting, textures, splashes, and layers that create the psychic palette so that no center can be discerned.

What if our emotional situation is enlivened by vulnerability, dependency, care, ethics, the enigmatic message, the passing of time, and fallibility?

Chapter 3

Turning to the Subject

"The One and the Many"

Between the years of 1959 and 1967, Theodor Wiesengrund Adorno published a series of searing addresses to the public, teacher educators, professors, and those students entering the teaching profession on the difficulties inherent in researching, imagining, and transforming the afterwardness of education in postwar Germany. Their titles are in confrontation with the residues of National Socialism and its "pedagogy": "The Meaning of Working Through the Past" (1959), "Philosophy and Teachers" (1962), "Taboos on the Teaching Vocation" (1965), and "Education after Auschwitz" (1967). And their words—*working through, philosophy, taboos, teaching, Auschwitz, education*, and *after*—are signifiers under distress. With each examination, Adorno charged pedagogy with building democracy from its ruins, but only if the enterprise of education can become intimately embroiled in and affected by the transformation of character formation and group psychology. The balance is nearly impossible to imagine since character had already been transformed to a function of a function and since, over the course of the horrific war, group psychology was either reduced to indifference to the other or dedicated to hatred of the other. That was how Adorno saw the problem of his time.

Adorno had to begin by recounting the devastations of fragmented emotional life presented as indifference, coldness, cruelty, pseudo-stupidity, and feigned innocence. And he had to link the situation of emotional deadness to the inheritance of regressed education that, for him and for psychoanalysis, had to begin in family relations that impressed our earliest childhood. Yet how difficult it is to approach this disclaimed history for those who come after. And how difficult it is to imagine psychic deadness that can neither know its own procedures nor recall its murderous drives. So, what is it to remember or work through education? What kind of education might be capable of symbolizing the inexpressible? And what kind of education can narrate the deferred traces of its own events, yet to be rendered as affecting the transformations of mental life?

Reading Adorno's work today, one may be struck by his efforts to speak of education at all, as its enterprise had dedicated itself to defending against the mental pain of transforming its own learning imaginary. The challenge of change is catastrophic and requires disquieting imagination in the service of working through an education that had already happened. I find in Adorno's work three conflictive dimensions of education true today: the cruelty of institutions as expressed through group psychology and the technological narrowness of functional language in cultural life; education as aftereffects in mental life; and the fracturing of ties of object relations between the one and the many that wreck the capacity to think and care. In each dimension, Adorno found the situation of "cold mentality," by which he meant a hardened indifference to the lives of others defended by the confusion of love with hate and good with bad. Cold mentality splits these distinctions in such a way that awareness of remorse, reparation, loss, and dependency become symbolically equated with weakness, narcissistic injury, deficiency, and retaliation. A change of mind is catastrophic.

My focus is on the third dimension of conflicted education as passage between the one and the many. I read Adorno through my preoccupations as university professor on matters of teaching and learning, where trying to communicate and listen is touched by both pathos and frustration, as researcher of the emotional world where, more often than not, inner life is rendered irrelevant, as psychoanalyst in clinical practice, where I hear more than I understand, and, as Jew, born in North America, mid-twentieth century and subject to anti-Semitism and a Jewish education. Adorno's papers, now over sixty years old, are used as an occasion to look back on what education has unconsciously inherited and project forward what education may create today.

As for Adorno, in placing education within the ostensible claustrum of psychosocial life capable of unspeakable involvement in social illness dedicated to genocide, his emphasis had to land on the analysis of the perpetrators' and bystanders' emptiness of character. A significant consequence of Adorno's approach, and what I understand as weighing down pedagogy today, is that in giving priority to the actions of perpetrators and bystanders, in attempting to instill guilt and remorse for those who chose destruction, he had to set aside both the humanity of Jewish life, before, during and after the war and the humanity of those who came after. My understanding is that humanity cannot be given away, though it can be lost, destroyed, and profoundly diminished. The indeterminate problem as history returns is that unless an appeal to human warmth and the dignity of the subject's restoration becomes the heart of pedagogy, we can grasp neither the loss of meaning nor the meanings of loss (Hassoun 1997).

In setting up the problems made from advancing a pedagogy of warmth, I need to break my discussion with a psychoanalytic question of why, when attempting to work through social breakdowns, the giving of priority to developments in object relations allows new approaches to recognizing emotional situations of repair and reparation. *Object relations* was Klein's (1940) term for wide-ranging internal phenomena, functions, phantasies, and defenses that signify mental states and their procedures of internalizations, identifications, splitting, and projections of both interiority and exteriority. While such functions of mental life can be identified, the deeper question arrives earlier. What comes before these defenses? Why do we have them at all? From the perspective of object relations, the other comes before any activity of defense. There is no such thing as an object without a relation to something and someone and there is no object without a subject's relation to anxiety over loss. The object is both the source and sinkhole of thinking, and given such precarity, object relations have priority in any conceptualization of what happens when learning. Complications ensue. There are many objects, or phantasies, that compose our mental constellation and its destiny: there are part objects, persecutory objects, and good objects threatened by bad objects. There are schizoid objects, paranoid objects, and depressive objects, all of which are features of the same mind as much as they are the characteristics of perceptions of exteriority. Given these constellations, where would learning settle and be felt as unsettling?

As the worried heart of the human condition, anxiety, for Klein, signals the emotional situation of object relations and its anxieties over loss, destruction, and annihilation. With the concept, function, and logic of anxiety Klein theorized the developments of inner worlds as open pathways to the pathos of intersubjectivity, the capacity for guilt, reparation, and gratitude, and susceptibility to aggression, envy, and hate. And Klein also thought the earliest yearnings of the infantile mind, with the emotional situations of pining for the other, created depressive anxiety and its feelings of loss of the other. These are the barest inklings that animate love against hate. The balance of internalizing the mind and externalizing the social world, Klein found, is precarious, and the pain for any integration is never complete.

Adorno built his theory of destruction from the other side of life. He had to survey the wreckage of an instituted education, felt as omnipotent and violently attracted to violence and the destruction of the mind, just as Klein had to sort through conflicts of phantasies of omnipotence and manic defenses on the way to depressive anxiety. Klein thought of the depressive position from the self's on-going awareness that while love can be lost in phantasy and reality, anxiety over loss animates the urge for reparation. There is something utterly human in our history of dependency and helplessness that includes a mechanism for overcoming persecutory thought. For Adorno, however, society lost its capacity for anxiety and the conditions for its overcoming of the externalization of the death drive. Klein and Adorno differed on the matter of what kind of knowledge opens awareness of destruction of loss when affected by the drive to destroy.

We should have in mind that any education is an emotional situation, that learning cannot proceed without anxiety, and that these factors complicate how we may accompany the uneven progression and indeterminacy of learning and thinking within the object relations of pedagogy. Much later, the psychoanalyst Cornelius Castoriadis (1994) proposed the paradox of pedagogy. Just as with the mother's care of the infant, the development of civic life must lean on an autonomy that does not exist: "Pedagogy has at every age to develop the self-activity of the subject by using, so to speak, this very self-activity. The point of pedagogy is not to teach particular things, but to develop in the subject, the capacity to learn: learn to learn, learn to discover, learn to invent.... Any educational system which cannot reasonably answer the question of the pupils, 'Why should we learn that?,' is faulty" (5–6).

And yet, what if the *why* is systematically abolished and replaced by taboo? That was Adorno's dilemma. When the why of learning is abolished, so too is the chance for doubt and for an autonomy that must also lean on questions of *Why learn?* and *Why care?* Essentially, Adorno's discussions on education had to address a cold public with an opening developmental paradox proposed by Castoriadis. Any approach to the vexing problems of *Why care for learning?*—which is another way of asking *Why care for others?*—must also give priority to the question of why there is learning at all. Why imagine what does not yet exist by attending to what exists in the here and now? A great deal of pressure gives birth to teaching and learning, since what exist are hesitations, ambivalence, moods, helplessness, anxiety, identifications, and disorientations. The teacher is already affected by a nexus of transferences to the fragility of knowledge exchange, the history of that reception, the students' anxiety, and the teacher's doubts over how to respond to questions or blank stares that seem to stop the passing of time and call for interpretation.

Those reading Adorno's papers on education today have not been spared from the experiences of social violence and are already affected by the estranging sway between the history of the reception of horrifying details of destruction and the agonizing contradictions in finding significance between the one and the many. Any turn to the subject, then, is a reach for contact with the fragility and creativity of intersubjectivity yet to become and already seeded in birth. The quest, then and now, involves an earlier dimension of Castoriadis's developmental paradox for pedagogy: to lean on a self-activity of warmth before it exists. Or perhaps, the paradox of pedagogy is one of absence: to remind others that something has been forgotten. Klein's (1940) formulation of object relations may state the pedagogical paradox through its emotional situation: the teacher's pedagogy leans on the self-activity of "the depressive position" before it can exist.

Adorno had as his focus the mentality of the perpetrators with the question of what has happened to them. But a pedagogy must also ask what it is to survive after the destruction. This question may be the basis of a new beginning and I draw from the writing of Hillel Klein (2012), a survivor, psychoanalyst, and contemporary of Adorno who emphasized the challenges of intersubjective revival. In so doing, Klein, along with other survivors, revised postwar psychoanalysis with a new understanding of the after-education of survival. His question to himself and to his patients was *What now?*

In 1945, Hillel Klein, like many others, was an adolescent survivor of many camps. At liberation, Klein was 22 years old. He had to rebuild his capacity for transference to living, wanting, and being while subject to the profundity of loss and despair. His focus then was on the individual difficulties of revival for both the survivor and those who came after. Klein's quest for life began with the emotional demands made from any encounter with humanly induced destruction and the fracturing of time. His dialogue with young people, adults, clinicians, and teachers resided within their initial building of interest as predicated on the fragility of learning that, at times, felt awkward, hesitant, ambivalent, and painful. Such on-going work opens the relational experiences of transference made from difficult knowledge: "The attempt to understand the psychosocial background of the Holocaust must be made in spite of the fact that in interpreting the events of the Holocaust, one exposes oneself to the pressures of one's own present conflict situations with their fantasized and real threats of extermination. Such threats and intra-psychic conflicts place psychological and emotional demands on the interpreter to view the past according to his present self-ideal" (H. Klein 2012a, 111). And it is with the depressive anxiety for attachment and disillusion of ideality that render learning so uneven and painful. Klein was one of the first postwar Jewish analysts to acknowledge that encountering the trauma of others meant that learners, clinicians, and witnesses of the archive would be affected by the defense of idealization and with transference to their own conflictive past. There would need to be a pedagogy that could focus on the receptions of both past and present responses to social destruction and survival. So as to interpret the play between learners, the material, and their lives today, pedagogy can be interested in the dreamwork's activities of deferral, displacement, substitution, consideration of representation, and reversal into the opposite. That is, pedagogy would have to be an activity of polyvalent listening and exchange.

Typically, in Adorno studies, commentators privilege his critique of Enlightenment rationality and its accompanying idealizing ideology. But in his papers on education, just at the point when Adorno asked what happened to thought—and just at the point when he tied disaffecting education to character structure—he extended Freudian vocabulary to social thought with the analysis of the gap between the compulsion to repeat what cannot be remembered and is thus acted out and his proposition that learning is both a turn to the subject and a working through of the past. The problem Adorno faced was immense and involved generations subjected to murder and expelled by an administrative order overseeing pedagogical autocracy. Within the mental constellation of educational relations qualified by authoritarianism, humiliation, sadism, persecutory anxiety, and violence, and when the enterprise of education was dedicated to the destruction of the mind, Adorno asked, is it possible to create the capacity to desire thoughtful citizens who want to restore imagination by affecting and even redirecting the consequences of their education?

Reflections on a Damaged Education

Adorno's ([1967] 1998) postwar demand for education "after Auschwitz" may be understood as articulating a triple challenge to educators: pedagogical relations must address knowledge and cultural mentality and propose interest in the depth psychology of individual subjectivity. The interminable tasks for both students and teachers are to develop from their studies of self/other interactions the means to think with moral character capable of withstanding the pains and incompleteness of historical memory and ethical choice. The questions Adorno posed for education concern the unconscious depths of its affective influence on character formation and how this may be known. If such demands can be made, and if warmth can become education, Adorno's turn to the subject may be understood today through the object relations of pedagogy in transference to intersubjective relations between teachers and students and between past and present.

Yet education is a dimension of the human condition as well as the condition for the human; it already contains an attraction to mechanisms of social and psychical alienation that shuts out the stranger and that sustains ideality, indifference, and the narcissism of minor differences. Given the magnitude of education's reach into emotional life, Adorno proposed that the key demand is that educational institutions, from early childhood through to the university and professional life, find the moral courage to invent, from the ruins of war, a new kind of human. The dilemma is that coldness or the turn away from the subject repeats the repressions of the original woeful disregard.

Adorno's discussion had in mind Freud's (1915b) "Thoughts for the Times on War and Death," written six months into World War I and penned the same year Freud published his metapsychology, "Mourning and Melancholia" (1917b). As a personal meditation on the death of a loved object, it was in "Mourning and Melancholia" that Freud made the distinction of the diminishment of self when love is lost. In the work of mourning, one feels the profundity of loss, and as the self's agony then identifies with that loss, there is a growing awareness that part of the self has come to an end. Indeed, the work of mourning involves both creating a past that is no longer and building a future that is unknown (Major and Talagrand 2018). The work involves rejoining the world and this, Freud argued, takes its own time. In melancholia one knows who and what has been lost but not what has been lost in the self. Freud's (1915b) "Thoughts for the Times on War and Death" was a turn to society. He emphasized two inexplicable melancholic responses—disillusionment toward life and an altered attitude toward death. Freud was addressing those who were not combatants, but citizens, civilians, and youth reduced to "a cog in the gigantic machine of war" (275). Each disillusionment and its attitude present what Freud called our double susceptibility to culture and to the internal drives. Together they create "a special capacity for involution—for regression" (286). "Thoughts for the Times on War and Death" ends with a variation on the old saying: "If you want to preserve peace, arm for war. It would be keeping with our times to alter it. . . . If you want to endure life, prepare yourself for death" (300). The problem, as Freud conceives it, is that we cannot prepare for the death wish. Indeed, we do not believe in our own death, and likewise, we do not recognize as a symptom of the death drive our own cruelty, desire for control and power, and hatred for the other.

But why bring to education the depths of these psychical matters? And why did Adorno think of education through to its failure to educate and, against these odds, continue to argue for the possibility that education can become the moral foundation for self-reflection and a desire for the gambles made from intersubjective emotional life?

These questions are those of today's education, where global migrations, the on-going histories of decolonization, anti-racism, human rights for sexual and gender subjects, and pulls of subjectivity in digital technology bring into education and its learning theories both situations and people never anticipated that include political refugees, displaced people, survivors of national atrocities, former child soldiers, the exiles of failed states, illegal migrants, Roma people, orphans, those fleeing from civil war, those without documentation who also are subject to a history of hatred and cultural violation, and young citizens who demand reparation for past national harm. Contemporary Canadian education, for example, is only beginning to face its own history of woeful disregard as tied to a quest for a better society. And any attempt of reconciliation to address the history of First Nations disenfranchisement made from governmental and Canadian church policy of residential schools must now be understood as an effect of longstanding First Nation demands for self-determination, reconciliation, and the development of an education for treaty people.

Adorno's writing on education proposed that individuals become invested in self-reflection on the most difficult, painful, and devastating events wrought by human actions. Yet how paradoxical are the demands for education to be in the service of humane public life and, dare I say, be on the side of sanity and its contribution to ethical reparation when humans have never lived in a world without violence and when dwelling in the failure of peace and in histories of war may invoke cynicism and hopelessness and forms of forgetting the past that unconsciously repeat what has happened. Since education already reflects the people it seeks to affect—teachers were once children needing education and generations would be unconsciously affected by massive deception and social repression—Adorno had to draw attention to those who teach. Teachers too are subject to regression, thoughtlessness, hostility, and compliance to authority. They too can become functions of the functions of administrative procedures. The most difficult work for teachers concerns creating a public that desires more education by asking more from their education.

The Depths of Education

Adorno's critical turn to education followed from his empirical studies on the authoritarian personality while in exile in the United States, and then, upon return to Germany, continued with "Experiments with Groups," his postwar interviews with German people, young and old (Pollock, Adorno, et al. 2011). For a brief time in the United States, Adorno passed himself off as a psychologist (Hullot-Kentor 2006), perhaps to gain funds, perhaps to legitimize his measurement, or even to assure his research subjects that he knew what he was doing. It was his turn to groups, however, where his research thesis stated unequivocally the problem of education:

> The indoctrination during the twelve years of totalitarian information, propaganda, and education went too deep for it to be wiped away through a defeat that not only caused disillusionment deriving from the fall of the Reich from its dominant position in Europe but conversely also produced legends of past glory.... In all of this, one has to consider not only that fascism was forced on people from the outside by a propaganda machine, but that the receptiveness to totalitarian systems was built into the psychology of the individual through sociological, technological, and economic developmental tendencies and continues to exist to today. (Adorno 2010, 138–139)

Adorno's study on group experience documented the currency of receptiveness and its psychical consequences wrought by the Third Reich's perversions of law, civic duty, medicine, culture, technology, religion, history, architecture, transportation, record keeping, child rearing, language, and education. The professions were both servants and planners of an administrated society of genocide, anti-Semitism, hatred of foreigners, the euthanasia of disabled children and the elderly, and the reduction of people to functions and then to worthless part objects. Adorno's work was not well received. In retrospect, he must have expected a poor reception given that he was writing on psychical and societal pathologies of denial, projection, collective delusions, splitting, forgetting, and disavowal, all defenses utilized to disclaim responsibility for genocides.

Adorno's studies then involved thinking more from a psychoanalytic notion of the human as subject to the acting out of aggressive drives, projecting pain into the other, and the excessive use of unconscious ego mechanisms that ward off guilt and being affected. Much later, Elisabeth Young-Bruehl (1996) classified these ego defenses as in the service of "ideologies of desire." Adorno's "Education after Auschwitz" ([1967] 1998) pointed to the psychosocial emotional constellation that suffers from cognitive indifference: cultural glorification of hardness led to the incapacity to feel and to coldness within emotional life and found its traces in the conduct of and social attitudes toward education, gender, culture, and race. It is here that his work leaves us with a question: how are we to identify with humanly induced catastrophe, acknowledge woeful disregard of its consequences, and work through what could be thought of as psychical allergy to truth, warmth, tolerance, softness, and civility? Yet in turning to the German institutions of pedagogy as still affected by their deeply entrenched history that expelled its Jewish students and teachers, taught the propaganda of the National Socialists, encouraged Christian children and adolescents to join the Hitler Youth, censored books, deemed music and art degenerate, and sent very young boys off to fight a losing war, what could transform the teacher and this devastating education?

Exile

Adorno's father was Jewish, and his mother was Roman Catholic; his middle-class secular childhood, he would later say, was happy. He held a "supernumerary" professorship in Frankfurt and, by 1933, was expelled from his teaching position, as were countless others due to National Socialism's early racist laws that prohibited Jews from working in the professions of medicine, education, law, and government (Müller-Doohm 2005). In 1934, he left for the UK to take a second doctorate at Oxford. By 1938, with his wife Gretel, he fled into exile to live in the United States, first in New York City, and then to Los Angeles. Those first chaotic years were dedicated to helping his family and colleagues leave Germany. He could not save his lifelong friend, Walter Benjamin. In retrospect, Adorno admitted he could not recognize the horrendous consequences of National Socialism (Müller-Doohm 2005).

By 1940, living in the United States, Adorno's work was dedicated to understanding anti-Semitism, the makeup of an authoritarian personality, analysis of individual susceptibility to fascist mentality, and what he saw as a culture industry of mass deception that contributed to loss of autonomy and thought. In exile, he composed perhaps his most enigmatic, ambivalent book, *Minima Moralia: Reflections from Damaged Life* (2005), spanning the years 1944–1947. The text runs 157 paragraphs, each ordered by a key word or phrase that leads to an ethical choice for private existence. Adorno called this work his "melancholic science" (15): it was his personal testimony to loss, grief, and the agony of contemplation. In his dedication, he wrote, "The violence that expelled me thereby denied me full knowledge of it. I did not yet admit to myself the complicity that enfolds all those, who, in face of unspeakable collective events, speak of individual matters at all" (18).

And yet, only by speaking from individual matters can we understand our relation to the lives and losses of others. There is never "full knowledge" of any historical catastrophe, and a large part of its affective incompleteness emerges from the anxiety to speak of such matters as having something to do with the self. For meaningful cognition to begin, we must not only face the failures of others but also recognize our limits of understanding, empathy, and historical memory. Perhaps this was why Adorno placed into the education of teachers, professors, and students something he, too, experienced, namely the problem of knowing and not knowing the contingencies of the present. He would begin by describing character as subject to defense mechanisms of projection, splitting, and denial: "thinking oriented along the dimensions of power and powerlessness, a rigidity and an inability to react, conventionality, the lack of self-reflection, and ultimately an overall inability to experience" (Adorno [1959] 1998, 94). He found these splitting mechanisms in the enterprise of a dissociated education, before, during, and after the war. The large questions for education involve how the world can matter if it cannot be meaningful to the self and what meaning can be without care for the worlds of others.

The Problem of Re-education

By 1949 Adorno returned to a devastated Frankfurt. He was then witness to the disastrous consequences of murderous National Socialism and, for the everyday citizen, the massive denial and disbelief of the genocide that had taken place under their name. Denial is not a disagreement with ideas. Rather, the ego defense of denial is the obliteration of meaning. Adorno's research turned to how individuals old and young refused to admit what had happened. The empirical study conducted in 1950–51, analyzed the rawness of the intersubjective legacy of National Socialism. The study concluded with a long essay, "Guilt and Defense" (Adorno 2010). One can see the roots of Adorno's ([1959] 1998) paper, "The Meaning of Working Through the Past," where he juxtaposed denial in the form of a mastery of the past that involved the defenses of forgetting, undoing, and disavowal with the Freudian model of "working through." Working through the past did not mean magically blowing history away or pretending that what happened is now over and done with. The Freudian concept would have to be interminable, an on-going project for mourning for education because the emotional appeal of National Socialism would have to be decathected bit by bit and memory by memory. Such disillusionment is needed to address the mechanisms of personality structure subject to the pathology of compliance, denial, and the hatred of the human condition expressed in public insistence that no one knew anything that happened. But something must have been known, for in Adorno's (2010) interviews on group life conducted in Germany in 1955, there were many opinions such as "Concentration camps are not all that bad" (133) and "The Jews themselves are to blame for everything" (152). He considered these diminishments through the defense of "projections" and as "archaic themes of hatred against the foreigner" (130).

Adorno's writing on education came about a decade after the Allied forces carried out a drastic military "re-education" and "de-Nazification" program that now stands as the vast pedagogical failure of the postwar years. The pedagogy involved forcing German Christian citizens to acknowledge the horrors of their concentration camps and death chambers. It had the consequence of continuing the psychosocial link of education with punishment and humiliation, experiences that repeated conflicts of authoritarianism in cultural life that rendered others and education as so hated.

Exposing the horrors of war and mass murder is a poor substitute for the slower and painful work of thinking from the ruins of social life and all that mattered. Some of this fallout returns in Philippe Grimbert's (2008) novella, *Memories*. Grimbert was born in postwar France to what he thought were perfect, beautiful, athletic parents. Philippe remembers being fifteen years old, in school, and having to watch *Night and Fog*, a black-and-white film shot just after the war documenting German civilians being taken to a concentration camp by Allied forces and required to bury Jewish bodies:

> The only sound was the whirr of the projector. Slagheaps of shoes, of clothes, great piles of hair and body parts. These weren't extras, or sets. . . . One of them had me pinned to my seat: a uniform soldier dragging a woman by one foot and hurling her into an already overflowing pit. That broken body had been a woman. A woman who had gone shopping for clothes, who had admired the elegant lines of her new dress in the mirror. . . . Now she was just this broken doll, dragged along like a sack. (52)

Philippe had been sitting next to a football captain, who jabbed him and made a joke. At first Philippe laughed but did not know why. Then he became sick to his stomach and began punching the football boy. The teacher stopped the film. Grimbert went home with a blackened eye, and his parent's friend, Louise, then told him the history of something he knew but had no words for: His family is Jewish, and his father survived the war in hiding but his first wife and their first son were murdered. Philippe's mother was his father's second wife. It was not information Philippe was after but a means to symbolize the affective silences of his parents and understand the broken ties between then and now, and how family secrets are always cultural affairs disguised with idealism, perfection, and silence. Years later, Grimbert would come to understand why he voluntarily failed his Baccalaureate oral exam. He was to discuss Laval, a French Vichy president during the war who signed off on the deportation of Jewish families to Auschwitz. As for the examiner, Grimbert writes, "convinced that I was talking to a Vichy sympathizer, I had gone mute which cost me a repeat of my final year" (139).

The Subject's Turn

Adorno's participation in re-conceptualizing education, through radio address and essays, attempted to reach deeper into the affective meanings of the lives of people. He tried to uncouple the unconscious symbolic equation of learning as punishment by authorities with "practical advice" on pedagogy, simply called "a turn to the subject" (Adorno [1967] 1998, 193). On the one side, Adorno argued that curriculum should create conditions for disidentification of National Socialism through focusing on the perpetrators. On the other side, discussions should encourage identification with the fragility of freedom, autonomy, and self-reflection, by which he meant rebuilding the capacity to imagine that one's perceptions of the world as still subject to desires for social compliance and their severance of associations. It may well be that even as Adorno implied the working through of dissociated affect, freedom does not necessarily follow from admitting social fractures.

The stage version of *The Diary of Anne Frank* began performances in Germany in 1956. By 1959, there was a resurgence of anti-Semitism, which strengthened social denial of responsibility for the murder of the European Jewry (Olick and Perrin 2010). Adorno ([1959] 1998) mentions the Anne Frank play in "The Meaning of Working Through the Past." Major intellectuals would comment on and argue over the *Diary*'s affective value in understanding genocide, and youth across the world would read the *Diary*. Adorno ([1959] 1998) quotes one audience member who claimed to feel sorry for Anne Frank and wished that she could have lived but could not see the larger totality of people sent to the death camps.

Indeed, the problem of denial persists through to our own time, when the teaching of Anne Frank's *Diary* keeps her safe at her desk and celebrates the adolescent girl's faith in the goodness of people to ignore the history of the *Diary*'s reception and pedagogical problems the *Diary* can never solve (Britzman 1998; 2000). Should the apprehension of the Shoah really have to lean on the shoulders of a young girl? Even the ever-crowded Anne Frank Museum in Amsterdam, with annual attendance of over 1.3 million people, must now ask this question of how the secret annex can become meaningful for those unaffected (Siegal 2017). The Museum curators know they must seek new ways to communicate with today's younger generation, whose inheritance is also with the question of relevance or how any address from history can be received. And still, the curriculum that includes the *Diary* seems caught between teachers asking students to recount what happened and say why the Frank family went into hiding while leaving students to wonder how these details of life and death matter to them today. The *Diary* is now over seventy years old, and for youth, seventy years can seem like *once upon a time*.

The Education of Teachers

After returning to Germany from his exile in the United States, and because his 1933 expulsion from teaching in the university disqualified him from being reinstated as a professor, Adorno's chief means of employment was at a teacher's college. He was assigned the charge of examining secondary teachers on the topic of philosophy (Hohendahl 2005). In "Philosophy and Teachers" ([1962] 1998), Adorno analyzed the new teachers' malaise: whereas most candidates could give the facts and adequate answers, they also admitted that philosophy meant nothing to them. They passed the exam by offering clichéd accounts and platitudes: "The test should... permit us to see whether those candidates, who as teachers in secondary schools are burdened with a heavy responsibility for the spiritual and material development of Germany, are intellectuals, or as Ibsen said more than eighty years ago, merely specialized technicians" (21).

Adorno's ([1965] 1998) "Taboos on the Teaching Vocation" tried to specify two sides of the effects of a socially disparaged profession. He linked public disaffection toward teachers to memories of teachers who chose cruelty over thoughtfulness, meaninglessness over meaning, and violence over peace. Through the ego mechanism of reaction formation, Adorno considered teachers' aversion to teaching as a transformation of the public's hatred of education. The teacher's aversion was not only due to the regimentation of institutional life and their disciplinary function. Hatred of teaching was closer to the affecting imaginary of the figure of teacher in the minds of the public that contributes to an unconscious attitude of suspicion toward the worth of teachers, doubts over the value of knowledgeable people and, ultimately, hostility toward the value of education as such. Adorno ([1965] 1998) located these unconscious attitudes within the "latent hierarchy" (186) of the school and university, where some are rewarded while others are punished. He named this as a part of the unconscious problem of education and asked how teachers understand the antinomies of their profession. "The pathos of the school today," Adorno wrote, "its moral import, is that in the midst of the status quo it alone has the ability, if it is conscious of it, to work directly toward the debarbarization of humanity" (190). Everything depends on *if* the teachers can be conscious for the sake of humanity.

"Education after Auschwitz"

A close reading of Adorno's essay "Education after Auschwitz" ([1967] 1998) reveals his deep ambivalence over whether teachers can meet a new categorical imperative: "The premier demand upon all education is that Auschwitz not happen again" (191). The complications of what comes before the demand render any simple response inadequate. Reason cannot account for education's fall into perverse violence and the rendering of ethics as meaningless (Bernstein 2001). Reason may even require the obliteration of others in its relentless goals of totality, systematicity, and transcendence, a central finding of the Frankfurt School and the basis for Adorno's (2000) claim for "the frailty of truth" (33).

The problem only grows. How are we to think within and act from an ethic for the quest for humane learning when the terrible truth is that as an authoritarian structure and as inculcation of the belief in compliance to authority, education's regressive tendency cuts off warmth? Adorno ([1967] 1998) called this compliance "the insane dimension" (194). So, is there a capacity for knowledge to touch and transform both the character of education and the characters in education? Or can character be affected by the desire for living with others?

Difficult Knowledge

Regression is a particularly difficult concept in the Freudian lexicon, for it only erupts as incapacity. Robert Hullot-Kentor (2006) developed the view that regression, closely tied to the violence of the return of the repressed, is a symptom of unresolved conflicts:

> Regression, as Adorno occasionally points out, is not to be understood concretely, as traveling back to an earlier period, but as the manifestation of conflicts that were never resolved in the first place. In this, Adorno agrees with Freud in emphasizing the infantile past of the individual and society in conflicts that continually remerge in moments of crisis that reveal the ongoing failure to solve these conflicts . . . as the enduring situation of the reproduction of incapacitating conflicts. (9)

The dilemma is that as returns, conflicts do not appear as unresolved experience. Nor does the social response to the breakdowns of civility. Traumatic repetitions do not feel as if anything is being repeated. Freud's (1914b) technique paper "Remembering, Repeating and Working Through" proposes that one consider repetition as regressions to earlier conflicts. That is, a tendency to repeat what cannot be remembered can be recognized through the transference of archaic agitations: "the patient does not *remember* anything of what he has forgotten and repressed but *acts* it out. He reproduces it not as a memory but as an action; he *repeats* it, without, of course, knowing that he is repeating it" (150).

The regressed past cannot become past because it is forgotten. For this reason, the return of history as unresolved conflicts and as reaction formations does create pedagogical regressions whenever incapacitating social conflicts in group life are repeated and acted out without a care for the fallout of meaning. Our current symptoms of social conflict in the form of trauma can be found in censoring of textbooks, literature, and libraries. In both compulsory education and university settings, current attacks on pedagogy, feminism, critical race theory, gender theory, queer theory, and sex education, and attacks against language, identity, and bodily dignity can be understood as agitations of unresolved conflict. And symptoms of the fallout of meaning are also found in the rigidities of character structure. Adorno first gave educators an analytic task that earlier I have suggested as the depressive position. Teachers and professors must be willing to conceptualize and interpret what incapacitates their cognitive awareness of both regressed pedagogy and the public reception of pedagogy. With students, teachers can create a warm pedagogy and not abandon people to the anxiety that nothing can change the vicious circle of regression and ideality.

What Now?

Adorno did not use the term "depressive anxiety," though he came close to depicting the paranoid-schizoid mentality of murderous culture. But to name the pathos of education, one must suppose the teacher's developing capacity for the depressive position needed to tolerate the frustration of trying to get to know the self who tries to get to know others. Depressive anxiety is founded in concern or pining for object relations made from the intersubjective world. Not only does the external world become the internal one, but also the internal world can become more than what is received because there is a good enough other, someone nearby, a *Nebenmensch*. There are inklings of a new kind of pedagogy in Adorno's ([1967] 1998) last essay, "Education after Auschwitz," where he concluded that teaching and learning only begins by addressing subjective life at the level of intersubjectivity. It was from the ruins of a damaged education and his memories of a happy one that Adorno came to the cusp of restoration that joined the desire for education to a desire to become a new kind of person. The tension is that if the reliance upon some kind of clarity can be made from the ravaging of life, everything depends on whether an individual can want more: "In the attempt to prevent the repetition of Auschwitz it seems essential to me first of all to gain some clarity about the conditions under which manipulative character arises, and then, by altering those conditions to prevent as far as possible its emergence.... This could be done only if they would want to collaborate in the investigation of their own genesis" (199).

In our time, the relations among knowledge, self-reflection, social thought, working through the past for new conditions, movements for a warm pedagogy, and conditions for moral activity are themselves unstable and subject to social regression. Given the vehemence of social splitting, one may wonder what sort of clarity can come from the rubble of unresolved conflict and what conditions may be created for affiliation across differences. To ask who can want more is to begin from the intersubjective fact that institutions of public education are where strangers meet and where individuals can experience not only the nature of constructing knowledge but also feel transformative human nature with the passing of time. Probably for this reason Adorno's writing was deeply invested in the study of aesthetics—literature, music, myth, and poetry—as expressing life's affective struggles and the indeterminacy of becoming a thinking subject with others. But only if we want disquieting imagination can memory bear the psychical weighing of mental pain with the desire to revive the search for truth, justice, and beauty. In this sense, educators always work within and answer to the address of the emotional procedures for apprehending intersubjectivity. Perhaps the force and responsibility of learning as an emotional situation is our most difficult knowledge and the indeterminacy of knowing one's mental acts is only the tender for imagining a psychoanalytic subject that can change its mind (Bohleber 2010). As historical subjects, our challenge is to auscultate the freedom to feel, imagine, and learn from the significance, vulnerability, and fragility of intersubjective life. Warm pedagogy may be a tonic to the coldness of regression.

Chapter 4

On the Pains of Symbolization

In the work of mourning, it is not grief that works: grief keeps watch.
—Maurice Blanchot (1986), *The Writing of the Disaster* (51)

Presenting Difficulties

Word for word, *oppression* and *depression* signify loss of inner and outer worlds. They share misery, exclusion, disappearance, anxiety, and those feelings that sway between intractability and inevitability. Both create an emptiness of affective life that unnerves the primacy of the subject's capacity to communicate, belong, and desire thinking.[1] If, however, we speak of the oppressor and the oppressed as out there, assume knowledge of social and material causality, and if we acknowledge discrimination and hatred as both mental and social facts made to wreck thinking and disclaim the significance of everyday interactions, within recessive depression a catastrophe has already happened and no such external couple exists. The self is unfamiliar, even hated, and psychical representations fail, or rather, they collapse into themselves. And yet, by design, how difficult it is to separate the transit between oppression and depression. Indeed, those who seek clinical relief from the agonies of depression identify their feelings as oppressive, deadening, and persecutory, as if for no cause at all.[2] And as political situations fuse with emotional life and as emotional life must reference its history of loss, such anguish affects the imaginary, practices, and reception of psychoanalysis and education. Psychical and social loss marks our work, loss of self and other unconsciously impresses our understanding of transformation, and all of this affects what we can symbolize as becoming transformed.

My inquiry into the pain of symbolization focuses on the emotional work of coming to know the world of others through the passage of one's history of attachments to loved and hated objects. I lean on a psychoanalytic reading of Paulo Freire's *Pedagogy of the Oppressed* (1988) and his call for a radical humanization to release the hold of oppression, and a pedagogical reading of two of Melanie Klein's affecting theories animating mental life, "Love, Guilt and Reparation" (1937) and "Mourning and Its Relation to Manic-Depressive States" (1940), both written as the world slid ever deeper into war.[3] Freire and Klein's respective titles insist on the startles of love and hate. These affects are primary, driven, and immediate. They arrive before understanding and are founded by the radical situation of relationality. Not only are we utterly susceptible to impressive thought perceptions and phantasies of destroying and repairing the external world, we are also subjects of depression.

Klein and Freire agree that life itself already proposes the problem of emotional transformation whereby loss, depression, and mourning are elemental, although why this is the case, and indeed what the necessities of loss bring to the transformation of affects, symbolization, and the social bond, is far from clear. Together, they make an odd couple and, at first glance, seem only to present the distance between the clinic of psychoanalysis (anti-depression) and the politics of education (anti-oppression). When placed in dialogue, Klein's terms for the inner world of object relations and Freire's call for the restoration of interiority to change the world create new approaches to the pain of symbolization.

Freire and Mrs. Klein, as she was known, experienced the difficult life of exile, war, and diaspora, though they traveled differently through the disparities of gender, language, religion, culture, generation, and profession. These histories partly account for their commitment to linking thinking and symbolization to bodily processes for a new kind of mental freedom. Their work in the world with others may also account for their theories of symbolization. Each wrote compellingly of failures and progress in their practices; their work challenges the ideality, certainties, and externalizations of practitioners even as they addressed two influential sides of life that do have more in common than is typically admitted. Klein built her theories from the infant's earliest emotional situation of helplessness, dependency, and anxiety and saw these affects taking the shape of object relations. Freire's theories of pedagogy begin with the adult world, built from his work within adult communities of the oppressed, subject to forced dependency, colonialization, illiteracy, poverty, and the breakdown of the social bond. Generationally, I imagine them as separated grandparents affected by the intertwined and incomplete revolutions of twentieth century life: decolonization, education, human rights, sexual freedom, divorce, and psychoanalysis.

Freire's pedagogy proposes the paradox that, if words call upon anxiety, they may also break open uncanny reality. Klein proposed the opposite: anxiety calls upon the expressions of object-words. Klein (1930) works within the imaginary realm of "unreal reality," or phantasies, as presenting the urgency of bodily drives attaching to (lost) objects, prior to words (221). She begins with two assumptions on the nature of life: birth ushers the infant into its emotional situation and the adult mind has its roots in infancy. Our earliest anxiety situations over loss of the breast, loss of love, and fear of annihilation, Klein speculated, create needed psychical defenses such as projection, introjection, omnipotence, splitting into good and bad, ideality, denial, and identification, all thought perceptions that are both constitutive of the mind and, at first, function *as if* they are emissaries from reality. She understood this early rushing anxiety as oscillating between the paranoid-schizoid and depressive positions. Klein then made a novel claim: our prehistory of loss and separation, beginning with the loss of the breast and felt as inexplicable and inchoate, becomes the basis for phantasy, then imagination, and eventually, for our capacity to think and symbolize self and other without having to deny the frustrations, losses, and uncertainties reality entails. Yet the frustrations do not disappear, and for this reason, symbolizing the world comes with a measure of pain or depressive anxiety. The pain of symbolization, then, is our plight and lifeline.

Admitting objections to the naming of affecting matters through to their unconscious impressions, however, animates moral anxiety. The worry is that in turning to the subject's inner world as the basis for relating to external reality, matters of historical reality, consciousness, and political life will be pushed aside and people, rather than the conditions they face, will be deemed pathological and dissolved into diagnosis. For both Klein and Freire, environmental, social, material, maternal, cultural, and political provisions of care and choice serve as elemental scaffolds for expressions of mourning and melancholia. Each provision carries the pathos of our incompleteness, our attitudes toward need and fulfillment, and the contradictions and conflicts of worldly affairs. But without an address to the inner world and a vocabulary of giving and losing that invites our dreams and fears, and our loves and hates, representations of both the self and exteriority collapse into meaninglessness. Indeed, both Freire and Klein insist on the transformative effects of symbolization from the inside out.

Depression

What then is this prehistory of loss and how does it repeat over a lifetime?[4] Freud's (1917b) metapsychology, "Mourning and Melancholia," remains a touchstone for psychoanalysis and now for cultural theory's turn to affect, the body, and social grief. His speculations are as much about the self's compulsion for introjection and identification with the lost object as they are about the functions of internalization and the ego's splitting in defense against loss. When a beloved object is lost, there is a comparable diminishment of psychical life. In both mourning and melancholia, the ego recedes from the world and becomes caught in a painful, persecutory negation that the object is not gone. Within "the crushed state of melancholia," Freud wrote, "the shadow of the object fell upon the ego" (248–249). The loss is incorporated or, as we would say today, the situation of loss is internalized. The only distinction Freud gives between the work of mourning and melancholia is that in melancholia, while the ego knows what is lost in the world, there is no awareness of what has been lost in the self. This is the case, Freud thought, because the incorporated object has taken over the ego, so to speak, and spit it into warring parts. Here the ego is itself an object relation and with the idea of mourning, Freud introduces the problem of identification with the lost object and the splitting of the ego. In a contemporary view, H. Shmuel Erlich (2024) specifies the encompassing challenge for the ego in times of loss, both conscious and unconscious: "The central issue and theme for humanity is not mere awareness, which can be gained and dismissed, but responsibility" (116). Loss, Freud supposed, can only be made significant through the work of mourning, and an acknowledgment and response that involves new investments in memory, symbolization, and interests in an unknown world. Mourning is highly symbolic work for readmission to the external world and a frame for what the pain of symbolization involves.

What then is it to listen to loss? Freud's (1914b) advice to psychoanalysts can be read as referring depression and oppression to his technical concept of "working through resistances" (155). He does not provide us with any pedagogy of the depressed. The analyst, Freud advised, must give up "the attempt to bring a particular moment or problem into focus. He contents himself with studying whatever is present for the time being on the surface of the patient's mind" (147). Within the slow mutual back and forth of free association, the psychoanalyst invites desire. Two types of emancipations for libido occur: emancipation from the dictates of external authority dedicated to the destruction of the self's desire to symbolize, imagine, and care for the social bond and, simultaneously, a psychical emancipation from the grip of internal persecutors that fragment the self and the world. Emancipation is never complete; constructions of memory continue to oscillate between the things done and the things yet to come.[5]

The oddest question Freud (1917b) raised in "Mourning and Melancholia" is why the loss of the object is so painful. Klein provides an answer as she imagines the earliest grief from the side of the infant. Mourning is painful because we have experienced the profundity of loss of love before. She turns to the situation of weaning, a primary separation that serves as her first model for depression, where loss of the breast is thought of as the infant's sense of persecutory anxiety. She deems weaning to be our earliest emotional situation that calls upon infantile defenses against frustration, just at the point when the premature ego is unable to tolerate "the task of mastering the severest anxiety" (1930, 220). The loss of the breast is akin to the experience of the adult's work of mourning and melancholia. Yet for Klein something more occurs. Losing the breast creates the lost object and then gradually gives way to a new relation: the desire for symbols and an awareness of the other. Identification, at first dependent upon merging and likeness, becomes "a forerunner for symbolization" (220).

Ten years later, Klein's (1940) "Mourning and Its Relation to Manic-Depressive States" lays emphasis on the mourner's reconstruction of the relational internal world as opposed to Freud's view on the ego's decathexis to death. One not only slowly comes to accept the loss: Returning to the world of others reanimates the experience of grief and feelings of being left behind. Klein departs from Freud with her claim that mourning resuscitates "the depressive position" first established with the breast in infancy. Her emphasis is on the destiny of early anxiety situations felt again in the mourner's heartache and despair over losing their good internal and external objects. Loss returns one to likeness, and in Klein's (1940) view,

> The pain experienced in the slow process of testing reality in the work of mourning thus seems to be partly due to the necessity, not only to renew the links to the external world and

thus continuously re-experience loss, but at the same time and by means of [loss] to rebuild with anguish the inner world, which is felt to be in danger of deteriorating and collapsing. Just as the young child passing through the depressive position is struggling, in his unconscious mind, with the task of establishing and integrating his inner world, so the mourner goes through the pain of re-establishing and reintegrating it. (354)

Divergences

The emotional situation of having to think draws Freire and Klein closer and while each of their theories analyzes the fear of language with views on dependency and relationality, their common words such as *internalization, castration, anxiety, guilt, depression,* and even *dependency* carry dissimilar experiences of the apprehension of loss. They diverge on the situation, origin, and destiny of relationality. I understand their difference as emerging from an on-going dilemma of meeting others in the work of taking in new objects. Klein's exemplary couple is the infant meeting the mother's breast while the mother gives (and loses) her breast for the infant. Freire poses this couple through relations between teacher and student, where the teacher too gives and loses what she or he most values: the good breast pedagogy. So, there is a kernel of continuity that belongs to these two sides of life. It may boil down to whether the teacher/mother remembers a novel relationality once upon a time, and can still be responsive to questioning freedom and capable of noticing its strangulations. It may boil down to the teacher of any gender accepting maternal transferences and responsiveness of warm care without malicious envy. Yet the divergence between Freire and Klein does not simply reside in spans of life or even that of relational developments. It begins with the question of how and why the outside world becomes like an internal world and then how introjection, identification, and projection render the boundaries of the self and other as porous and antagonistic.

Freire sought the adult's apperception of historical reality that he argued is the basis of consciousness of human relations. Klein invested in the unconscious fate of the prehistory of infancy and then had to cast her lot with the early phantasies that constitute the mental oscillations she eventually named as the paranoid-schizoid and the depressive positions. Freire too pointed to a Manichean world of terrible splitting and projective identification as he worked his way toward a dialogic pedagogy that, for the sake of creating a thinking world, can tolerate the dissonance of working through the compulsion to repeat suffering, injustice, and cultural invasiveness. His great topic was liberation as tied to a critical pedagogy for freeing the mind from the persecuting orders of worldly others and the dehumanizing history of colonization. His interest was with the human subject as a process of humanization and often argued that the term "object" could only signify an objectification of the subject.

Klein, however, considered "objects" as mental representations of loving and hated relationships, beginning with the breast, and with her theory of object relations, as forming the mind and its functions. Introjections, projections, and identifications multiply object relations that then become the basis for our emotional situations and their sources of anxiety, phantasy, and defenses over loss of love. For Klein, the most devastating defense is the denial of psychical reality that she believed could be found in inhibitions in education, family, and creative arts. She built her theories of development not from a culture of silence, as did Freire, but from where we all begin within the wordless helplessness of infancy, bereft of historical reality. While spectacular in dependency, the infant, Klein argued, is readily engaged in an emotional situation of object relating. In taking in the object, the growing infant wants to know what is inside. The tiny creature begins her epistemophilia with a desire for the good breast along with an inchoate primal agitation, frustration, depressive irritation, and hatred and fear of bad objects.

Symbolic Equation as Defense

If we are subject to the force fields of depression and oppression, how then are we ever able to think of these situations and symbolize loss? In Klein's (1935) view, only with numerous anxiety situations over what to do and why: "To quote only a few of them: there is anxiety how to put the bits together in the right way and at the right time; how to pick out the good bits and do away with the bad ones; how to bring the object to life when it has been put together; and there is the anxiety of being interfered with in this task by bad objects and by one's own hatred, etc." (269). While Klein did not make this leap, with Freire, affect also belongs to the pedagogy of adult literacy. The confusions Klein summarized also give us a picture of the anxieties of learning to read. These anxieties are heightened when instructions reduce words to the decoding of letters, to the sounding out of part objects before the struggle for meaning can begin, and when instructors ignore the terror of confronting signs without knowing why. Reading, after all, is about putting things together.

Klein found anxiety as somehow linked to the work of tethering thoughts to what presents as inexplicable disasters. For Freire, thinking too emerges from a painful confrontation with how the world affects mental life and involves a twofold relation: (1) dissembling emotional attitudes that disparage literacy, intellectual processes, sexuality, and social change and (2) consciousness of social structures and social relations of inequality as historically created and as situations that can change.

Untethered thoughts, at least for Klein and her colleague Hanna Segal (1952), begin the bare stirrings of a needed defense against the unknown. Through the psychical mechanism of projective identification, the compulsion to send out parts of ourselves into the world is a prelude to as well as a quality of transformation. Klein's model for thinking about projective identification is the child at play who bestows inanimate objects with their frustrations of life. At first as defensive structure, language is treated as physicality. The child is on the verge of another weaning, itself an anxiety situation. If language is not unhinged from the confines of the thing, if the body remains an empire, the self has no means for transforming phantasy into imagination and language play, needed to become a creator of symbolization.

Klein also names the mash-up of psychical and external reality as symbolic equation, a melancholic identification whereby concrete objects become fused with functions of the mind.[6] In his study of the enigma of schizophrenia, Christopher Bollas (2015) suggests that the procedures of symbolic equation are a defense against a terrible invasion and thus serve to eliminate the alterity of the object and the self: "The word stands in for the thing, the thing stands in for the function of the personality, hence the word stands for the personality function. To use the name of the object is therefore very nearly the same as physically handling it" (131). And to physically handle the word is either to crush it or become crushed by it. Such feelings of despair over introjections are one account of why reading is hated and why symbolic equation should be thought of as the subjective basis stereotypical thought and for collapsing the other's identity into the disparagement of whole groups of people.

Anxieties

Klein (1946) theorizes anxiety through its dispersals, stated most emphatically in "Notes on Some Schizoid Mechanisms": "The feeling of being disintegrated, of being unable to experience emotions, of losing one's objects, is in fact the equivalent of anxiety" (21). She specifies an emptying out and a taking in with her two positions of anxiety that she thinks of as constituting the mind: the paranoid-schizoid position dedicated to splitting and self-preservation, and the depressive position oriented to care of the self and the other. Klein understood anxiety as "phantasies," or delegates for bodily drives (satiation, frustration, and aggression) that function as a constellation of defenses against fear of annihilation. For the infant, the nature of panic over loss lends unreasonable reason to the earliest splitting of the object relation into the good and bad breast, felt as love against hate. Between three and six months of age, the infant perceives the world of whole objects that help usher feelings of ambivalence. Only gradually do we become subject to the pain of integration, an admission of the mind's oscillations, a coming feature of the work of mourning and symbolization and, by nature, integration is always incomplete.

Susan Isaacs (1952), a colleague of Klein, gave us a picture: "the mind as a small society of relations to objects" (38). Isaacs identified the dilemma with the notion of phantasy as constituting the mind: we "deny to psychical reality its *own objectivity as a mental fact*" (81, emphasis original). For this reason, Isaacs proposed the fraught relation between phantasies and words: "At first, the whole weight of wish and fantasy is borne by sensation and affect" (92). Words, Isaac thought, follow along the lines of phantasy, and phantasy always has to do with the body: "pains and pleasures directed to objects of some kind" (99). Both pleasure and hostility are projected onto objects in the world and the processes of introjection and projection serve Isaacs's key claim: "*The external physical world is in fact libidinized largely through the process of symbol formation*" (110, emphasis original). Recall that Freud's discussion on mourning as a working through homed in on the freeing of libido to restore our world.

How then does libidinal reach grow capacious when the world is so subject to destruction? Kristeva (2001) raised the interminable question in her discussion of Klein: "Under what conditions are the anxieties that tear us apart amenable to symbolization? That is the question that Klein uses as she reformulates the analytic problem, a question that places her work—unwittingly so since she was most notably a courageous clinician and in no way a 'master of thought'—at the heart of humanity and the modern crisis of culture" (14).

Dialogue: Inner and Outer

The difficulty of dialogue, a key condition for opening Freire's pedagogical project, also belongs to the psychoanalytic situation, though the clinical dialogue proposes the problem of the analyst's transference with free association and empty thoughts. Listening does not occur without the conflict of counter-transference, and the analyst must wean herself from education's goals. For Freire, dialogue can contain the shock of unexpected replies, provided that the educator weans herself from treating knowledge as a possession to dispense. I understand dialogue through the allegory of the pain of weaning and so as the capacity to tolerate the frustration of not understanding and of having to lose preordained meaning while questioning the wish to know and the meeting of the unknown.

Dialogue thus contains an intimate dimension and even an intrinsic irritation that cannot be extricated from intersubjective life, though what is personal can be denied, diminished, silenced, and rendered useless. Green's (1999) discussion, "On the Edge," admitted the startling complications of psychoanalytic listening and speaking. The human is utterly affected and subject to paralysis: "According to psychoanalysis, whichever side of the couch one is on, man is conceived of essentially in relation to the disorder which is intrinsic to the human condition and which, in certain cases, may develop in such a way that the person who is going through it has the feeling that the incredibly complicated consequences resulting from it cannot be solved through the means, opportunities or situations which he has at his disposal during his life" (258). Dialogue can both contain and question the limits of knowledge, experience, and relations to authority, love, and desire and be felt as unbearable and invasive. The vulnerabilities of symbolization are affected by a certain discord that escapes consciousness and returns as the oppressed or as fatalism that nothing can change. Freire (1988) proposes the interminable problem and its illnesses: "While the problem of humanization has always, from an axiological point of view, been man's central problem, it now takes on the character of an inescapable concern. Concern for humanization leads at once to the recognition of dehumanization, not only as an ontological possibility but as an historical reality. . . . Both humanization and dehumanization are possibilities for man as an uncompleted being conscious of his incompletion" (27).

Klein's (1930) "inescapable concern," anxiety—of a being ill at ease—births something terribly human: phantasies, identification, symbolic equation, and the symbolization of incompleteness. Her description begins with the terrors of losing organs and the fate of destruction:

> Since the child desires to destroy the organs (penis, vagina, breasts), which stand in for the objects, he conceives a dread of the latter. This anxiety contributes to make him equate the organs in question with other things; owing to this equation these in their turn become objects of anxiety, and so he is impelled constantly to make other and new equations, which form the basis of his interest in the new objects and of symbolism. Thus, not only does symbolism come to be the foundation of all phantasy and sublimation but, more than that, it is the basis of the subject's relation to the outside world and to reality in general. (220–221)

What does dialogue open if psychical reality and historical reality are always in an uneven and conflictive relation and what is opened if the line between consciousness and the unconscious is far more porous than waking life admits? If psychical reality is the basis of our incompleteness, and much is unconscious, and if historical reality is tied to consciousness, memory, and forgetting and thus more than brute facticity, then dialogue opens with the pain of symbolization as an experience of working through anxiety and its seemingly relentless personifications.

Whereas public dialogue exhibits noise, conflict, and confusion, the state of internal dialogue, such as found in dreams and in thinking, is clandestine. What is internal? Alix Strachey's (1941) "A Note on the Use of the Word 'Internal' " argues that while the word is commonplace, there are at least three different experiences conveyed. First, *internal* is used as a metaphor for functions, structures, and workings of the mind. Strachey links the term *internal* to defense mechanisms, states of mind, imaginative processes, free-floating and invasive or persecutory thought-feelings, and even dreams. A second use lays stress on the objects, situations, and events that go on to make the imagination. As fictions or phantasies, they seem to run with parallel feelings projected to the external world and introjected into the internal world. Strachey's third use comes closest to Freire's sense of an oppressor housed within the oppressed. Situations, events, and other people are felt to be inside the body, gnawing imagoes that are frightening, persecutory, schizoid, and insistent. With the third use, we are within Klein's (1935) formulation of the paranoid-schizoid position where the world and the self are in bits and pieces.

Pedagogy's Depressive Position

We can conceive of both psychoanalysis and education as a treatment of thought, language, and desire. The challenge of education, however, as Freire (1988) argues, turns on affiliation and whether there can become a social bond created from the ravages of experience with others: "Pedagogy makes oppression and its causes objects of reflection by the oppressed, and from this reflection will come their necessary engagement in the struggle for their liberation" (33). His method of treating key words as unlocking consciousness to its existential activity for new demands continues to influence diverse struggles such as patients' rights, LGBTQ politics, feminism, teacher education, national liberation, and the education of the human professions. Before these struggles, however, are the painful predicaments of acknowledging loss and disassembling the defenses of symbolic equation. Freire supposes that education, amidst these conflicts and given its history, is itself conflictive.

Thinking with Klein's notion of the depressive position, I find the means for a warm pedagogy: from the beginning of life there is always already an affected and affecting interiority that wants more of the world. On these terms, the fragmenting of the ego already supposes that the ego and the other exist, not as causality but as a matrix of intersubjectivity: psychical life beholden to the other. Indeed, it may be said that the infant faced with weaning and separation first experiences the stirrings of the depressive position, perhaps a response to the mother's giving and losing of the breast. And if this concern for the other with self is disturbed, if the self is confined by symbolic equation, then the depressive position, so needed for anyone's symbolization as a subject, dissolves into a paranoid-schizoid world.

Freire and Klein developed the claim that putting together a fragmented world includes the self's deep awareness of two sides: what tears it apart and what it tears apart without knowing why. On the one side, radical relationality. On the other side, radical responsibility. Their vocabulary on these matters differs and can conflict in the sensate world of temporality, gender, development, and idiom. For Freire, it is the struggle for national liberation, and for Klein, it is concern for the internal world and a liberation from persecutory superego demands. Together they bring pedagogy and psychoanalysis a measure of resignation due, in part, to over-determination, to the unconscious, to the oscillating paranoid-schizoid and depressive positions, to human incompleteness, and to accepting the slow work of symbolizing the aftereffects of a history of loss agonized both by structurally induced impoverishment and injustice and by fear of vulnerability and dependency. I place the interminable work of mourning and melancholia within these inner and outer dialogues on love and its loss. My claim follows from a psychoanalytic paradox on the fate of inchoate loss: constellations of attachment to loss met by its social and psychical disavowal render inexpressible the work of mourning and drive its internal and external expressions into meaninglessness. Grief calls upon symbolic equation (a collapse of subject and object) and the pain of symbolization (the depressive position as contingency without certainty).

The idea of education for liberation will have to be rethought and, at the very least, serve as a challenge to the educator's paranoid-schizoid anxieties and its defenses of idealization and symbolic equation. The educator's depressive position involves her/his pain of symbolization with an abiding cathexis to constitutive human helplessness, vulnerability, and dependency. There are, to quote from Steven Cooper (2016), "melancholic errands" (47).[7] The pedagogue and analyst are affected. Side by side, each wander into transference thickets between the psychical and the social and between what has happened and what is yet to come. Even our interpretations carry traces of inchoate loss, along with attempts to auscultate the heart. We are back as well to Kristeva's (2001) pressing question in her discussion now directed to the terrible uncertainties and violence of our own time: "Under what conditions are the anxieties that tear us apart amenable to symbolization?" (14). And then, "under what conditions," and without being "a master of thought," do we lean upon the work of symbolizing humanization?

Chapter 5

Before and after Misogyny

In the Spring 2016, the Toronto Advanced Training Program in Psychoanalytic Psychotherapy held its 44th Scientific Meeting on the topic "Misogyny in the Clinic." Immediately, those present were asked to think of the destiny of hatred of women, girls, and femininity as unconsciously impressing the analyst's education, practices, and our discussions. The request was to understand the history of our thinking and analyze how our clinical imaginary is affected by normative, sociocultural, familial, and personal idealizations and disparagements of femininity, masculinity, sexuality, and gender spectrums. In terms of the politics of education, the meeting resulted from the demands of students and analysts participating in the training program to open the parameters of the clinic with the crucial question of how the psychoanalytic field is also affected by movements of civil and human rights, social conflicts, and the contemporary therapeutic imaginary that follows from the existential critiques of psychic life proposed by feminism, decolonization, queer theory, critical race theory, and transsexuality. From these views, thinking is at once pedagogical, existential, anthropological, political, and biographical. Being in the world, then, is to be taken personally and as a perspective that also insists that our relationship to ourselves is the most difficult relation for us all.

Our presenter, Dr. Leticia Glocer Fiorini, a senior training psychoanalyst of the Argentina Psychoanalytic Association, is internationally known for her pioneering books and papers on affecting psychoanalysis with new theories of sexuality, gender, and social thought. Ironically, her research is not typically considered to be central to the education and training of clinicians (2007; 2017). Her discussion raised the urgent question, "Are psychotherapists immune from misogyny?" (2016, n.p.). The answers involved wide-ranging critical assessments of how the psychotherapeutic field enacts mechanisms of sexual and gender normalization through theory, through transmission of paternalistic social attitudes, through cultural prejudices, through the history of psychoanalysis, through clinical education, through modes of diagnosis, through techniques of listening and interpretation, and through public perceptions of why to have therapy at all. What then is to be undone?

Dr. Glocer Fiorini's main communication was that meta-theories of social, political, cultural, and psychical life carry on the ego's defenses of splitting through binary logic, idealization of the phallus, and, in the context of the clinic, through the imposition of authoritarian relations of power and control. Glocer Fiorini answered her initial question: No one is immune from the insidious social pathologies of misogyny. Glocer Fiorini proposed on-going efforts to reconceptualize sexual difference beyond binary splitting of femininity from masculinity. I was a respondent to her presentation and my inquiry now traces the temporalities, sequences, and receptions of misogyny with an interest in the education of analysts. Given the contentions, obstacles, and ambiguities of its naming, I ask, *What comes before and after misogyny?*

Disturbances

Misogyny involves us all in urgent and seemingly intractable conflicts within gender and sexual relations that, for both life and the clinic, present as difficult, challenging, disturbing, and painful to address since we must speak of hatred of feminine bodies along with phantasies of disgust and shame for human origin. How may we intervene within the claustrum of misogyny and transform practices of education and psychotherapy, particularly because the pain of symbolizing the advent and vicissitudes of such destruction is a disturbance to narrative cohesion and requires on-going self and social analysis? Indeed, all at once, the disclaimed emotional logic of misogyny erases the subject. After all, misogyny is the destruction of the birthing of human meaning: by word and action, by family, upbringing, and education, and by institutional and cultural designs of inequality, discrimination, and denial. Anyone is subject to attacks and to attacking those fragile links to singularity, freedom, dependency, autonomy, and, perhaps most of all, to the mother who gives life. Motherhood, as Jacqueline Rose (2018) puts it, "is the place where we lodge, or rather bury, the reality of our own conflicts" (1). But motherhood is also our fact of existence and where each of us begins.

Narrative disturbances emerge in any attempt to admit the fate of broken relations from birth and speak of those strangulated affects that drive pernicious misogyny. There is neither a single entrance point of discussion nor an exhaustive account of misogyny's condensations, displacements, substitutions, distortions, and regressions. As a hatred of bodily life and thinking and as an attack on linking, misogyny somehow confirms itself, collapsing psychical procedures of splitting, projective identification, envy, and denial with the cultural functions of exclusion, degradation, and sexual violence. In trying to speak of misogyny, ontological difficulties challenge the very possibility of understanding, relationality, and communication as we know them (Pitt and Britzman 2015). And our constructions, too, are subject to the symbolic collapse of nature and culture, leaving only a seething morass of denial and hatred of psychical reality. Misogyny destroys our capacity for depression, freedom, and imagination. We must then ask, how does symbolic equation, or the collapse of difference between subject and object, leave us with the affectivity that feeds on and sustains misogyny? And how do we work through the rigidities, instructions, and defenses as searches for emotional freedom necessary for new mental constructions of the right to embodied existence?

At the most elemental level, misogyny is a revolt against life itself, and life comes before misogyny. Mass rape, sexual enslavement, humiliation, burning, disfigurement, the murder of women and girls, and attacks against transgendered and queer people are misogyny's obscenities. Its aftermath leaves survivors and those who can witness such socially induced and denied terror with traumatic grief. Our age of worldwide wars and failed states, of global displacement and masses of stateless people, of the burning of libraries, schools, and hospitals, of the destruction of art and the censorship of ideas, and the assassinations of journalists, human rights activists, lawyers, teachers, and students brings us to ask, as the political theorist Arendt (1993) asked, why are human rights, as the right to have rights, so disparaged? Some of us are brought to relate the failure of human rights as fuel for misogyny.

Even as I gesture toward crimes against humanity, the tension between the one and the many blows away the question, *What now?* We seem better prepared to list an avalanche of failures and find ourselves rehearsing a litany of despair, just as the opening of this chapter did, as if to convince ourselves and those who turn away that destruction does hold terrible significance for how anyone can live. And in these excruciating accountings, helplessness overtakes understanding while individual stories slip away. The complexity of defending the inner world is shoved aside and then so too are efforts in analyzing everyday dissociation and doubts over meaning. How do we find the words to say that in body and spirit, we too are affected? Can we, too, imagine the location of culture, as D. W. Winnicott ([1967] 2001) imagined through "the potential space between individual and environment"? (100). If misogyny is so unrecognized in our own work, how, as Dr. Glocer Fiorini asks, "is it possible to detect something that is also naturalized in the psychotherapist?" (2016, n.p.).

Dr. Glocer Fiorini's urgent questions also belong to the fraying of education and lead me to treat subterranean misogyny through two intertwined psychoanalytic temporalities that constitute revisions of psychical life, memory, and the potential space of education: themes of "before" and "after." These conceptions of time and sequence draw from psychoanalytic thinking on the paradoxes of temporality known as deferred action and delay in meaning, or more technically, memory as an activity of *Nachträglichkeit* that signifies the psychical belatedness of apprehending the first event (what happened before conscious apprehension) that is already overwritten by the second event (the struggle of creating meaning from what comes after). "Before" and "after" references the psychical operations of revision and forms the basis for symbolizing both the fallout of representation and the aftereffects of witnessing as expressed in literature, pedagogy, and psychoanalysis (Felman and Laub 1992). Since I am mainly addressing the problem of education, near the conclusion of my discussion I suggest the ties between thinking and reading. I ask two questions. First, what sort of thinking can we manage if we can imagine the question, *What comes before thinking?* Second, what can it mean to think after misogyny?

What Sort of Thinking Before Thinking?

Misogyny sutures ideologies of desire with pathological stupidity: as negation, its confusion of libidinal ties provokes ideality and its disparagement; and through denial, misogyny conceals its aggression through phantasies of fusion and exclusion. Such woeful disregard may be at work in our clinic and classrooms. Dr. Glocer Fiorini's critique is that our clinical work is badly compromised when we ignore, deny, or diminish the contentions, disagreements, contradictions, and uncertainties within the psychoanalytic field as tied to the larger world of political rights and spheres of domesticity, community, culture, language, and nation.

So, what are we analyzing when we negate? For the literary critic Lyndsey Stonebridge (2015), the analysis of negation, in her insightful discussion, "Statelessness and the Poetry of the Borderline: André Green, W.H. Auden and Yousif M. Qasmiyeh," begins with thinking of what is not there, surely a work of poetry and a situation of political displacement, as much as it is a view of psychoanalysis. New thinking, Stonebridge writes, "is not a once and for all narrative moment in the development of the ego. . . . We cannot recall that first scene of taking in and spitting out or that judgment and separation. Negation must be grasped retrospectively as an act of thought that has to acknowledge not just the 'no,' but the state of merging that preceded it" (1337). Perhaps that first scene can only be recalled by way of its negation. Freud (1925b) handled negation as a technique of ego defense, met by the analyst's way of listening to desire by taking away the "no." Negation is a partial lifting of repression. But look who is pushed away. The "no" refers to someone and the thought is discounted, giving novel meaning to the phrase "never mind." Freud introduces negation with a patient's response to the analyst's question: "You ask who this person in the dream can be. It's *not* my mother" (235). The time of negation is almost unreachable since the mother's act of giving and taking away her breast creates the infant's experience of presence and absence. Both are needed. Klein took the relation of negation further back, to a time before, where "no" comes to partly signify the depth of our lost impressions of the earliest object, namely the emotional relationship with the breast, the cause and project of our earliest anxiety situation. The sentence might be, *Oh no! It can't be true that the breast was taken from me.* Klein's (1959) main idea was to root infancy in the adult mind, perhaps still shocking for those who treat adulthood as a progressive development away from one's earliest and most helpless prehistory. The negation, then, is directed at the maternal environment, provisions for the infant's dependency, helplessness, fusion, and love and, significantly, the founding relation from which selves emerge. This environmental provision also involves the autonomy of the mother, who must disillusion omnipotence, her own and that of the baby. Indeed, the thinking that comes before thinking is beholden to a curious fusion and nondifferentiation as an infantile contingency and sustained by the maternal mind, body, and spirit and then taken away. That is, at a primal level, the regressed emotional logic that fuels the vehemence of misogyny erupts from the paranoid anxiety that something of mine is being taken away.

Klein considered anxiety as a contingency of loss of love and as separation anxiety. Such foundational loss, she argued, is the basis for the self's aggression and its source of two mental positions or orienting phantasies that compose psychical life and where love and hate of the maternal imaginary play their part. Whereas the paranoid-schizoid position expels frustration, splits the object into good or bad, and creates the talisman principle of attack and revenge from this phantasy of persecution, the depressive position emerges as beholden to thoughts of the other, a pining for lost love and a position of ambivalence needed to link good with bad. The depressive position is an area of concern for the self and other accompanied by the desire to repair what phantasy has destroyed.

Sometimes, the negation comes as bare sentence. I'm thinking of six-year-old Erna, one of Klein's (1932) young Berlin patients. In their first session, Erna tells Mrs. Klein, "There is something about life I do not like" (35). It is an extraordinary sentence made from the pathos of six years of life. Erna's play, Klein interpreted, was filled with the warring factions of object relations in despair and enacted with small toys as delegates of violent scenarios of murder, revenge, and manic triumphalism. With Erna, Klein had to create a new kind of story made from her play technique that both called upon anxiety, phantasies, and defenses and somehow still invited new conditions for becoming, also understood as the depressive position dedicated to the links among freedom, imagination, and care of self with others (Britzman 2016).

What Stories Today?

Rose's (2014) *Women in Dark Times* proposes that we need more than new stories that can tell us what the old ones destroy. Our work is to create the conditions for political imagination that involves sorting through the rubble of lies and idealizations that cut thinking short. Rose considers the pain of integration when she argues for "a scandalous feminism, one which embraces without inhibition the most painful, outrageous aspects of the human heart, giving them their place at the very core of the world that feminism wants to create" (ix). And the scandal is a turn to the agency of the subject in confrontation with the constraints of compliance, violence, and denial. With great courage Rose returns to the historicity of history and just at the point where women's lives serve as warning signals for the dangers faced and as a challenge to the erasures and lies of national pasts. Her cases are built from a history of the reception, creativity, affiliation, and transference to women such as Rosa Luxemburg, Marilyn Monroe, and Charlotte Salomon, and to Shafilea Ahmed, Heshu Yones, and Fadime Sahindal on the horrors of honor killing. "It is time," Rose demands, "to return to what feminism has to tell us . . . to make the case for what women have uniquely to say about the perils of our modern world" (ix).

And the perils of both the said and the unsaid in our world are exponential. Ken Corbett's (2016) *A Murder Over a Girl* is a psychoanalytic report on the *real* of racial and gendered school violence where unspeakable things are enacted, where misunderstanding is mistaken for belief, and where presence is felt as too much. Readers are left with more questions on what is most inexpressible within enactments of phantasies of destruction. Corbett's study is at once crime reportage of a fourteen-year-old white boy's murder of a fifteen-year-old brown boy who had just begun to identify as a girl, Leticia, and a psychoanalytic mediation on the profundity of social failure, the confusion of bodies, and the breakdown of potential space. The murder occurred February 2008 in a first-period junior high school English class in Oxnard, California, a day after the fourteen-year-old white boy, walking in a school hallway, may have become unhinged with the question of the fifteen-year-old brown girl, Leticia, who may have said to him in passing, "What's up baby?" Was this an address of passion and a calling out? Was this the unspeakable thing spoken? And can one know what was in either of their minds just before all had to be lost?

The murder had already occurred when Corbett arrived. Day after day Corbett sat in the court room of the murder trial, listening to lawyers, witnesses, and the judge. He interviewed parents, teachers, and adolescents about what each had seen, felt, and missed in their respective attempts to make sense of a senseless murder. Readers face what is ordinarily terrible and terribly ordinary: the town's symbolic equation that "boys will be boys" as justification or perhaps as naturalization for inchoate gender rage. Gender violence is never just that and Corbett's analysis opens onto the larger context: violence as the aftermath of corrosive poverty, the disorders of racism, sexism, homophobia, and transphobia, and the negligence, hostilities, and negations of education to find any meaning in distress, ambivalence, or desire.

Those few townspeople who supported and joined with Leticia were treated as abettors. Many blamed those who loved Leticia as the cause of her murder. There was the female teacher who had given Leticia the gift of a dress and a lesbian teacher who complained to the school administration of homophobia. There were adolescent girls who took pleasure in Leticia's happiness. And there were other boys who tried to ease the growing tension. Yet the volatility of ideologies of hatred played out in school life refracted the psychological failures and the turning away that accrue from family and community indifference. Beneath the indifference one finds the chaos of and defense against helplessness. Corbett's layered narrative is unsettled by a conflict of stories lived by boys and girls, teachers and parents, and principals and judges. Who is the girl? In the wasteland that is murder, meaning is killed off, lives are lost, desire is ruined, and reasons only sustain paranoid logic and conspiracy. The families, teachers, welfare system, and other young adolescents were all involved in what none of them could think, namely the collusion of gender transitions and libidinal desires with the tragic failure of erotic imaginations. Corbett deftly analyzes the slow unfolding of this classroom and courtroom crime scene and how the passion for denial, on the part of the adults in the town, sustained a fantastical hostility toward gender variability aggravated on one side with rumors, magical thinking, and blunt paranoia, and on the other side with the ideality stew of masculinity excited by the attractions of gun culture, Nazism, hardness, and fear and loathing of queer love.

Our clinic, whether of psychotherapy or education, is challenged to be responsive to social revolutions that demand new ways of relating and thinking. We are, after all, intimately affected by gender fluidity, queer sexualities, choice, and invention. There are new words to learn and more rights to create, all of which have to do with the entanglement of bodily lives. When the world of others matters, we encounter more than what any one of us can know, including what Kristeva (1995) termed as "new maladies of the soul" tied to human desire in conflict with its limits. Our clinics, whether for psychotherapy or the classroom, are charged with responding to situations that we cannot anticipate but that nonetheless bring our thinking to a crossroad.

"Fugitive States"

Once again, what sort of thinking comes before thinking? In one of his last and perhaps most compact papers directed to psychoanalysts, "An Outline of Psychoanalysis" (1940a), Freud turns to the ego's fragile boundaries and so to consciousness as "fugitive states" (159). "What is conscious," Freud wrote, "is conscious only for a moment" (159). The self is always in contiguity with influences of the past, the unconscious, the imperatives and aggressions of the drives, and the entanglements of cultural histories of love and hate, first conveyed by the phantasies and prohibitions of family life, later as expressions of superego and cultural anxiety, and, with phantasies of education, subject to professional and religious idealities. As borderline creature, this bodily ego, as projection of its own surface, is affected by its anticipation of reception in the world of others. If early on, Freud described the unconscious as the empire of omnipotence, by the end of his life his "Outline" left us with something new: "The process of something becoming conscious is above all linked with the perceptions which our sense organs receive from the external world" (161). Even if we intellectually know that perception does not equate with reality and even if we sometimes know that the internal world of others is largely unknown, these mismatches and their tendency to collapse characterize the broken heart of gender and sexuality. As a means of defense against so much uncertainty, the body, Freud wrote, can "take the place of the external world" (161). Klein made the same assessment when she identified weaning as a crisis for symbolization. Phantasies of taking the place of the world also mean that the body becomes its own omnipotent empire. When the difference of the world disappears, all that is left is the urgency of inchoate and aggressive drives and with terrifying negations: no potential space, no other, no alterity, no otherness, no enigma, and no interpretation.

Bion (1993) took a further step. Becoming conscious requires an apparatus to think. Otherwise, there is only "a thought without a thinker" (165), or a bodily urge without the containment of mind. Bion writes, "I shall use the term 'thought' to the mating of a preconception with a frustration. The model I propose is that of an infant whose expectation of a breast is mated with a relation of no breast available for satisfaction" (111). Bion references our most intimate education, the mother's capacity for reverie, containing the infant's agonies and returning manageable experience. His formulation is that thinking is a retroactive experience that contains or translates thoughts, which he saw as frustrations. Thinking is our afterward. From this requirement of breast and no breast, or preconception, frustration, and absence, we can learn to accept the meeting of emotional and mental constructions, or what Klein (1932) understood as the emotional situation of symbol formation. In different terms, symbolization, or more simply, affecting words break open the defense of omnipotence (O'Shaughnessy 2015). Education alone could not have done this work. Indeed, it became the crime scene.

After Misogyny?

My second question—*What is it to think after misogyny?*—follows from Dr. Glocer Fiorini's challenge, "Is it possible to detect something that is also naturalized in the psychotherapist?" (2016, n.p.).

My associations to the difficulties of symbolizing misogyny and the need to link its destructive features to the denial of fluidity in gender as spectrum and to otherness in sexuality are deeply affected by my libidinal history and two of the many worlds I share with others: the university and the clinic. Between these worlds there are urges to think from within the limits of knowledge, culture, and psychical life while having to lean on the binds and pulls of transference. Whether in the classroom or the clinic, I witness the startles of ambivalence over whether emotional life should have any privilege or meaning and whether a new vocabulary that has the tendency to repeat learning's dilemmas have any place at all (Britzman 2015). One cannot speak of anxiety without experiencing its expressions and dangers. Feelings are hurt and omnipotence takes hold of an emotional logic caught between compliance and pride (Green 1982a). Yet selves are neither poster people for social disorders nor flat characters serving plot devices. Life is far more contradictory; so much happens without our awareness.

In our education, we can be charged with thinking our thoughts and finding ways to nurture our tender minds. As small as it may appear, the solitudes of reading may serve this purpose. Being with words is of a different order, a giving oneself over to the work of becoming immersed in an author's world and with what is difficult to see. In reading between the lines, we give up our own empire of meaning, only to slowly lean on the feats and failures of language, the consequences of mishaps in not being able to communicate, and still in the twilight zone of reading, the reader is witness to what can happen when phantasies are given their due and can go no further. A similar intimacy may be had with writing. Between the pen and paper, we become narrators of our incompleteness. Kristeva (2000) begins with the fractures: "What are the stories that Freud asked his patients to tell? Stories full of gaps, silences, awkwardness—in a way, novels deprived of an audience" (65). Even the hesitations of narrative invite a paradoxical creation: words as the audacity to signify the things we unconsciously set in stones and words that can crumble.

What then is the clinician's involvement with knowledge beyond the clinic and what then is the educator's involvement with knowledge beyond their education? Bion's (1993) conception of knowledge involves getting to know emotional experience; perhaps the primal experience belongs to the on-going nature of getting to know the self. Bion posits the pain of learning from not knowing and raises the question of how we engage psychoanalytically with interdisciplinary views that pressure our sensitivities and may lead to the frustration of not understanding while still needing to know. We have a strong model for opening disciplinary boundaries in Freud's work as he too extended his ideas to be moved by the expressive arts and the aesthetic conflicts. Kristeva (1995) too gives us the idea that if one is to tolerate the variations of mental distress, including our own, and learn from "the inability to represent" (9), and if we are to be affected by the swirls of variability that Henry James, in *The Spoils of Poynton*, called "the germs of life" (1987, 23), then all this life is best read with very long novels. There the reader sits in place and will experience their own sense of reading life's accidents, blows, failures, reprehensions, and incompleteness. There the reader experiences their waiting mechanism. But then, to read psychoanalytically brings notice to an insisting absence in the presence of things.

Difficult novels, plays, poems, and art leave us speechless, saddened, and incomplete. We become affected by words that carry our aesthetic conflicts, made from the wonderment with the enigmatic breast as inaugurating the thirst for beauty, truth, and knowledge (Meltzer and Harris Williams 1988). Certeau's (1993) thinking with the Freudian novel asks, "Does one read a text as if it is lying on the couch?" (52). His answer is affirmative: "Psychoanalysis takes up the definition given to fiction as being a knowledge jeopardized and wounded by its otherness (the affect). . . . In the analytic field this discourse is effective because it is 'touched' or wounded by the affect" (27).

The analytic principles of construction, deconstruction, and reconstruction—activities Freud (1914b) described as "remembering, repeating, and working through"—serve as the symbolic means to narrate resistance to resistance, analyze the collapse of time and space, link a time before to what comes after, and interpret negations of mental life as already touched by affect in search of objects. The analysis of the patient and analyst's speech is then an open book to be written and a page to be turned. If childhood and adolescence naturalize or idealize what will need to be historicized, then the act of becoming a historical subject involves disillusioning the absolute mythologies of ideality and disparagement (two sides of the same coin) that denies and negates gender fluidity and sexual otherness. What comes after is the counter-depressant of words. I find generative ideas with Dr. Glocer Fiorini's view that analytic work emerges from attending to constructions created to think the enigmatic within sexual difference. Even more. Perhaps it is in encountering what is most unexpected that any enigmatic construction is given its emotional tenor and freedom to break through the mesmerizing phantasy of part objects. The work is excruciatingly slow and subject to the pain of symbolization. But it is also in affiliation to what Oren Gozlan (2015) develops as "the art of transitioning," that sexual difference opens bodily experience to new expressions.

I think we can accompany our patients' phantasies along with our own through to the broken heart of our respective speechless agonies. It means going to where neither of us knows, while destroying what we know too well, namely a syndrome of ideality and disparagement that characterizes misogyny and the negation of gender fluidity and sexual otherness. Young-Bruehl's work as teacher, analyst, and writer provides invaluable resources for our thinking. *The Anatomy of Prejudices* (1996) traces the bodily roots of prejudice as secured by adolescence, an area of life subject to ideality and splitting and more difficult to reach in treatment and in life. Young-Bruehl proposes that, since post World War II, any approach to addressing the activities of prejudice requires that social discourses, literary revolts, and education become polyglot. This is so because prejudices are based on the "marks of difference" that sustain "ideologies of desire." (28). Along with adolescence as the flowering for the syndrome of ideality, Young-Bruehl has made the stunning argument that we have to go back further to think about something that comes before and has no name: prejudice against or hatred of children. Her last book, *Childism* (2012), provides a stringent critique of the helping professions of psychology, medicine, education, and law. Young-Bruehl too rehearses the doubts that follow from accepting that there are more *isms*: "When childism pervades a society, however, even people who genuinely want to make the world better for children may find it hard to realize that it exists" (4). No one is immune from having to be a child and perhaps pretending that childhood is over. And no one is immune from having to be born.

Perhaps the main communication, then, belongs to how we answer for ourselves the psychoanalytic questions of sequence that link meaning to meaninglessness: "What does this have to do with that?" and "What has happened before?" If misogyny fractures our capacity to think and to tolerate otherness, both yours and mine—if its hatred of femininity can be apprehended as the disavowal of gender and sexual transformations—free association can be our greatest ethic for breaking through the boundaries of negation and omnipotence and for lending signification to the repetition compulsion of meaninglessness. What comes after holds no guarantee. For education and the clinic, our desire for freedom yet to come may well depend upon welcoming the audacity of the thinking breast.

Chapter 6

The Times of Friendship for Mrs. K. and Richard

Just before the start of the Freud-Klein Controversial Discussions held in London by the British Psychoanalytical Society and that would last from 1941 to 1945, Melanie Klein, then fifty-nine years old, conducted a four-month analysis with Richard, a ten-year-old English boy. Due to the war, Klein had already moved her clinical practice from London to a small town in Scotland in 1939. There, she rented a Girl Guide hut where the analysis took place. Richard and his mother would stay in Scotland during the week and, when safe, bus back to London for weekends. From the beginning of their work Richard knew they would only have four months together and that Mrs. Klein would have to end the analysis. Perhaps such knowledge confirmed his suspicions. And there were many: Mrs. Klein's thick German accent, Richard's visible and invisible enemies, his worries about the war theatre, and something entirely new, the improbability of their friendship. The transference, then, was immediate. Years later, thoughts on countertransference would affect Klein's writing on her mistakes, mishearing, and wishes. Near the end of her life, in a seminar on technique given in 1958 to candidates with the British Psychoanalytic Society, Klein described countertransference as indicating the analyst's feelings: "I have never found that the counter-transference has helped me to understand my patient better; but if I may put it like this, I have found that it has helped me understand myself better" (J. Steiner 2017, 103).

Richard and Mrs. Klein met in 1941, a particularly difficult year for them both. In one of those strange psychoanalytical coincidences, the analysand's anguish was not far away from that of the analyst. Klein, too, must have been preoccupied with enemies, visible and invisible, who were suspicious of her theories. Her longstanding arguments with Anna Freud on the nature of child development, the technique of play, and child analysis had come to a crossroad by 1938 when the Freud family and other Jewish Viennese analysts fled Austria in exile to London. Due to the war, once in London, these refugees were termed "enemy aliens" and not permitted to travel freely beyond their residence (R. Steiner 2000a). Klein's diasporic life was different: from Vienna to Hungary, to Berlin. She immigrated to London from Berlin in 1926 and took British citizenship by 1934. By 1938 she was a well-established training analyst, and it was known that she wished the Freuds would move anywhere else but London. At the beginning of her work with Richard, Klein was in preparation for her defense to the British Psychoanalytical Society's Controversial Discussions. The debated question became whether one Psychoanalytic Society could contain significant differences over the status of phantasy, aggression, infantile life, and the drives (King and Steiner 1992). Klein's letter on August 29, 1941, to Clifford Scott forecasted heartache and she mentions Richard:

> We are only at the beginning of making people understand the importance and meaning of depression—I am afraid it will be a lengthy and difficult job. I now analyze a boy of ten.... It is surprising and gratifying to see how much the knowledge of the depressive position has advanced technique and theoretical and practical understanding.... I am afraid however that most of our colleagues are extremely reluctant to accept these new things—this may retard progress but should not altogether hold it up. (quoted in Grosskurth 1986, 262)

Nineteen years later, around the age of seventy-six, Klein returned to her boxes of notes on an analysis cut short and wrote her most affecting case study, published posthumously: *Narrative of a Child Analysis: The Conduct of the Psycho-Analysis of Children as Seen in the Treatment of a Ten-Year-Old Boy* (1961). It runs 496 pages, and her concluding remarks noted her reason for publishing the case: "[to] throw light on the basic principles of my technique of analysing Children.... And I believe this book ... should prove helpful to the student of analysis" (464). Klein's extensive footnotes, written years later, continued to justify her psychoanalytic technique. Many of her comments responded to longstanding contentions over her style of addressing anxiety with deep interpretations. By the time she returned to her clinical notes on the Richard case, Klein had refined the designs of her psychoanalytic concepts on the sources and conflicts of the mind's developments that also served as the basis of her techniques for interpretation. These techniques and their mental functions included projective identification, the paranoid-schizoid and the depressive position, envy and gratitude, the total situation of the transference, the centrality of phantasy to early anxiety situations, and the infantile roots of the adult mind. She continued to maintain that early analysis of young children was the royal road to knowledge of adult psychoanalysis. How else, after all, without the clinic of early analysis, would she be able to reach into the convincing reality of emotionality as the source and object of thinking, and how else would she be able to address the object relations in mind?

My turn to Klein's late work attends to the fate, or perhaps vicissitudes, of the good object with the provocative claim that beyond the insistence on the designs of theory, the heart of the psychoanalytic situation proposes to the analyst and analysand a question of their friendship. Such friendship is unlike any other: as appeal to fleeting scenes of appearance, disappearance, and the art of compromise, and as caught in the thickets of transference, psychoanalytic friendship must bow to its incompleteness and to the time when the analyst and analysand no longer meet. Now, while the field of psychoanalysis contains significant commentary and dispute over the analytic couple, the analytic relationship, endings and new beginnings, free association, and the significance of the transference-love; while Freud suggested that the analytic alliance is dedicated to the destruction of the symptom as played out in transference between the couple; and while the analyst's ethic of neutrality may serve as warning to the unavoidable volatility of handling the transference—what today is discussed as the analyst's self-disclosures—the hovering question of friendship and its *Nachträglich* effects as a contingency of technique and the art of libido is hardly discussed. With Klein, the question of friendship belongs to the fate of the good object, theoretically incorporated inside, to become an internal friend for the psychical world of object relations. Her emphasis on the inner world of object relations as friendly and unfriendly and as good and bad opens new awareness for why the desire for friendship is so significant to the holding lifeworld of the mind and the moral capacity for symbolizing the depressive position that keeps watch over feelings of loneliness, sadness, and thoughts of gratitude for the other

(Klein 1963). Made from scenes of likeness and regard for affiliation, and made in the exchange of play and words, friendship then is theorized as those threads of identification in the service of psychical binding. On these matters, André Green (1982a) turns to Freud on how we come to terms with the exigencies of life that involve abandonment: "According to Freud, identification is then the sole condition likely to make this loss of the object acceptable" (24).

I also place into the folds of my discussion on psychoanalytic friendship the desire to write about our work and to note why justice to the uniqueness of style and the singularity of listening occurs when we receive the words and sufferings of others. Friendship put into words can bear the desire for the human bond when there seems to be no friend. Jacques Derrida's (1993) "Politics of Friendship," republished in *American Imago*, holds a mediation on friendship as "thoughts of the other" (362), "as something yet to come" (368), and as "an experience in waiting" (386). Such is the character of the psychoanalytic affair.

Before, during, and after the psychoanalytic situation, and even between sessions and on weekend breaks, thoughts of friendship may flounder on anxiety over loss of love. The friendship yet to come belongs to the psychical experiences of wanting, wishing, and waiting for an actual other who also suffers yet still welcomes the workings of phantasy, the unconscious, imagination, interpretation, and the urge for reparation. What then does this psychoanalytic friendship propose? On offer is the gift of transference. For Klein and Richard, their question of friendship is tied to the promise for the good object and worries of how easily it can slip away.

Klein's last book differed in four extraordinary ways from her 1932 study, *The Psycho-Analysis of Children*, as that first book could only present the rapid brushstrokes of her techniques and grand theoretical leaps of what she termed "early analysis." That book, made from a series of 1927 lectures in London, included her Berlin work. Klein's theory of psychical life as the self's emotional development and situation served as the royal road to her play technique. She argued that her techniques and theories of development are inseparable (J. Steiner 2017). Just as with her 1961 Richard case, Klein worked from her telegraphic notes and her method of reconstruction (Frank 2009). By 1961, however, twenty years had passed since she saw Richard. And this last case worked from the psychoanalytic time of retroaction, benefiting both from Klein's developing the technical aftereffects of her theories and from a writer's method of portraying novelistic time.

Second, the *Narrative* unfolds with literary devices such as first- and third-person voice, foreshadowing, suspense, dialogue, personification, retroaction, and the illusion of the first time. It is a case filled with characters, drawn from historical actors, dictators, strangers, battlefields, mothers, school bullies, dropped bombs, and Richard's and Klein's baby talk. Footnotes serve as her conservative Greek chorus while her index proposes the radical mash-up of phantasies put to wordless things. Richard's apprenticeship in transference lit the flame for Klein's narrative liberties.

There follows a third difference from her earlier case studies: Klein seems to have invented a new genre of writing, named as narrative, and a new genre of reading as returns. Readers experience Mrs. Klein and Richard's strange volley of discordant words spoken to each other, words that may be witness to a love play made from misunderstandings, confusions, and unaccountable anxiety. Psychoanalytic writing and reading are given over to their emotional situation, birthing what Patrisha Salah (2018) graciously termed as "literature of libido" and what I am suggesting as friendship.

Klein hardly comments on a fourth difference and one that continues to cast a shadow on contemporary understanding of psychoanalysis and from where its theory comes. The *Narrative* responded to one of the most difficult criticisms leveled at psychoanalysts generally and Klein quite specifically: many have argued that her psychoanalytic approach and theory of object relations cares nothing for the forces of the external world. Richard's analysis proved otherwise. It occurred within an extraordinarily urgent context: the frightening world at war—bombings, terrible suffering, displacement, destruction, death, and what seemed like endless waiting. In her introduction to the work Klein notes that for purposes of the analysis and due to the London Blitz, Richard and his mother stayed during weekdays in a hotel in a Scottish village. Five to six days a week, he took the bus to Klein's rented playroom for their fifty-minute sessions. When they could, over weekends, each returned to their London homes. They meet for ninety-three sessions. Klein (1961) begins with the key theme enacted in his play: "The outbreak of the war had greatly increased Richard's difficulties. . . . The war stirred up all his anxieties, and he was particularly frightened of air raids and bombs. He followed the news closely and took a great interest in the changes in the war situation, and this preoccupation came up again and again during the course of his analysis" (6). Richard's attention to the war is almost an understatement: really, the war intruded upon Richard's life. His father and older brother were soldiers and just before he met Klein in Scotland, his London neighborhood was bombed by German planes. So too with Klein, who was able to leave her London home to set up her work with Richard and others. Indeed, the question of war was inextricable from the lives of psychoanalysts, the rise of child analysis in London, and the theories and language of the psychoanalytic movement from Sigmund and Anna Freud onwards (Kahn 2023; Rose 1993; Segal 1997). European Jewish analysts were affected by the ravages of anti-Semitism, displacement, and too the reparations of World War I and II. In the post-war years, Sigmund Freud's early emphasis on war neuroses transformed into a medical and psychoanalytic consideration of the nervous child (Roper 2016; Shapira 2013). Klein seemed to be a bridge between these transformations: in her view, the only war that could be subject to symbolization and that could address the child's inner world belonged to the psychoanalytic situation. And this was hardly a justification for the unfolding of their work, but it was where Richard and Klein could meet.

Klein was instructed by Richard's striving to understand his own mind and, even as she accepted the harsh fact that her theory tags along, to learn more from Richard and more of her own experience, she had to break her own rules of analytic comportment. Two were broken: she answered Richard's questions and at times reassured him. Given her technique of needing to respond to what she called "intangible factors and the most urgent aspects of the material," Klein's countertransference was inevitable (Klein 1961, 13). She worked for and against her theories, a common and crucial conflict in the developments of human sciences and in the writing of case studies. As the analysis proceeded, Richard begged for their work to continue. Even as Klein knew this was not to be, she gave into a faint hope for their future. Perhaps she, too, held a wish for the fate of the good object, or even to become that good object-breast for Richard to use and enjoy.

In session 65 Richard's anger toward Mrs. Klein came in the form of a monstrous portrait of her. Drawing 55 is titled "Mrs. K." She is a triangle body with glaring eyes, gigantic breasts, a V on the stomach, hair on the head, and a line to the genitals, perhaps added as an afterthought. Then, Richard "picked up the drawing suddenly and put his lips to one breast" (Klein 1961, 323). It is the only picture he would be embarrassed over, and one of the few times Mrs. Klein would try to appease his worries. *Appeasement* is the key term, and in a note on that session Klein expressed her bother: "I have repeatedly remarked that, in spite of not deviating from my technique, I sometimes answered questions, which had the effect of reassuring Richard . . . which I on the whole deprecate" (325). She then presents their shared dilemma and what could have become lost when Klein attempted to take away his bad feeling. While Richard seemed relieved, his associations said otherwise and his doubts over Mrs. Klein's goodness were now displaced into another scene:

> His very next remark referred to the girl on the road who, although of quite harmless appearance, looked to him like a monster. . . . Idealization of the analyst—the patriotic and not foreign and suspect Mrs K.—had not resolved the doubt in her; but this doubt was deflected and transferred to the girl passing by. . . . We find again and again that mistakes of this kind are unconsciously—and with adults sometimes consciously—resented and criticized; and this is true in spite of patients longing to be loved and reassured. (326)

"Go Right into the Depths"

Donald Meltzer's (1998) lectures on the *Narrative,* covering their sixteen weeks and given to candidates at the Institute of Psychoanalysis, London, and The Tavistock Clinic, begins with the heart of Klein's technique: "The first week of the analysis opens like a Chekhov play—immediately all the characters are introduced and all the themes and subplots are hinted at. What can be seen happening in the first week is that, intentionally or not, Mrs. Klein has set about mobilizing anxieties, rather than diminishing them. And the technique she employs for mobilizing Richard's anxieties is really no different from one for diminishing them: that is, to go right into the depths" (148). These depths of anxiety are murky and express the stirs of love and hate, conflicted feelings of loneliness, envy, gratitude, and jealousy, persecutory phantasies of destruction and being destroyed, Oedipal conflicts, and a constellation of defenses that cue the denial of psychical reality. And with so much affect at stake, Klein had to call Richard's anxiety into words. But Richard was so much more than an announcer of his anxiety, and one of the treasures of reading this case is how alive and invested in the work they both seem.

Klein presents Richard as an articulate, intellectually gifted, and charming boy; at times he deploys his talents to manipulate others. He is both excessively polite and terribly worried. Richard becomes lost in his circuitous reasoning and then, as a way out, to bouts of paranoia, depression, and spectacular sadness. He is at war with his useless feelings. Around 1939, due to his fear of other children and his anger at being without friends, at the age of eight, he stopped going to school and his mother took over his education. His mother reported to Klein that Richard was anxious, overly affectionate, and worried about their separation. Then too there were Richard's paranoid fears of being poisoned by the cook and of being watched by strangers, and his compulsion to be on guard. Whenever Mrs. Klein and Richard went outside, he required her to whisper. Everything was dangerous.

The playroom too became a character world. It had a kitchen and lavatory and Klein provided small toys, paper, paints, pens, chalk, and a little table with two chairs. Klein would take his paintings home and return them the next day. Occasionally, Richard would bring his own fleet of toy soldiers and warships. Leaving toys home meant a loss of trust in Klein. The rented playroom was used for other purposes, and for each session, Klein had to unlock the outside door. Much of their time Richard arrived early and stood outside waiting for her. When the sessions ended, no matter how difficult, they walked away together. Richard would have last words while Mrs. Klein kept her thoughts to herself. Interpretation of Richard's anxieties only occurred during the session.

At their first meeting, Klein asked Richard if he knew why he was seeing her. He said he had some difficulties and wanted to be helped and then filled the room with his worries about Hitler's cruelty and whether Mrs. Klein, like Hitler, was Austrian. He worried about boys and tramps who might hurt him, he worried he would be overheard by enemies, he was concerned over his mother's health and whether she would be kidnapped, and then something more must have peaked Klein's listening. Richard worried what he was like on the inside and what other people's insides were like. Through the characters of his mother, father, Mrs. K., Mr. K., the cook, terrible Hitler, and genitals and breasts, that first session belonged to Richard's battles with persecutory objects. And this was how Klein heard his fears: everything stood in for something else. Mrs. Klein felt that Richard's transference to her began as soon as he stepped into the room, and immediately, she gave deep interpretations to his anxiety, explaining that his worries brought him to terrifying thoughts on parental coitus, father's violence, mother's helplessness, and Richard's guilt at wanting to have his mother all to himself. So much was happening, and in a footnote on that first session, written years later, Klein (1961) tips her hat to the chaos of the session as well as to the liberties of narration: "But often I did not or could not record the fleeting effect the interpretations made on him. The child would seldom have been sitting silently, while I was speaking. He might get up, pick up a toy or a pencil or pad. He might interject something which was a further association or a doubt. Therefore my interpretations may frequently appear more lengthy and consecutive than they in fact were" (25).

By the fortieth session and after a holiday where both Klein and Richard returned to London and its air raids, Richard's anxiety was palpable, as was his resistance to their work. Their separation had turned everything bad; Mrs. Klein described him that day as "a picture of unhappiness" (1961, 191). He had difficulty settling, ran outside, stamped on poisonous weeds, and finally pulled from a shelf a book to read. His restlessness matched Klein's interpretation of that session; it reads as brutal: "Mrs K. interpreted that his silences and his reading expressed his wish to escape from his fears about the poisonous and dangerous father-genital and the dead babies inside Mummy—the toadstools and nettles which he crushed under his feet. The playroom, the garden, and Mrs K. had turned bad and poisoned in his mind. He wished to find out about Mrs K's insides by looking into the book. This seemed less frightening than looking around the playroom" (191). However terrifying Klein's interpretation of Richard's anxiety can seem to readers, Klein reports that after the session, they walked side by side into the world. She made a long note on Richard's capacity to sustain a double attitude of both anxiety and hope. And as if concerned about the readers of the case, Klein turned to her technique of addressing the urgency of anxiety situations: "It seems striking that interpretations which are most painful such as those of destructive impulses directed against the loved object or even—as will be seen in later sessions—of anxieties relating to internal dangers and persecution by dead and hostile objects, can yet lead to great relief.... I discovered that progress in analysis was bound up with interpreting whichever anxieties were most acute, whether they were of a psychotic nature or not" (192–193).

"Do You Really Know What I Think? How Can You Really Know?"

Mrs. Klein's interpretations called upon Richard's anxieties and his doubts over their work. At a certain point, his doubts appeared as if anxiety took the form of punctuation. However, doubts may also function as challenge to internal and external scenes of authority. Until Richard could question his thoughts, affects remained split off from their symbolization. The capacity for doubt, as the analyst Marion Milner (1996) described in a 1942 lecture given to the Institute of Education in London, begins with an awareness of the relation between inner and outer reality with the idea that "thoughts are different from things" (13). The child, as well as the adult, must learn to doubt magical beliefs and disillusion not only the illusion of what feels like absolute knowledge. External authority, such as the school, must also be rendered as human and as capable of being questioned.

In the psychoanalytic situation, doubts serve another purpose: The analyst is not omnipotent, only a participant with congealed feelings that chime in with the insistence that drifting thoughts release an overabundance of feelings. So, one of the large issues that became the work involved inquiry into how and why the analyst disillusions her seeming omnipotence or breaks open the phantasy that minds can be read and thus controlled. Technique itself cannot be omnipotent, and countertransference points to our limits of self-understanding. There must be an eye toward freedom as well as an address to the paranoid anxiety that stops it short. Indeed, the other cannot know too well and uncertainty over meaning is as much an operation of language as it is a quality of affect. The doubts begin with the question, *Is it true?* Or, *How can you know?* Milner's (1996) open question turns toward feelings, terminable and interminable: "How far does it help the child to realize the inner reality as process, if this recognition does, in fact, require the ability to tolerate doubt and the willingness to wait in uncertainty?" (14). From Klein's view, thinking itself would become a container for mental pain, a waiting mechanism, an avenue into narrative adventures, and an act of love and reparation.

Their twenty-fourth session occurred on a Saturday when Richard began with his doubts and what they could mean for Klein. He was drawing a picture, one of a starfish series, where each arm represented Mummy, bad Daddy, Mrs. K., brute-Hitler, and the empire. As he colored in the arms, he was singing marching songs. Richard was worried about the invasion and whether Mrs. K. would still be able to see him. The drawing was one of attack and destruction and Richard did not believe he harbored bad feelings toward his parents. He stopped and asked Mrs. K., "Do I really think this of all of you? I don't know if I do. How can you really know what I think?" (1961, 111). How anyone can know anything expresses a feeling. Mrs. K., in third-person voice, then acknowledged his relation to his doubts: "from his play, drawings, and what he was saying and doing she gathered some of his unconscious thoughts; but he had just expressed his doubts whether she was right and could be trusted" (111). Klein related these feelings of mistrust to his worries about his mother and that Mrs. K. would give Richard to Mr. K., who he thought was an enemy. "Recently," Klein added as an aside, "he had unconsciously expressed death wishes toward Mummy and Mrs K, and found it very painful and frightening when Mrs K. interpreted this. . . . It seemed that he experienced both trust and distrust more strongly" (112). It is Richard's double attitude that Klein held close when he demanded, "Was Mrs K. a foreigner or not?" (113). Is Mrs. K. now on his side?

Just as they were ready to take a weekend break, Richard seemed more relaxed. Klein noted Richard's affection: "Turning off the electric fire he said, 'Poor old radiator will have a rest'" (114). Richard wanted to make sure Mrs. K. would bring his drawings back next time. Then, looking over the room, he said, "Poor old room, so silent. Then he asked Mrs K. what she was going to do over the weekend" (114). Klein's last interpretation drew the personification of the room into a personal narrative of reparation: "Mrs K. interpreted his fear that she might die at the weekend—the poor old silent room. That was why he had to make sure about her bringing the drawings; this also expressed his wish to help in the analysis, and thus to put Mrs K. right and preserve her. This was why he wished for Mrs K.—the poor old radiator—to have a rest, not to be exhausted by her patients, particularly by him" (114). Klein's note on this session attended to the mechanism of denial as a way of dealing with anxiety: "In this instance the internal danger situation consisted of the good mother being attacked and destroyed by his hatred, and this gave rise to depression and despair" (114). As Richard's anxiety diminished, he could face the external world as more than a delegate of his hostile feelings.

"Do Psycho-Analysts Go to Church?"

Mrs. K. and Richard met for their fifty-second session on a Sunday. Richard was most curious about what Mrs. Klein did when she was not with him. The session turned to Richard wondering about Klein's beliefs about

God and country. Then, while drawing a German airplane on the ground hit by lightning, he asked if he could raise something personal: "Did she go to church? Do psycho-analysts go to church? And at once, even before Mrs K. could have replied, he said that she could not go because she was too busy" (1961, 253–254). Mrs. Klein opened his question through what he could not ask: Did Richard think it wrong not to go to church? Then, "Mrs K. asked was he afraid of punishment by God?" (254). Richard changed the topic by announcing he wished to give a performance with a rope that he swung between his legs and told Mrs. K. to be the audience and clap enthusiastically. The play became manic, and Richard then asked Mrs K. to perform with the rope. She too swung it around:

> Mrs K. then interpreted that when Richard held [the rope] between his legs, it represented Daddy's genital, which Richard had taken away and now possessed. Mrs K. performing with the rope meant that Mummy, too, should have a powerful penis which would make them all equal. The rope play—both Richard's and Mrs K.'s—expressed also his wish to have sexual intercourse with her; at the same time this was the wish he had been so afraid of and for which he felt that God, standing for Daddy, would punish him. (254)

Richard kept returning to his drawing of the downed airplane, blacking the sky. He then walked around the room aimlessly and Mrs. K. told him he wished to escape from his bad thoughts. The last turn was to his urgent dilemma: Richard felt it wrong that they met on Sunday. Moreover, he had severe doubts about psychoanalysis and felt it too as wrong. The sexual talk was improper, though Richard did have the dangerous wish to have sex with Mummy. But it was improper of Mrs. K. to speak of such desires, as they were tempting him. It is worth quoting the range of emotional experiences involved in such a quick exchange:

> These desires seemed all the more dangerous to him because they were connected with hate, jealousy, and destruction of his parents, whom he also loved. He had always been struggling to get away from such hostile feelings which he felt were 'bad' and wished only to experience love. But Mrs K., when he was afraid of her tempting him, represented Mummy as well, who was tempting him by allowing him to sleep in a room alone with her. He also suspected her, whenever she showed him

love, of being disloyal to Daddy, and of encouraging Richard's bad and hostile desires . . . he felt Mrs K. should not have given him this session on Sunday; she and he should have gone to church. . . . At the same time he did want Mrs K. to give him an additional session. (1961, 255)

At this point Richard told Klein he felt the analysis was helpful.

What changed his judgment? In Klein's view, putting into words the disorder of painful, clashing persecutory feelings provided Richard with a means to symbolize anxiety and his ambivalence. His anger and worries mean something. When bad things can be put into words the authority of phantasies diminishes. The analytic dialogue was now deep into the heart of Richard's worries, though when they walked out together into the world Richard turned back to the playroom and said it was good for the playroom to have a rest.

Here we can summarize Klein's play technique. She listens to the child's disparate utterances and sees in his drawings depressive pain and his hopes; she observes Richard's walkabouts as eruptions of anxiety promoting the defense of denial of any meaning unconscious communication holds in store; and she works from inside Richard's questions. Technically, Klein's interpretations are meant to call forth both anxiety and new ideas. Richard's activities, drawings, doubts, questions, and refusals became an index of his emotional attitude toward his inner world, his transference to Klein, and what he cannot bear to imagine about the outer world. Paradoxically, the mechanisms of defense—omnipotence, identification, projection, splitting, and denial—carry the means to know them. Klein is then proposing a new kind of psychological knowledge capable of containing inchoate elements of the emotional world and the moral quandaries involved. Then too, the unconscious communication that Klein conveyed between the lines of interpretation belonged to their friendship. Still, the analyst must be willing to be a magnet for love and hate, become the poor radiator, the sad, silent, empty room, and then the playroom that needs a rest.

"Must We Say Goodbye?" The Sadness of Parting

The last sessions were those of parting as much as they were an inquiry into the sways between security and insecurity and between friends and no friends. Klein (1961) felt that Richard's manifest wish was to end his analysis in a friendly way. There were, however, new pains: headaches, tummy aches, and demands that Mrs. K. leave her other patients and work only with him. His distrust of Klein resurfaced in the form of doubts over her and his goodness. Richard is manically drawing pictures and tearing them up. In the seventy-fifth session Richard asked could Mrs. K. cure "dopey boys?" (383). He also wanted to know when she became a psychoanalyst. Was it before or after she married Mr. K? Was Mrs. K. loyal to the German enemy? "Then he asked whether Mrs K. really did not mind his referring to her nationality" (385). Have Richard's questions hurt Mrs. K.'s feelings?

Feelings of persecution, rage, and resentment returned in session 83 and Klein's notes reflected on Richard's growing anxiety expressed in his scribbling and throwing objects around the room. It seemed as if Richard was attacking Klein:

> Richard's state of mind in the last two sessions, in which the need to tear out bits of me was expressed in his attempts to break open the floor—and his increased urethral attacks were shown by pouring much more water than he used to—had given me the feeling that he had regressed to the attempts of young children who are unable to draw a complete figure, for complex reasons such as lack of skill, lack of integration, and feelings of guilt about having torn to bits the mother's breast and the mother.... The regression to early attacks by tearing, biting up, and the corresponding persecutory anxieties, were therefore used in order to get away from depression and despair. I have pointed out generally speaking that the incapacity to cope with the depressive position often leads to a regression to the earlier paranoid-schizoid one. (1961, 424)

While Klein's notes can appear to be using Richard to explicate her theories, they also register her heartbreak over his suffering. She knew Richard was worried over his safety and her safety in having to return to London and the air raids. The drawings, Klein remarked, were like temper tantrums and Richard's fury, she thought, expressed his deepest worry that he was destroying her in the drawings. Klein then observed how difficult it is to contain one's sorrow: "It became very clear that his incapacity to put right or retrieve his injured or dead loved objects changed them into persecutors. His strong sense of guilt about his dangerous hate and jealousy made him feel completely responsible for the analyst's expected death; the sorrow about this, together with his guilt, were unbearable.... At the same time, he tried to build up and preserve internally the good mother—the photograph of me he had taken" (425).

The "dopey boy question" returned in session 92 when he asked whether Mrs. K. was "a doctor for the mind as others are doctors for the body?" (1961, 459). Then, "Richard said that the mind was even more important than the body, though he thought that the nose was very important too" (459). Klein's interpretation returned to his worries over the insides of his body and whether Mrs. K. could be a helpful figure: "That the nose also stood for Richard's genital, and that he was afraid that something was wrong with it, that it was damaged and would not develop properly, and this was the reason why he was afraid of becoming a 'dunce.' He doubted whether Mrs K. could actually cure the genital as well as the mind" (459–460). Everything stands for something else and threatens to collapse meaning. Bad objects threaten to destroy good ones. Richard seems to be asking what Klein can really do for him. And in their last three sessions, the large question was whether, in the sorrow of parting, everything good would disappear forever.

In their last session, Richard wished to caress, kiss, and hold Mrs. K. and agreed that touching her was his way to keep her inside of him. He was afraid he could not keep her but had hopes that he could. Klein's (1961) last comment concerns Richard's worries of parting and his wish to preserve the good object: "Richard's mood during this was on the whole much like that of the Ninetieth Session, with much unhappiness and tension. His increased desire to be cuddled showed repeatedly in his touching Mrs K., and he dropped things so as to be able to touch her legs when picking them up. He was obviously all the time trying to restrain his aggressiveness because of the fear of injuring his loved objects" (461–462). It seems all along Richard was both desperate to keep in mind good objects and deeply worried that just as the world was being ruined by war, he too would destroy his capacity for love and friendship. But now there were at least two Mrs. K.'s: His psychoanalyst he wished to kiss, who played with him, and accompanied him in his troubles—and because of their work he was determined to keep her alive—and his internal Mrs. K., who witnessed the comings and goings of his emotional world and who Richard felt might be destroyed. Klein (1961) considers, then, the fate of the good object and the glimmers of the depressive position, there all along: "The growing predominance of the life instinct in the fusion between the two instincts and the ensuring mitigation of hate by love were the ultimate reason why he could remain hopeful in spite of the very painful experience of breaking off an analysis which he consciously and unconsciously knew to be essential to him" (466).

Klein insisted that only by addressing anxiety—calling it forth and giving affects a story with symbols of embodiment to aid in the freedom of dispersal—would the child invest in the lifeworld of the mind to create libidinal bonds needed for symbolization and thinking. But we also learn that children, too, not only create the analyst they can bear, but are also analysts in the making. Such an important tie to the transference dialogue affects both the course of psychoanalysis and Klein's working style. In contemporary terms, Kristeva's (1995) figure of "The Inexpressible Child," caught between biology and meaning, provides a fine description of the child and analyst at work: "The therapist's task is twofold. First, the therapist must be an analyst who fosters desire (including of course the desire to speak) despite inhibition and depression. Second, the therapist must be a speech therapist who maps out an individual program for each child (since 'theoretical givens' do not apply to everyone) and then helps those children understand the linguistic categories that will allow them to add symbolic productions to their subjectivity" (105–106). Klein's principle for an affecting psychoanalysis, then, may go something like this: Where deprivation was, there frustration, aggression, phantasy, anxiety, defense, depression, gratitude, reparation, and friendship shall become. Step by step and side by side, human tolerance for the exigencies of life and the mental freedom to think walk hand in hand. And Klein insists upon narrative, now as negative capability, as our finest resource for working through the schizoid defenses and their denial of the relational, infantile roots of the emotional world.

It must be said that the need for anxieties, while our human condition, is perhaps our most dangerous feeling, for anxieties are only known through their ego defenses and inhibitions. In a 1958 interview with candidates in training at the British Psychoanalytical Society, Klein was asked about this danger and her reputation for calling on anxiety to interpret aggression. Her response seemed to be history's return, perhaps with thoughts of Richard and the Controversial Discussions of the British Psychoanalytical Association:

> There was a time when I felt very badly because my work on bringing out the importance of aggression led some analysts to

behave as if they could see nothing but aggression. I was quite in despair. All I heard in the seminars and at the meetings of the society was aggression, aggression, and aggression. Now you can't do anything with that at all, because the point is that aggression can only be tolerated when it is modified, and mitigated, and this happens when you have brought out the capacity for love. The fact that the conflict is so great is because it is a loved object that is being destroyed. (Steiner 2017, 112)

So narrative, like the desire for love and friendship, as we have seen in many of their sessions, is a double-edged sword. The words themselves can be mistaken for taunting objects. They may also become a symbolic scaffold for new thoughts to be cared and loved. Klein understood her vocabulary would be shocking to her readers. At the start of an elaborate index for the Richard case, Klein (1961) writes an unusual prefatory note: "This book is written in three distinct languages: the first expresses the child's material, in concrete every-day terms and symbolic meanings; the second, the chapter notes, is written in the terms of an ordinary psycho-analytic book or paper; the third, however, seldom appears in the index, and when it does it is usually for the purpose of illustrating chapter notes" (469). But how daunting it is to index the effusions of psychical reality as theory that performs its functions, styles, gymnastics, dreams, transferences, and directions for the theatre of object relations. See under babies: "Babies/baby (see also Children and e.g., Chicks, Eggs, Fish, Flies, Sailors, Salmon parr, Seed, Starfish): birth of; desire for; desire to be; desire to give mother; desire for mother to have; desire to restore mother's; fear of children as; greedy; hostile internal; inside mother, attacked or dead; inside mother, fear of; mixed feelings about; shared with mother" (472). Only in the index do we feel the collapse of the three registers of psychoanalysis: affect, phantasy, and technique.

Postscript: Richard's Recollections of the Analysis

If some people may wonder what happened to Richard, I believe this question stems from Klein's aesthetic depiction of the work in its immediacy and that it is difficult for readers to say goodbye, even when the book ends. Readers are deeply involved session by session and in transference with Richard's wishes for safe passage. Or perhaps readers are even angry at Klein's approach to Richard's anguish. They may wonder, did Richard survive this treatment? Or who is Richard now? It is one of the paradoxes of psychoanalytic treatment that what happens after only belongs to the analysand. Klein reported some news that he returned to school, though she knew there was no way to forecast the afterwardness of endings. In 1958, in her talk to psychoanalytic candidates, Klein admitted the other side of help and the defense against helplessness: "The question of can I help also leads to the issue of failures. Of course, one is discouraged by one's failures if the failures are predominant.... One accepts the fact that one can't always cure everybody.... That is why experience is important because we realize we are not omnipotent, one can't change everybody, but one can help quite a number of people. Sometimes even the most difficult patients can be helped" (Steiner 2017, 116).

And where is Richard? He appears briefly in another book. Phyllis Grosskurth, a biographer of Klein, somehow found the adult "Richard" 40 years later (Grosskurth 1986). Grosskurth reported on their three meetings. In their first encounter, she faced a fifty-year-old man who did not know of Klein's study and of course did not respond to the name "Richard." But he remembered Mrs. Klein and recollected the toys, the analytic room, the bus he traveled on, his fears of other children, the kisses he wished to give her, and then, his temper, still active, he admitted. In their second meeting, Grosskurth gave him a copy of *Narrative of a Child Analysis* (1961). She describes Richard holding the book: "He glanced at the photograph of Klein on the back cover. 'Dear old Melanie,' he murmured. Then he suddenly put the photograph to his lips and kissed it affectionately" (275).

It was the third meeting, after he had read the *Narrative*, that Richard expressed what his analysis felt like: "The Adagietto from Mahler's Fifth Symphony more perfectly than any words I could use sums up the complete truth of my feelings at that time" (Grosskurth 1986, 275).

Gustav Mahler's Fifth Symphony was written between 1901 and 1902. He had fallen in love with Alma Schindler. With music he created what Jens Malte Fischer (2011) described as "a vocabulary that seems familiar and sometimes even intimately colloquial. Mahler expresses all that is unheard of and uncanny, all that is unsettling and upsetting. What was alien sounds familiar, and what is familiar now seems alien" (387). The Fifth Symphony is a vast and stormy sea of the soundings of the drive to reach and express the elusive pathos of emotional life. Some musical commentators have described the opening of the symphony, known as the

Funeral March, as hysterical: crying horns, loud blasts that insist upon their hearing, and *Sturm und Drang*. It is difficult to listen to without feeling anxiety. Is that first movement an ode to the past or a foreshadowing of a future of war? The second movement, too, is stormy and Mahler directed it be played with "vengeance." The Scherzo is a frenzied dance that Mahler described as both giving and destroying birth (389). The fourth movement, Adagietto, is best known through Luchino Visconti's use of it in the film of the Thomas Mann novella of the artist's crisis with art and love, *Death in Venice*. It goes right to the depths and is to be played with excruciating slowness. Fischer describes the Adagietto as one of love and elation. And what is one to do with all this poignancy? How shall it end? The fifth movement cannot give an answer, only a compromise that Fischer noted as "a papering over of the cracks" opened by the first four movements (391). It is as if Mahler's symphony understood the pain of integration as never complete.

Near the end of Klein's life, close to the time she was working over her notes from the Richard case, she wrote a last paper on the fate of anguish. I discussed this paper in my study of Klein (Britzman 2016), and in thinking again of her work with Richard, it seems fitting to quote from that work. Klein was seventy-eight years old when she wrote "On the Sense of Loneliness" (1963). As with the case of Richard, it was published a few years after her death. Perhaps her turn to loneliness gave new poignancy to her views on "the pain of integration" (304) now imagined as existential companionship and keeping watch over the self's loves and losses. Just as with the Richard case, the apprehension of mental pain would be another term for anxiety, initially experienced as a terrible conviction that no one can help. Klein's consolation or perhaps compromise is found in her phrasing on the need for "a measure of resignation" (310) that accompanies the pain of integration. In my view, Klein's late work can also be read as admitting into her theories the pain of incompleteness when she wrote, "Full and permanent integration is never possible for some polarity between life and death instincts always persists and remains the deepest source of conflict. Full integration is never achieved, complete understanding is not possible and this continues as an important factor in loneliness" (302).

As for the psychoanalytic situation, the plays of passion while trying to know the self with the other take instruction from movements of anxiety, vengeance, aggression, love, and symbolization. These compose grand psychical themes of friendship, belonging, pining, and loss. Klein provides an uncanny vocabulary that is both utterly familiar and estranged. Such words may bear the weight of a multitude of object relations and open the art of compromise: symptoms, weaning, the psychoanalytic situation, transference, the endings, the pain of incompleteness, a measure of resignation, and still the reparative urge for a narrative. All express the flux and flummox of emotional attitudes toward someone or something. Klein also teaches that the self—as everything good and bad—also serves as "the papering over of cracks" (Fischer 2011, 391). Phantasy will be our best and most fragile threading and, subject to the wears and tears of life while narrating the fate of depressive anxiety, will be our lot. But so too will be the wonders of an unrepeatable friendship that can bear the question of hope for a moral psychology dedicated to the good object, whatever that may be. Klein's parting gesture would come as her last book and in her paper on loneliness. It would remind a fifty-year-old Richard of those long-ago years of yearnings of love and loss that return with great poignancy when looking back. His parting gesture in receiving their book was to seal his friendship with a kiss. To stay with this phantasy a bit longer, it would be in friendship with his own mind, a friendship like no other.

Chapter 7

H. G. Adler and Themes of Uncertainty, Transformation, and Binding

Exigencies

Commentary on the author H. G. Adler (1910–1988) begins with his history as a survivor of the Shoah, his isolation as a writer in the postwar years, and the difficulties of publishing his work. Only slowly and only in part is his life work available to English readers. He was one of the few Jewish German writers producing novels, poetry, philosophy, and sociology of the ghettos and camps just after the war. Jeremy Adler's (1997) entry in *The Yale Companion to Jewish Writing and Thought in German Culture* describes his father's novels as "one of the last exponents of the Prague school of German literature, which brought forth Rilke and Kafka" (599). Through the estrangements of modernist aesthetics H. G. Adler confronts the raw immediacies of life *in extremis* with the subject's urgency for human dignity. Difficulty seems his byword and his efforts have come at great cost. In an interview given in 1981, and quoted in Jeremy Adler's entry, Adler had this to say: "The experiences of a German writer of the Jewish nation who comes from Czechoslovakia, belongs to the Austrian cultural sphere, and is a loyal British citizen are not particularly pleasant. Someone like me does not belong anywhere. That is my fate."[1]

H. G. Adler's two postwar novels, *Panorama* (2011) and *The Journey* (2008), experiment with his fate and now with ours.[2] From the ruins of life they are dedicated to the creation of emotional meaning and return to memory what historiography defers, namely matters of affect, the horrors of regression, and the sorrows of those who come after. For these reasons, Adler's novels exceed plot: disrupted lives worded from the dredge of experience threaten the narrative frame. And like the characters, readers too are caught between the lines of what they know and why that knowledge, supposed as security and guardian of goodness, is insufficient. *Panorama* unfolds ever-widening scenes, perceptions, experiences, and thoughts of the lifeworld of one Josef Kramer, from his early childhood and its mysteries of education into the devastations of forced imprisonment and then survival. *The Journey* plunges readers into the Lustig family's forced confinement in the ghetto Theresienstadt, then to their deportation to Auschwitz, and ends with the survival of one member, the son Paul, who must also question where he belongs. In both novels, survivors ask, *What now?* What does it mean to go on?

As novelist of incontrovertible history and writer in exile, Adler seeks what comes after fate by questioning where memory and aesthetics can belong. Today we may read his novels as challenging the anticipatory temporality—indeed, the anxieties—of critical thought and aesthetic theory that attempt to enter and instruct what is said "After Auschwitz."[3] As a question of belonging, memory animates a retroactive and often deferred emotional predicament. Our cogency of understanding is disrupted by the combine of historical facts, the history of their reception, and the affecting affairs of the emotional world, subject to the defenses of splitting, dissociation, ideality, confusion, undoing what has already happened, and even kitsch (Kahn 2023). Adler exposes these psychical dimensions in theory and aesthetics, and he tells us why it is not enough to represent the Shoah through the confines of anxiety and the guilt that accompanies trauma's return. Paradoxically, the dilemmas of the return of historical memory are what aesthetics direct, and to face the writer's dilemma with handling the deferrals and resistances to affecting history, we are challenged to imagine what comes before and after aesthetics.

My inquiry emerges from the question of how we may bind history's return to our challenges of working through the past and do so for the sake of human dignity and the desire for freedom. I wish to imagine the difficult history of Adler's reception from the side of its delicacies: the affective qualities of memory articulated by struggles to symbolize emotional meaning as opening psychical boundaries to what must threaten our sense of cohesiveness, reality, and knowledge of self and other. I believe a study of psychical weighing lends new significance to a theory of learning found in Adler's aesthetics and provides the means to symbolize the frustration and uncertainty Shoshana Felman (1992) named as the crisis of education and transference. The paradox is that the emotional procedures for apprehending knowledge needed for historical memory can only become affecting if one can come to terms with that which destroys thinking, namely, denial and the discharge of unbound hatred and aggression. And anxiety that is expressed as denial may only serve to defend against acknowledgment of the terrors of loss, unimaginable vulnerability, and the horrors of annihilation.

The writer, however, creates meaning from the ravages of experience through binding of thought to its competing realities. Green's (1982b) frame of "the work of the negative" presents the following parameters for representing any theory of thought: understanding involves an awareness of limits, a representation of psychical experience, a discussion of binding and unbinding of the drives, and a capacity for abstraction (39). These ushers of symbolization can be identified in the writing of Adler and in psychoanalytic responses to the pathos, terror, and beauty of the unanswerable question of what it means to go on. Hanna Segal's (1952) early paper on psychoanalysis and aesthetics, written just after the war, dramatized the writer's and perhaps her own passage: "It is when the world within us is destroyed, when it is dead and loveless, when our loved ones are in fragments, and we ourselves in helpless despair—it is then that we must re-create our world anew, reassemble the pieces, infuse life into dead fragments, re-create life" (47).[4] Segal turns to the inside of mental space and imagination to envision the self as the struggle to bind affecting words to all that is lost. Her address from the writer's crisis may now be read as asking, *What comes before aesthetics and what carries aesthetics forward?*

As novelist, Adler enacts the transference of life into aesthetics. Life comes before and carries aesthetics forward. Adler gives words over to the question of uncertain meaning, presses inner thoughts to vie with the fracturing of external deception, refuses anonymity by naming the madness of the persecutors and points to the devastating denials that carry hatred. Symbolizing the clashes of dense reality, however, creates a paradox for imagination. There is no direction into the brutality of confinement and death, no way to grasp the devastation of the human reduced to waste, and no order to the unspeakable except to admit what memory feels, observes, fears, and turns to, and except to honor the decency of spirit and the desire to protect the love of the mind as the core work of witnessing. The estranging forms of Adler's novels remain true to the process of suturing the fractured fault lines of continuity; that is to say, through the prism of aesthetics Adler presents a self that contains dissonance with history and that his biographer, translator, and poet Peter Filkins (2019) names as "A Life in Many Worlds." What breaks through the claustrum of National Socialism is the narrator's story of survival, or what Adler ironically names on the first page of *The Journey* as "Augury," or signs of what will happen.

What has happened today involves a constellation of depression that Eve Kosofsky Sedgwick (2011) tied to a flight to pedagogy: "('pedagogy' not referring, for me, to the academic institution so much as a mode of relationality—not only in the classroom, but equally around it and, especially for the writer)" (139). For readers, researchers, teachers, students, and parents, depressive anxiety is a symptom of feeling the undertow of the return of devastating history. There are anxieties and fear of affect, worries of being misunderstood, strong feelings of helplessness, and even anger at those who are caught in history. Yet as a mode of relationality, both historical facts and literature that enliven their complexities and ambivalent experiences provoke transference, and what I have described through the frame of "difficult knowledge," as a clash of temporality that unsettles epistemological, ontological, and relational bearings (Britzman 1998; 2000). A further difficulty is that approaches to difficult knowledge mirror the breakdown of meaning, and professors and teachers may unconsciously project into students our own depression, anxiety, helplessness, and the mutating avoidance. Surely the Shoah has transformed what may be said about transference to loss, even as the contemporary gap between the terrors of apprehending historical facts and the fragility of being affected remains an open question for both pedagogy and psychoanalysis.

Within the imaginary of psychoanalysis, the authority of affect belongs to the psychosomatic pain invoked. While there are many entry points into describing anguish, Melanie Klein's (1946) depictions of the mind as made from the mental constellations of the depressive and the paranoid/schizoid positions suggest the blurring of intra-psychical and intersubjective processes. Both positions create the mind and symbolization and imagination lean on their variations. Adler exposes these psychic dimensions in theory, sociology, and aesthetics, and he tells us why it is not enough to represent the Shoah through the confines of anxiety and guilt that accompany the aftermath of trauma. When history returns, aesthetics directs the dilemmas of symbolizing the receptions of memory. To face the writer's struggle with the deferrals and resistances to affective history, we, too, must imagine resistance to what comes before, during, and after aesthetics.

In pedagogical encounters "After Auschwitz," both teachers and students may experience a sudden wish to console, rescue, protect, and give a lesson in courage. Or there may be identification with meaninglessness, the incapacity to act, the collapse of then into now, and then the move toward guilt, still defended against by clichés or evasions made from facile comparisons of catastrophes or competitions of suffering.[5] Or, discussions of representations of the Shoah may be reduced by expectations of how one must feel or who can speak. From any angle, identifications with the wish for understanding or with the failure to understand obstruct the work of binding what it is like, then and now, to encounter the work of thinking and feeling, and what it is like, then and now, to question what stops significance short or why the mind gives itself away. These pedagogical challenges belong to the aesthetics of learning and our capacity to represent the predicaments of thinking that contain and are guided by themes of uncertainty, transformation, and binding. Adler was involved with these pedagogical problems with a keen eye to the developments of the new modes of address with his focus on the history of reception. He performed the dilemmas of understanding by creating relations to history and memory with the survivor's quest, *What now?* Adler's work creates the conditions for belonging with an emotional vocabulary that enacts, contains, and symbolizes the vulnerability of becoming subject to historical memory.

Between Adler and psychoanalysis there is something unavoidable that involves encountering deep regard for the complexities, perplexities, and impressions that belong to psychical life and its right to interiority. My dialogue with Adler, philosophers, writers, and psychoanalysts is loosely woven from three psychoanalytic themes and their methods that, given their emphasis on the exigencies of life, love, and containment, serve as a counter-depressive to apathy, trauma, and dissociation. Each theme has a share in my handling of the backdrop of affected history as the unconscious and conscious ways we bind our lives with others. Approaching affected history, then, involves a radical relationality I later describe as "aesthetic conflicts," or profound questions the self gives over to the impact and meaning of beauty, truth, and knowledge.[6]

The first theme registers the arrival of uncertainty. It emerges from reading Adler's novels as profoundly psychological and as a challenge to psychology; they are literary expressions of human explorations of experience as sensation, impression, and impact and they perform the utter difficulty of responding to what has no precedence. They formulate what it feels like to move closer to events without reason. Even in ordinary times, the mind's capacity to compose its inner world from object relations and with actual others is always in ambivalent flux with the obscurity of external reality and with attempts to know what is real and unreal, what is good and bad, what is true and false, and what is generative and deadening. These searches for meaning lean on the depressive and paranoid/schizoid positions and express the mind's aesthetic conflicts. But Adler's novels, symbolizing the imposition of traumatic reality and the afterwardness of perceptions of deep psychology, ask more from the search for beauty, truth, and knowledge: What can life mean, what should it mean, and what means are available when its purposes are denied? In symbolizing the fragmenting worlds of historical catastrophe into their aftereffects in thought and writing, his novels propose to psychology the uncertain question, *What now?*

A second theme of transformation belongs to contemporary narratives of the postwar history of psychoanalysis. Perhaps best described as a psychoanalysis of afterwardness, the main claim is that the modern history of anti-Semitism and the Shoah has transformed the imaginary, theories, and techniques of psychoanalysis. Werner Bohleber (2010) develops the idea that the Shoah has affected the imaginary of psychoanalysis in ways that the field is just beginning to acknowledge. He points to two conflicted elements at work, trauma as the fracturing of meaning and the problem of acknowledging historical truth: "the traumatic experience disrupts the network of meanings for a human being, it is impossible to describe in a way that is bound to meaning.... [And] aside from an empathic listener, a social discourse about the historical truth of the traumatic events is also needed, and about its being denied and warded off" (94). Indeed, as trauma theory has become joined to the experiences of witnessing testimony, and as testimony has been joined with the crisis of education as developed by Felman and Laub (1992), the field of psychoanalysis now returns to its own archive to understand how the world has in fact shaped its understanding of interiority, intersubjectivity, and group psychology on the one hand, and transference and counter-transference on the other hand.[7] Both dimensions bring consideration to the work of mourning as conscious acts (Kahn 2023) and as the working through of collective wounds in political life and aesthetics (Soreanu 2018; Soreanu, Staberg, and Willner 2023).

Themes of transformation emerge from the experiences of displaced people. Freudian psychoanalysis in Germany, Hungary, Poland, France, and Austria was nearly destroyed by National Socialism; by 1933, the Jewish European psychoanalytic diaspora began for those who could leave and escape.[8] Continental psychoanalysis had to be rebuilt after the war. Many analysts who did such work were survivors in exile. Through the Jewish figure of the psychoanalyst Hillel Klein, contemporary psychoanalysis responds to the survivor's call for witnessing as transformation of the self with others.

A third theme concerns the tension of memory as belonging, not to place, but to the psychical work of binding the past and the present. Binding is a bringing together or a linking with what presents as split off, disparate, or repressed. It is created from the psychoanalytic ethic of free association as an invitation to extend the reach of words into affecting and faraway experiences that bring likeness to what first presents as dissociated and discarded. Free association renews the life of narration and the power of listening in unexpected ways. As a technique for bringing into play what is furthest from the mind with what the self would never say, free association releases the experiences of aesthetics from the judgments of taste and disinterestedness. Another term for binding is linking, a bringing together or an association of ideas and affect for the work of construction and significance. Through these signifiers we may imagine aporia, dispersals, and unconscious relations among ideas, experiences, people, and affects.

Uncertainty, transformation, and binding are also elements of historical memory and perhaps even constitute and express their pedagogical principles. This is due both to the problem of symbolizing trauma beyond the repetition compulsion and to experiencing the history of its reception, part of which includes working through denial, disbelief, and a turning away from the pain of relationality called by witnessing. Thus, a notion of belonging to and affiliation with the past one has not experienced is needed to imagine what can be shared, discussed, and affectively desired. In reading clinical literature on survivors' testimony and dialogue in treatment, I am struck by their thematic resemblance to the struggles presented in Adler's novels. Their resonance is uncanny and follows along the lines of Adler's images of his experiences. While no survivor experience is the same, when the survivor speaks and writes from what is elemental to the self, there is an address to the other, both within and without, that releases an affecting emotional imaginary through signifiers that link us all: *mother, father, home, friendship*, and *love and hate*. The survivor remembers ordinary life before its traumatic fracturing. In narrating what has happened, the primal meaning of these intimate signifiers is stretched to their breaking points, not only by the temporality of before and after, but also in breaking the frame of the here and now with expressions of anguish and hope over the nature of loss, forgiveness, atonement, and mourning. And, yet, when words are forced to carry the burden of incontrovertible historical facts, the survivor may be lost, or reduced to an object of history. Here, themes of uncertainty, transformation, and binding are highly charged with what comes before and after.

What Now?

The psychoanalyst Hillel Klein (1923–1985) has written on the relational complexity and emotional legacy and trials of "the survivor" as they play out in Jewish life in Israel, Europe, the United Kingdom, and the United States. Klein was a Polish Jew, captured in 1942 around the age of 18. An adolescent survivor of many camps, at the age of 22, he was liberated from the ghetto Theresienstadt by the Soviet Army. In a note, "Liberation, May 8, 1945," Klein (2012a) expressed the pain of losing his friends and family: "I could not feel joy. The intense hatred changed into a numbness and amnesia, and there were no feelings at all. Despite the long years of yearning and anticipation, of experiencing freedom in fantasy (the fantasies of 'Messianic times,' or *Machiach Zeiten* in Yiddish), and of the joy that would overcome me, there was only sadness and embarrassment. What to do with my freedom? What to do now?" (252).

After the war, Klein trained as a psychiatrist in Munich and took his psychoanalytic education with the Institute of Psychoanalysis in London, studying with two leaders of the Middle Group, Michael Balint and Donald Winnicott. Klein immigrated to Israel in the early 1950s and held his psychoanalytic clinic in Jerusalem. By 1933, a small group of German Jewish analysts had emigrated to Palestine and formed a psychoanalytic society. They attempted to establish psychoanalysis in the Hebrew University, began translating Freud's work into Hebrew, and held educational workshops for teachers with the view of bringing psychoanalysis to children in schools and the Kibbutzim experiments in social upbringing (Rolnik 2012). Much of their early work was dedicated to the building of a psychological Zionism. When Klein moved to Israel, he began to develop his ideas on "the Holocaust syndrome" as the incapacity to relate to the destruction of European Jewry in Israel, Europe, and the Jewish Diaspora. Late in his life, Klein (2012a) concluded that self-understanding and the undoing of the defense against being affected is key to the rapprochement with destructive history: "Widening the scope of our knowledge by means of self-scrutiny will enable us to reduce the repressed areas and the resultant defensive measures and thereby lessen the tendency toward self-hatred on the one hand and the magic approach of chauvinism and denial of reality on the other hand" (124). Near the end of his life Klein visited Germany to begin a dialogue with Jewish and German Christian analysts.

Klein is perhaps the first psychoanalyst to discuss the importance of play in the survivor's life and he gave attention to the power of literature and theatre as resources for emotional restoration. Given his emphasis on restoration, creativity, play, and rebuilding a life, Klein broke from the dominant psychiatric emphasis on the pathology known as "the survivor syndrome" (209). He treated this diagnosis as distancing, as a consequence of social silence, and ultimately, as indicating the practitioner's fear of the survivor. More intimately, Klein argued that therapeutic distance is impossible because "the difficulty lies in the universal guilt that besets us—the therapist as human beings" (209). The syndrome belongs to the counter-transference of the witness, by which the survivor arouses feelings of unbearable loss and helplessness. Earlier I suggested this dynamic as the pedagogical syndrome. Klein (2012a) also shifts commonsensical views from guilt as wrongdoing to that of an urge for consciousness of life when he identifies the intricacies of disparate relationality: within those who survived, with those who did not or would not help, with the children of survivors and perpetrators, and with those who learned to witness the witnesses and create communal rituals for the elaboration of social memory. Given such radical relationality, Klein preferred not to use the term *Holocaust* but "rather refer to it as 'Human Trembling' in association to Kierkegaard's concept of Abraham's trembling when he was commanded to sacrifice Isaac" (209). He then proposed that survivor's guilt is not necessarily harmful and is to be understood as regret for the other's sake, as an emotional tie to the past before the disaster, as a sense of continuity with the Jewish people, and as hope for the care of the social bond yet to become.

As for the work of witnessing, Klein's (2012b) "Problems of Countertransference in the Psychotherapy of Holocaust Survivors and Their

Children" considered intergenerational transmission and obstacles to emotional responsiveness. He named seven counter-transferences: "(1) detachment tactics, (2) the need for general conceptualization, (3) over-identification, (4) anger, (5) helplessness, (6) the guilt of survival, and (7) doubts about one's own capacity as a therapist and doubts about one's own profession" (208). While Klein's work specifically focused on how the psychoanalyst is affected by the patient, it is not such a stretch to relate these counter-transference defenses as a frame for assessing the qualities of resistance and identification across the spectrum of pedagogy, experienced between teachers, students, and the public, and in the emotional encounters in group psychology, with humanly induced destruction, social hatreds, competitive suffering, and the contentions over reparation.

The key question Klein brings to his discussion, however, belongs to recognizing the relational situation of survival. Klein (2012a) asked: "Who are the survivors? They have become the historians of their own fates as well as the objects of history. They are monuments to man's destructive power untamed by centuries of European civilization. But they are, as well, symbols of rebirth and of man's efforts to preserve within himself an image of God" (31). While Klein does not specify, and no one can, what image of God is to be preserved, his concern is with the aesthetics of rebirth emerging from Jewish spirituality that permits questions and doubts across a larger universe of meaning that is unknown. He proposes the difficult aesthetics of rebirth and relates the pain of becoming an object of history to the persecutory guilt that divides the subject, agonizes the wish to belong, and denies the pain of response. But through the refractions of its competing meanings, Klein understood guilt as a fragile tie to the other and, on this view, only as the beginning of a sense of one's responsibility for psychic change. The contention is that guilt serves as an entry into psychical conflict and, perhaps, the undoing of society's defenses. And as contiguity, guilt becomes an index for the impact of what the survivor's witnessing of life in extremity may come to mean today.

Ten years separated Klein and Adler; they may have never met, yet their lives crisscrossed the stormy currents of history. Klein was an adolescent survivor with a childhood still recent whereas Adler, prior to imprisonment, had already accomplished an education, was married, and had worldly interests. Each lived in the forced ghetto of Theresienstadt, and for a while Klein, like Adler, lived in London. Their meeting may only come in the work they left behind and through common questions. How can the emotional world be apprehended, symbolized, and responded to without unconsciously repeating the victimization and violence? What does life want? And while their methods and styles differed, both gave free admission to life as an on-going relation with the other, founded on emotional ties made from the search for beauty, truth, and knowledge. Within this search aesthetics becomes instructed by what life presents.

What life presents stands before us, and an earlier introjected history with our mothers is projected forward, to be incorporated and played between the lines of love and hate. Donald Meltzer and Meg Harris Williams (1988) have developed the view that early in life the infant apprehends the mother's beauty through her enigmas. They imagine this meeting as overwhelming, "as an emotional experience of a passionate quality" (22). Passionate, because the mother, our first love, is so unknown and creates for the infant a new form of uncertainty and even the pain of suspicion toward what cannot be seen: the future of difference and interactions between the inside and the outside, between essence and appearance, and between presence and absence. Meltzer and Harris Williams name this primary emotional situation "aesthetic conflict...in terms of the impact of the outside of the 'beautiful' mother, available to the senses, and the enigmatic inside which must be constructed by creative imagination" (22).

Aesthetic conflicts propose a paradox: existence as both a fundamental relation between the self and the other, earlier described as the depressive position, and existence as "the failure of apprehension of beauty through emotional response to its perception" (1–2) described as the pain of the paranoid/schizoid position. The failure scatters feelings of persecution, splitting, and the terrible paranoia that belongs to anxiety and the self's defense against loss. What makes this conflict aesthetic, however, is the element of uncertainty as to whether the inside that cannot be seen can be known and whether what cannot be known, can be brought closer. And this ambivalence, or depressive anxiety, creates the desire for imagination to symbolize and bind affects that agonize. It may be that there is a drive to aesthetics, or a drive to beauty created between mothers and babies. For Meltzer and Harris Williams, the work of art and psychoanalysis elaborates these conflicts with the difference of providing a container for their symbolization.

The Journey

The psychoanalytic mythology of the earliest impress of maternal care influenced my reading of H. G. Adler's two novels, *The Journey* (2008) and *Panorama* (2011). Both are full of grandmothers, mothers, fathers, brothers, sisters, aunts, and friends. The family as a loving container gives substance to being that usher its members into the humanity, faith, and desire Adler witnesses and remembers. Here are the first sentences of *Panorama*: " 'There's a new program today. We're going to the Panorama.' Josef hears the voice of his grandmother and looks up from his toy" (3). The novel opens into a loving scene that binds the goodness of grandmother's voice and a child's play to a new adventure. The narrator creates the child's associative mind: thoughts rushing to take in the mysteries of the family, then the adolescent desire for truth, beauty and knowledge in nature and the world of new ideas. Later, readers meet Josef Kramer's disillusionment, involuntary confinement, the horrors of the camp and the desire to keep his own mind from going insane. With survival, readers follow the agony of rebuilding the self. It is as if Adler demands that, for readers to face what is devastated and what survives, they too must first remember a time when sense was made, and life was both enigmatic and filled with promise.

Binding to a time before also unsettles thoughts of what is and will become. Nothing can protect us from the reverberations the past gives to the future. In an extraordinary passage in *The Journey* (2008), where Adler's style nearly collapses from the pressures of competing temporality, Aunt Ida's fate is to be both precious in life and reduced to an object. She is waiting with her sister in their ghetto home for the authorities to arrest and deport her. She has already packed a small suitcase, marked with her name and date of birth. Her sister, Caroline, both knows and does not know what will happen and is deeply preoccupied by their forced separation. Each has reveries. Ida's mind drifts back to happier times even as she reassures her sister that she will be fine. The narrator breaks in to explain the rules: "One talks about what is nearby and thinks about what is far off" (154). Adler handles the sisters' illusions tenderly. What is "far off" is before the war: Aunt Ida was born, welcomed lovingly into her family, married, gave birth to a good son now safe in America, survived her husband's sudden death, and was welcomed into her sister's home.

Near the end of this passage, Aunt Ida has been reduced to a name and date on a suitcase. Suddenly, the narrator breaks open time and voice, yanking readers into their future inside "a museum of technology": "What will happen to the treasures of the departed? Everything is displayed in glass cases after it has been cleaned and conserved, the neat writing explains everything.... The teacher leads the children into the museum and has to explain everything in detail" (2008, 158). The details are harrowing, and it is no accident that Adler returns the detached objectifications of material evidence to the education that will fail teachers and students. And readers are jarred, disoriented by the chaos of time, voices, addresses, intentions, characters, places, and Adler's effort to write. The children ask the unbearable question: Where are the bodies? And the more the teacher explains the more the narrator insists upon what is still missing. Adler's narrator protests: "How did this happen? . . . We won't do it! We don't want luggage, we want our life back!" (161).

It is as if, in repeating the word *everything* three times, Adler anticipated the crisis of education as being overwhelmed by the inconsolability of people and their stolen objects now housed in museums. Perhaps he already knew bearing witness would have to involve two opposing realities that occupy the same space: representations of unjustifiable violence, criminality, and indifference; and recognition of a human who was born, loved, cared for others, and hated dehumanization. Conflicts may inaugurate a passion for imagining incompatible realities, one that pedagogy inherits and must find a way to contain and bind. Such imagining also carries failure that capsizes into despair; as Meltzer and Harris Williams (1988) warn, there are "the constant dangers of both objects and values sliding into degradation" (80).

Letters

Between the years 1948 and 1950 and before his work was published in Germany, Adler exchanged a series of letters with the German Jewish author Hermann Broch.[9] They had much in common: home, friends, philosophy, experimental literary style, and the desire to name and transform what they saw as administrated man and the disintegration of human decency. Both writers were living in exile, Broch in the United States and Adler now in London. Broch wrote to Adler after learning from Elias Canetti of his outline "on life in the concentration camps" (White and Speirs 1999b, 145)[10] and asked for the manuscript with this warning: "one must of course be prepared for the fact that publishers here [in the United States], particularly in the currently bad business climate, take fright at massive works like this, especially as the public would prefer to read friendly stories rather than concern themselves with such an unpleasant topic" (Letter 1, July 23, 1948, 145). Adler replied a few days later with appreciation and an acknowledgment of how Broch's early novel influenced him: "The interpretation of the *Sleepwalkers* revealed to me for the first time the necessary prehistory, as it were, of the cultural and more general social decline which was bound to ensure and which I then witnessed directly in its symbolic culmination in Auschwitz" (Letter 2, August 7, 1948, 145–146).

Adler sent the thousand-page German manuscript on the ghetto Theresienstadt to Broch in early August and received a reply dated September 10, 1948. There was another prehistory that Adler could not have known and, too, a post-history that Broch would never know. Eventually, Adler's magnum opus, *Theresienstadt 1941–1945: The Face of a Coerced Community*, was published in German in 1955 and was one of the first reports on Jewish life in the camps; it was only later translated into English in 2017.[11] Adler was thirty-three years old when he was deported to Theresienstadt in 1942 (Filkins 2019). The English edition of his 875-page ethnography detailed life in the ghetto—documents, maps, data, statistics, food delivery, medical care, burials—with commentary on the designs of history, sociology, culture, and psychology. Adler's biographer and translator, Peter Filkins (2019), began his discussion of the ghetto by signaling its contradictions: "To understand Theresienstadt, one needs to understand what it was and what it was not.... Theresienstadt, ultimately, was too many different things at once, part ghetto, part old age home, part death sentence, part cultural oasis, part depot for transports, and part alibi for atrocities in the east" (103, 108).

Broch's prehistory was stated simply. "You see," Broch wrote as an explanation for his delayed letter, "my mother died in Theresienstadt, so that the first reading stirred me up rather too much, in fact to such an extent that I skipped over some things which I now need to go back to" (Letter 4, September 10, 1948, 147). Adler wrote back immediately: "How often and how clearly I saw you in my mind's eye in Theresienstadt ... how intensely your understanding of recent history occupied my thoughts as I dwelt, quite ignorant of the fact, just a few houses away from your mother whose life had to end in that merciless place. Perhaps I would have been less bold in approaching you if I had had any inkling of this circumstance" (Letter 5, September 24, 1948, 148).

What Adler could not have known as well was that Broch was turning away from writing novels. Broch had strong doubts over literature's ethical effects and questioned whether the survivor's emotionality lends to those who come after any understanding of the mechanisms of history. Looking back, it is difficult to know the nature of Broch's disappointment with literature. Perhaps a combination of the loss of his mother and his wish for a more distant, objective approach affected Broch's other responses to Adler's novels and poetry. As the correspondence progresses, their commonality frays and the exchanges grow exceedingly polite and distant. Broch's ambivalence toward literature forecasted contemporary debates on what Felman (1992) developed as the crisis of education opened by history's return in novels, art, poetry, and cinema and what I named, in my work on contemporary psychoanalytic pedagogy, as encounters with "difficult knowledge" (Britzman 1998).

Broch is ambivalent about Adler's fictional work and after a long silence writes Adler to ask how his novels have gone beyond Kafka's work. Adler did have Kafka in mind when, a year earlier and writing in 1947 to Wolfgang Burghart, he described his intent with the Theresienstadt study and perhaps more generally what he hoped his novels would create: "No one has ever written a work of this kind about a concentration camp.... At the same time it is readable and vivid, a Kafka novel in reverse, in that it evokes a real world. Anyone who makes the effort to read its thousand or so pages will really have been in the camp" (White and Speirs 1999a, 136). For much of the rest of the correspondence with Broch, Adler defends his literary approach:

> In order to say what I had to say, however, I could not use a discursive technique, i.e., I could not choose a scientific method because I had results to present which were indeed written from knowledge of and out of attention to philosophy and science but which had in no way been arrived at by such means or by means of them alone.... And I could only present my views and attacks as I experienced the process, and in the manner in which I could create it. (Letter 14, July 4, 1949, 159)

Adler may also be saying that something has happened to knowledge and its governing rules and writing that witnesses this collapse of meaning and decency must do so not with impartiality, distance, and reason.

The writing must pass through the force of affect and its aftereffects of shattering experience. What repels must be brought closer.

With the correspondence and the loss of a friend, we too confront an unavoidable problem of encountering conflicts within the reception of historical memory that binds Adler's time to ours: the on-going argument as to whether writing of the Shoah, or writing of any genocide for that matter, must be direct and factual or whether the obscurity of experience must instruct literary knowledge, ethnographic reportage, and their uneven receptions. These conflicts of relating belong to our present and what it is to be instructed by and instruct affected life. Broch had also been struggling with Adler's then unpublished novel, *Die Ansiedlung* (The Settlement), described as mythical allegory. The novel for Broch defied reason, and he felt at a loss to understand it. In a letter dated December 9, 1949, it seems as if Broch had given up or had left Adler hanging on to a history no one was ready for: "At any rate—this I know and this too expresses a generational difference—you are already in quite a different sphere from any that I could reach artistically; for this reason you should carry on writing.... But precisely because you are so far ahead you will probably have to wait a long time for the effect on the outside world" (Letter 17, December 9, 1949, 164). Adler's reply is an argument for the writer's aesthetic freedom that he attached to a "messianic principle." Limits must be mobile, and Adler quoted what he felt from his doctoral studies before the war: "The spirit of limitation must be defeated" (Letter 18, December 16, 1949, 172).

Broch asked whether literature was relevant to the task of truth: could literature have any ethical effect on the public; or just by virtue of its imaginative genre, just by virtue of its trespass into subjectivity, and by virtue of its liberties, constructions, and free associations, might literature also teeter into misunderstandings or denial? These anxieties are also glimmers of why psychoanalysis has been avoided: how, the rationalist might ask, can self-knowledge on the sources of thinking lead to social transformation? Isn't phantasy a dead-end street? Why consider obstacles to understanding? Broch may have felt that literature only serves to obscure the facts of historical devastation and its structural and material causes. For Broch, practical empiricism must come first, as there could be no mistaken interpretation for the reader. Adler believed otherwise. He wished aesthetics to come closer to what life feels. In one of his last and longest letters, Adler poses his question: "What can you do in a world like this which has acquired such a monstrous and often clownlike, de-ranged countenance and which, *cum grano salis*, is your world?" (Letter 20, July 17, 1950, 181).

Life Wants More Life

Adler completed his doctorate from the German University of Prague, the German-speaking branch of the Charles University, in 1935. There must have been many philosophical and literary influences (and one can sense these in his novel *Panorama*), but one that seems to be in the backdrop of the movement between literature and life can be found in Adler's admiration of the German Jewish philosopher and sociologist Georg Simmel (1858–1918). Simmel's (2010) last publication turned to a testimony of metaphysics, not by way of explication but as an address to the spirit or totality of life more than determinacy.[12] He depicted this life as "the reaching out of life beyond itself" (9) and presented his readers with the problem of boundaries—those of reality and historical fact and those of concept, ideality, and the sensible world. He saw each as strands that tie knowledge and ignorance. Simmel seemed to rework the meaning of binding when he wrote, "The inherent displaceability and displacement of our boundaries means that we are able to express our essence with a paradox: we are bounded in every direction, and we are bounded in no direction" (2). His aphorism on childbearing expressed a similar sentiment: "Childbearing tends to be imperfect because with each of its particular acts it must serve two opposed tendencies: freeing and binding" (177). Leaning on the faith that life is more than life and that life wants more of life inaugurates a terrific uncertainty: we are free to search for the beauty of meaning and are free to be beholden to what life presents. For both Simmel and Adler, the mutative boundaries belonged to the life of the mind and sensate life is more than bodily boundaries.

Adler's friendship with the writer Canetti permits more comment on the intimacies that stir subjective life into metaphysical discussions and that take a generative shape into friendship. Elias Canetti (1905–1994) also wrote novels, sociology, and memoirs. They would be close friends in London. Canetti's (1999) long memoir of his literary life that joins the love of his mother to his love of language ends in the year 1937 with two events: the death of his beloved mother and his meeting with Adler, then a young man. Canetti had come to Prague by Adler's invitation. They spoke to each other in German. And Canetti remembers Adler as a sensitive guide:

> He was intensely idealistic and seemed out of place in the damnable times to which he was soon to fall victim.... But he realized what it meant to me to hear all sorts of people speaking a language I did not understand, to hear them *for myself*, without anyone translating what they said. My interest in the effect of words I did not understand must have been something new to him. It was a very special sort of effect, not at all comparable to that of music, for one feels *threatened* by words one does not understand, one turns them over in one's mind in an attempt to blunt them, but they are repeated and in repetition become more menacing than ever. He was tactful enough to leave me alone for hours, though he worried about my getting lost.... When we met again he would ask me about my impressions and it was a sign of great sympathy for him that I found it hard not to tell him everything. (826–827)

Perhaps the great sign was Adler's empathy for the stranger, an emotional binding crafted from his attunement for what boundaries could not hold: the emotional turmoil of being affected by the struggle to understand. Adler, I think, understood the joys of language and the inchoate pains of its destruction. Like Canetti, he permitted what is not understood and what is uncertain to pass into the beauty of writing. The mother tongue, our first container for words, also carries this enigma, or aesthetic conflict.

Binding

The endings of both *Panorama* and *The Journey* present the slow, painful rebirth of a survivor. *Panorama* (2011) carries the burden of consciousness—the mind observing its own thoughts while trying to escape them. Josef Kramer is absorbed in the search for essences and their enigmas. Time hurtles Josef along, Adler changes scenery and countries, and Josef is now sitting on a hill in rural England, looking down at the ruins of Thomas Cromwell's castle where George Fox was imprisoned. Josef thinks of the association of home with prison and the state's unparalleled power to confine. He also replays the scenes from his life, which have taken form as passage through philosophy and the failures of the absolute, only to arrive at what is inescapable: "nothing more than the question, 'What now?'" (431). There are attempts at binding a broken history and in reverie, Josef thinks, "Grief exists but so does gratitude" (437). But that is not enough, and Adler's sentences become longer. No one sentiment, no one memory, no one viewpoint, no one feeling is enough for an awakening. All he can do is attest to his existence.

Adler gives more narrative structure to the conclusion of *The Journey* (2011). The torturous philosophical problems of going on have now become tender with the question of the pain of incompletion and the narrator's attempts to integrate feelings with life. Paul is the only survivor of the Lustig family, and his "liberation" from the camp begins with great chaos. He is looking for his family, their names, and proof of existence, theirs and his. What happened to them? Paul wishes to enter the inside of an apartment to see if it really exists, though he is asking about his own existence: "it is not that easy to go back to how things were. One must begin more slowly, from the bottom up" (252).

A stranger tells Paul of an empty military barracks; he can stay there. It is between these walls that Paul slowly emerges: he wills his legs to become his own legs, permits the grace of sleeping and then awakening, takes a bath, puts on a military uniform from the closet, sets a dinner table and decides to live. When Paul catches a glance of himself in the mirror, he is repelled.

Yet there is the desire to look and to remember. Adler's composition is reminiscent of the mirror stage, that phase of early development when a young child first recognizes its reflection in the mirror and feels the self as unity.

> Paul wants to flee this wretched image, yet his gaze is completely spellbound, something bothers him about it, he doesn't really know why and feels ashamed, though he cannot resist nor can he prevent himself from sobbing constantly and crying helplessly and watching his own tears fall.... What's he crying about? Is Paul missing or is he what he used to be, has he been taken away or is he standing here alive? No, it's not an old man, it's not a child who is crying. It's a silent, unstoppable weeping, an infinite sadness that has no reason at all and cannot cease.

> Paul feels the glass with the tips of his fingers. He wants the mirror in front of his eyes constantly to touch it and recognize himself. Soon the face quietly becomes more real, a sense of safety making it possible to feel that a new era is to begin. Years ago Paul had not liked mirrors and had avoided them. He doesn't like the way his gaze is trapped here as well, but he will take this mirror along with him when he leaves this room. Then a decision begins to dawn inside him. . . . The journey will have to take him back to where he was hauled off against his will. . . . Paul wants to go farther, yet he knows he has to travel to Stupart, because only there will he find what was taken away from him on this journey. Finally conquering the storm of tears, Paul smiles at himself. It's not a happy smile, but rather an end to this keening. (259–261)

This mirror stage belongs to an adult who must contend with pieces of the self through the refractions of loss and all that once constituted a capacity for wholeness but is no longer there. Unlike the infant receiving her image from the mother, the second mirror stage for the adult involves symbolizing the consequences of fragmentation and rebinding as means to revive the self. What repels must be brought back closer. Through Paul's words, readers rediscover history as body, as image, sensation, experience, other, as mirror to the present, and then, as decision. We are also privy to the emotional turmoil of facing the self with questions of beauty, truth, and knowledge. And as with the self, readers, too, must bind again pieces of a life into renewed meaning and become, not an object of history, but a subject who proposes the reconstruction of history from the ruins of what has already happened.

What Now?

The work of apprehending knowledge needed to enliven historical memory cannot be accomplished without symbolizing anxiety while also experiencing expressions of life as the unexpected groundswell for history's return. What must be brought closer is witnessing the witness's interest in auscultating the freedom to feel, imagine, and learn from what is already there: the significance and vulnerability of the emotional world and the need to ask, *What now?* Yes, the reception of history leaves us with the pain of incompleteness and attempts to hold what has happened to others as affecting how it is we live in our own time. Another way of posing these relations belongs to psychical experiences and themes of uncertainty, transformation, and binding and the intimacies of symbolizing the intersubjective struggle in remembering life as coming before and after aesthetics.

Chapter 8

Once Again, but This Time with Feeling

> A text, like a dream, has its 'day's residues.'
>
> —J.-B. Pontalis (1981), "Between the Dream as Object and the Dream-text" (39)

Reservations

There waits between the lines of each author's work a reserve of learning, inheritances on hold nearly remote from conscious motives and perhaps best described as remainders of life's illegible experiences. To release this reserve into writing and affect the startles of a sharable reality, the writer must gamble with her own scenes of incoherence that still contain the means for piecing the self together again. Communicating these matters brings the psychoanalytic claim that the act of writing is mirror to unconscious impressions of our earliest infantile learning now to be felt as appeals to the writer's inheritance. For the writer, inheritance carries the weight of the other's givens, contentions, and longings replete with the pathos of those loves and their losses.[1] Writing then appears where experience and communication fail, leaving the writer to ask, *What is missing?*

Of course, the writer may have reservations on hold and not only with how the choice of topic can be conveyed and received. There are also the writer's phantasies that follow from ambivalence made from having to begin with her own feelings of doubt, uncertainty, and hesitation. The unarticulated dilemma involves what comes before writing because *that* writing is also an appeal to sensate life with its designs of emotional ties readily entangled in the unconscious, imagination, the day's residues, and the world of others. From this view, try to consider the writer's inheritance through the delicacy of its many psychical transitions: with the birth of the body; with the emotional situation of infancy as inextricable from the mother; with the relational apprehension of phantasy and anxiety as the basis for creation of symbols; with a curiosity for the stirrings of loved and hated delegates of psychical life; and with the capacity for cathexis to a wider world.[2]

If writing has a great deal to do with the animations of our uneven development and the transference dispersals of our most affecting transitions, then a case can be made for the writer's question *What is missing?* I understand these psychical dynamics as the soft foundation for imagination and thought, as the bare elements for reading and writing, as pathway to self/other relations and, too, for commentary on affecting dream life. My title, "Once again, but this time with feeling," serves as the emotive scenery of inheritance and, as a referral for our emotional ties, carries the added appeal for sympathy.

The Day's Residues

While writing this essay, I turned to reading what others had to say about their writing. J.-B. Pontalis's (1981) psychoanalytic discussion of the writer's reveries gave me a metaphor: "A text, like a dream, has its 'day's residues'" (39). While so much of our life appears and disappears into our writing, the cast of day's residues, as they affect the text, can be imperceptible and prone to disguise, distortions, and condensation, just as with the dream-work. Indeed, while Freud (1923a) considered consciousness as a barrier to overstimulation—and perhaps writing holds this function as well—he also permitted the opposite experience: due to the unconscious, the human is utterly receptive to fleeting impressions of life and their notice without attention. Freud supposed the borders between the conscious and the unconscious are porous, just as are the boundaries between the self and the world and the writer and the words.

Freud (1900a) developed a trodden path to our most private subtext with the idea of returning to the day's residues as a method for free association and the interpretation of dreams. While not the only method, it is the one that keeps the dreamer in charge, and recounting the day's residues brings into awareness the dream's ties to the stream of life through what Freud called "consideration of representation" (310). Not any image or dream object will do. But its enigmas cause us to fill in the missing parts and narrate the dream as if watching a motion picture replete with plot, changing scenes, good and bad characters, familiar and strange locations, and fade-outs. As our nocturnal transference to the day's residues, the dream-work urges visitation rights to these left-over impressions and pushes the dream into the currency of our preoccupations and wishes however disguised, condensed, or displaced. Dreams, with the help of the day's residues, open the dreamer to narratives of a forgotten past and to what is absent. They may even begin to index the agonies, disappointments, and failures of political life (Sliwinski 2017).[3] However arbitrary the dream feels, and however far away it takes the dreamer from the logic of narrative conventions, associating the *as if* of dreams to the day's residues calls us back into the world, but now in place with conflicts and promises of untold experience and meaning. In this sense, dreams are not simple messages to decipher; they are appeals to someone.[4]

Since dreams are our most personal productions made to release the reserves of learning, they can be handled with Pontalis's (1981) other metaphor, "as staging a private theatre that provides a permutation of roles allowing one to assume none of them" (33). Yet for these transitions to be taken as variations on the theme of the personal and come as close to the pining for the object that we can bear, we do have to speak for the life of the mind as threaded by our emotional ties to others that also are the pulls of anticipation over their loss. We go far afield before we can care for the claims of the day's residues. Only later, when narrated once again to someone else, do we experience the movement from the phantasies and persecutory anxieties made from "memories in feelings" (Klein 1957, 234) to the witnessing of memories in construction, but this time as feelings for memories.

A Psychoanalytic Challenge

I understand our earliest learning, say when we learned to point, crawl, talk, walk, and eat, as something like a dream come true. Like dreams, learning does not appear out of the blue; yet in the beginning of our lives, we are permitted this illusion, and the mother makes that so: the infant creates and discovers what is there to be found (Winnicott [1967] 2001). Indeed, the borders between infant and mother are, at first, porous, mutable, and unconscious. The transformations from the immediacy of gratification to the experience of frustration, to the capacity to wait, and then to feelings of gratitude take a great deal of time (Britzman 2016). It is as if the subjective figuration of our earliest learning emerges from an illusion of fullness or magical thinking and then, due to the other, is subsequently an emptying out, needed to take in the world already there. Not until we try to relate to the other as separate, not until we symbolize the anxieties that urge us to go further or perhaps warn us to turn back, and not until we can acknowledge what is gone, destroyed, and what survives, may we play in the field of learning with actual others (Ogden 2016). As we move from the question *How does that work?* to *What is it?* we find ourselves struggling with inheritance just at the point that we grasp the ways we are charged to transform the objects of learning into personal significance and a shared reality.[5]

There are always traces of others whose stories bear the weight and feel of how their history has been first received, met by our phantasies of what it means to convey something of the self to another. Learning as inheritance is thus greater than a march of succession, more than accumulation of knowledge, and more than acquisition of technical skill. Its excess comes from the other and so is best apprehended through its psycho-cultural developments that themselves are transformations of continuity (unity of self) into contiguity (alongside others who are separate) (Winnicott 2001, 101).

As our libidinal dials turn toward the world of others, learning gains momentum through its double action: involvement with the self's objections and the self's creation of "narrative revolts."[6] Objections, readily found in pedagogical relations, may take the form of repudiation for all that is *not me*. Narrative revolts undo defenses with an exploration of the personal as an appeal to the world. And yet, there is no clear division, and these positions may occupy the same space. The tenders of transformations are indeed difficult to grasp, and not only because psychoanalysis proposes that consciousness is an exception in mental life. I think the dilemma is found in the on-going question of the shock of affect and its tendency to collapse subject with object and destroy the capacity to tell time and accept difference. By design, feelings are immediate; their transference urges blur the lines of anticipation with the defense of projective identification. The other part of the difficulty of knowing one's narrative acts belongs to the exquisite force of the other that can be felt or feel as threat, affirmation, or estrangement.

In figuring the density of our emotional logic and what is held in reserve we may find ourselves struggling to admit the force of personal investment with our mesmerizing attachments to a topic. Stephen Frosh's (2016) inquiry into his interests in psychosocial developments begins with that conflict: "It would be hard to wiggle out of the admonishment that an attachment to psychoanalysis always happens more for personal than for intellectual reasons" (469). But attachments are always personal, and if that is felt as admonishment, that can only mean the subject is in some kind of danger. But which subject and what kind of danger? It is as if the personal is beyond justification, and Frosh considers how quickly its entanglements become our means of disguise: "What is hidden from us is what matters most; and the more we explain, the more likely we are to become tied up in evasions and false trails" (470). Negations inevitably follow: It's not me.

The depth of our attachments creates a paradox for awareness: while much is unknown about the ephemeral self, while our reasoning is also caught within our emotional logic, and while the self's permit is to dream, to forget, to lose in order to find, and then to create, question, and doubt sensate thoughts and the desire to know, when giving an account of the compulsion to feel, the self tends to attribute emotional cause as coming from outside of itself (Aulagnier 2015). We seem to forget why that outside world becomes an inside one and how it happens that the unconscious registers even the tiniest events as appeals to earlier impressions. Perhaps the best one can say is that the effusions of emotional ties are like the air we breathe as well as that which takes our breath away. And the binds of emotional ties become more perplexing when approached from the angle of inheritances and how it is that historical memory presents as humane appeal. What is the nature of personal involvement then? And, within the biddings of the day's residues, is there a touching account for the affectivity of interests?

The Long Reach of the Day's Residue

One cold day in early March 2017, in the middle of struggling with writing this essay, I went to the movies to see *I Am Not Your Negro*, Raoul Peck's (2016) documentary film based on James Baldwin's plan for a book, "Remember This House." In 1979, Baldwin proposed to write a personal account of the lives and deaths of Medgar Evers, Dr. Martin Luther King, and Malcolm X. I was drawn into the work of the personal account, the incomplete manuscript, passing time, and my love of Baldwin.

Baldwin's manuscript could only be imagined, and Peck's film signaled that incompleteness. Perhaps this is how it must be, due not only to the unfinished manuscript but also to Baldwin himself. His (1985) critical essay, an autobiography of going to the movies as a child, adolescent, and adult, carries the title "The Devil Finds Work." The Peck film brought me back to Baldwin's writing. That long essay is a meditation on race and racism in films and novels and the personal account has to do with Baldwin's history of identifications with and anger for the disheartening portrayal of whiteness and blackness. Parts of that essay were read as the film's voice-over. What strikes me today about that essay is Baldwin's focus on why the social fractures of identity are simultaneously personal and relational: "An identity is questioned only when it is menaced, as when the mighty begin to fall, or when the wretched begin to rise, or when the stranger enters the gates, never, thereafter, to be a stranger: the stranger's presence making you the stranger, less to the stranger than to yourself" (606). The beauty of Baldwin's long perfect sentences still affects me: how he began with the day's residues and stretched these into a panorama of teeming life, saturated with desire for presence and its competing despair of loneliness. There was always feeling as much as there was his appeal to feel. Peck's film captured the cadence of Baldwin's prose: the slow burn of his words and the wake-up from the monstrosity of white disavowal; to see that this hatred was not a passion for ignorance but an unleashing of a sadistic force of destruction of self and other. Hatred, Baldwin insisted, is quite personal and, whether ingrained by the drive or the agitations of the failure of the social bond and the stultifications of injustice, the hatred of unleashed aggression wrecks us all and leaves those who come after to say what is difficult to tell, what is impossible to accept, and what is fragile to repair. But so too must we say whether we are believed or not, what it is to love.

Untimely Methods

It is difficult to decide whether methods for writing from the self to the other are led by postulates of experience or by what is missing and incomplete. I began with some reservations that circle the question of how the writer can grasp remainders of life's illegible experiences and still manage to admit a kernel of incoherence as a quality of the reserves of inheritance. The method emerges by asking *What is missing?* If writing is the return to what has been missed and to what is no longer there yet nonetheless insists on our beginnings, then the topic, however paradoxical, is an appeal to the emotional situations of absence and emptiness. I see in this approach a new theory for conceptualizing the appeals of learning through movements from transference to mourning, and from intersubjectivity to the capacity to be alone.

D. W. Winnicott's ([1963?] 1992) "Fear of Breakdown" regards the situation of "being" with an affecting kernel of incoherence, "that fear of breakdown is related to the individual's past experience, and to environmental vagaries" (87). Winnicott described the urgent response to what is unnamable with five of its primitive agonies: falling forever, fragmentation, depersonalization, de-realization, and isolation without any means of communication (89–90). These are not empty states but the experience of not being there, one of missing an experience that has already happened and without a witness. To grasp the fate of such agony, Winnicott ties the fear of breakdown to learning, a surprising turn since we tend to imagine learning as filling up with knowledge and rarely ask, *What is it? What happens before learning?* The enigma is found in Winnicott's observation: "The basis of learning (as well as eating) is emptiness. But if emptiness was not experienced as such in the beginning, then it turns up as a state to be feared, yet compulsively sought after" (94–95). In the mania that is the compulsion to seek, fear is mistaken for experience and experience is mistaken for force feeding and then, nothing. The breakdown has already occurred.

Winnicott proposes that only from non-existence does existence begin, and his method for understanding such an elusive claim is involved with his further thought: "Now emptiness is a prerequisite for eagerness to gather in. Primary emptiness simply means before starting to fill up. A considerable maturity is needed for this state to be meaningful" (1992b, 94). Tucked into this statement are the elements of time and someone. We need time to find our meanings. And our meanings need someone. Our earliest research is beholden to the passing of time, to wanting to be fed, and to thoughts of those who feed us. We have here the challenge of learning as inheritance. There is experience of meaningfulness and meaninglessness, of envy and gratitude, and of reconstituting the self, once again, but this time with the inheritance of emotional ties that gradually bind us to the creations of the third space of culture.

"W": Exemplars for the Method of Association

Twenty-eight years after D. W. Winnicott's death in 1971, his wife, Clare Winnicott, and colleagues gathered many of his papers and unpublished notes for an edited volume titled *Psychoanalytic Explorations*. It runs over 600 pages and spans his writing between the years of 1939 and 1969. Clare Winnicott's profession as child social worker brought her and Winnicott together and the volume begins with her (1992) "D. W. W.: A Reflection." Clare's thoughts end with a dream she had two and a half years after Winnicott's passing:

> We were in our favorite shop in London, where there is a circular staircase to all floors. We were running up and down these stairs grabbing things here, there, and everywhere as Christmas presents for our friends. We were really having a spending spree, knowing that as usual we would end up keeping many of these things to ourselves. I suddenly realized that Donald was alive after all and I thought with relief, "Now I shan't have to worry about the Christmas card." Then we were sitting in the restaurant having our coffee as usual.... We were facing each other, elbows on the table and I looked at him full in the face and said: "Donald there's something we have to say to each other, some truth that we have to say, what is it?" With his very blue eyes looking unflinchingly into mine he said: "That this is a dream." I replied slowly: "Oh yes, of course, you died, you died a year ago." He reiterated my words: "Yes I died a year ago." (18)

Clare concludes: "For me it was through this dream of playing that life and death, his and mine, could be experienced as reality" (18). *Playing and Reality* was D. W. Winnicott's last book.

Clare's dream takes poetic license with time, space, and numbers: there is a madcap dash, a spending spree, a holiday, a usual routine, a quiet rest, and a question, "some truth that we have to say, what is it?" (18). Readers are left with the subtractions of time: the time of death in the dream ("of course, one year") and that of the dream's appearance ("two and a half years later"). In their difference, only one is left, perhaps for us all, the most difficult number.

I am reminded of D. W. Winnicott's ([1968] 1990) address to teachers of mathematics, "*Sum*, I Am," a title, he admitted, that scared him. Winnicott began, "What bit of myself can I give you, and how can I give you a bit without seeming to lack my wholeness?" (55). There, he supposed that everything, including the unit one, begins with the capacity to develop a self, or what Winnicott slyly called "unit status" (61), without which one cannot enjoy bits and pieces. Yet humans do not last forever, and it may not come as a surprise that Winnicott had things to say about death: "There is no death except of a totality ... the wholeness of personal integration brings with it the possibility and indeed the *certainty of death*" (emphasis original, 61). Clare's dream of playing enjoys those bits and pieces of life no longer that led to reality, to say the "yes of death," his but also hers. In her reflection "D. W. W.," (1992) Clare adds a coda to her dream. She quotes a passage from Winnicott's notes as he tries writing on his death. It is titled *Prayer*: "D. W. W. Oh God! May I be alive when I die" (4). So why does my attention stay with Clare Winnicott's dream and her mistiming?

In late July 2016, my mother died. I was left with the force of grief, emptiness, the loss of a capacity to tell time, confusion over the date of her death, the hope that I was mistaken, and the overwhelming feeling of being lost to the world. Baldwin's descriptions of the fractures of identity that leave the self as stranger seem fitting. From my home in Toronto, a few months later, in November of 2016, the US presidential election concluded with Donald Trump's victory. That event felt so far away. A Canadian friend, who knew I was American, said to me, "You must be sad." I said, "Yes, I am sad." My friend asked, "How did this happen?" My first thought was, *well everyone dies*. It was only then that I realized my friend was speaking of the US election of Donald Trump and not my mother's death. When I described this conversation to another friend, she retold this to her mother, who replied, "Oh. Deborah does not believe her mother has died." I thought, yes, this is true. What felt intolerable is forgetting why I had such difficulty in trying to hear the abbreviation *U.S.* There are no longer us, only me.

The letter "W" repeated in the Clare Winnicott dream brings another association, this one to Georges Perec's (1988) *W or The Memory of Childhood*. Repeat the letter W and you will hear: double you.[7] I came to Perec's work accidently; I am not an expert, but really, is it surprising that I kept finding orphans and authors engaged with describing the intricacies of remembering a time no longer? The psychoanalyst Henry P. Schwartz (2016a, 2016b) wrote two compelling articles on Perec: one concerned a little-discussed topic, the analyst's identification with the patient; while the other was a close reading of Perec's book *La Boutique Obscure*, a collection of Perec's dreams between May 1968 through to August 1972 that occurred over the period of his writing of the autobiography, *W or The Memory of Childhood*, and to his four-year analysis with Pontalis. Schwartz (2016a) points to passages in Pontalis's clinical writing that referred to Perec's analysis and speculates that Perec had read that work with anger. He frames his discussion on the analyst's identification through the strictures of counter-transference and speculates that Perec as writer influenced Pontalis's turn to memoir. With great delicacy, Schwartz opens the ways in which the analysand analyzes the analyst, which appeals to the analyst's identification with that experience and creates inheritance: the analyst's "debt" to her or his emotional ties and to the analysand (152).

Like a dream, Perec's writing gives readers the challenge of how to describe their reading experience, with questions of what is being read and what history is being written. Anat Tzur Mahalel (2022) considers the dream-spaces of history, places like one's childhood home that both exist and do not exist. In memories of the quest for history, the childhood home is "strongly attached to as centers of our wishes and dreams" (876). Dana Amir (2019) turns to the writer to ask what difficulties bearing witness to trauma creates and how Perec, and now the reader, discerns the "passage of the story" (25) and the movements between the personal and world history. Amir points to the tension that Perec set in motion: "It is so easy, the narrator suggests, to use the objective history in order to erase the subjective one; so easy to use *history* to erase *biography*. When the inner witness is fragile and unstable, History with a capital H offers a means of escape, holding out articulation and expression, and providing an artificial coating and context" (25). Schwartz (2016a) wrote of his readerly difficulties: "Reading Perec is absorbing, but it is also like entering a maze: one often feels lost in a confusing landscape. Only with effort does one arrive at the center: a center that is nameless" (150). And Perec's biographer and translator, David Bellos (1993), attempts an exhaustive account of the far-reaching language games, mathematical structure, strategies of disguise, writing constrictions and rules, preparations for writing, and Perec's personal routines, summed up in the biographer's title, *Georges Perec: A Life in Words*.

Perec's *W or The Memory of Childhood* (1988) begins with not being able to remember. The text was written over a twenty-year period and completed after his analysis with Pontalis ended. There is a mystery to be solved, some mistaken identity, someone who has his same name but has disappeared, and then there is a terrible inheritance of the loss of his parents and the question *What is it?* Perec's memoir moves between the present and the past and is broken by a long sadistic childhood phantasy, as if to perform the shattering time of autobiography. Perec's opening is eerie, and he anticipates our struggle to read: "In this book there are two texts which simply alternate; you might almost believe they had nothing in common, but they are in fact inextricably bound up with one another, as though neither could exist on its own, as though it was only their coming together, the distant light they cast on each other, that could make apparent what is never quite said in one, never quite said in the other, but said only in their fragile over-lapping" (1). After warning his reader of the unsayable within what is said and of a needed incoherence within the writing—his method of alternating stories—his last observation, or perhaps appeal, is a condensation of it all: "In this break, in this split suspending the story on an unidentifiable expectation, can be found the point of departure for the whole book: the *points of suspension* on which the broken threads of childhood and the web of writing are caught" (1).

One part of his memoir is an allegory on the unspeakable terrors of deportation of Jews to the death camp Auschwitz. The phantasy gains its momentum in cruelty, sadism, violation, and inexplicable violence. It is painful to read. He began writing this phantasy around the age of twelve, seven years after the war ended. Occasionally he returned to it, forgot it for thirty-seven years, and then continued working on it as an adult. In an interview about his writing of W, Perec (1999a) said, "What I am trying to get at in my work is the manner in which that childhood is given back to me. The work of writing is always done in relation to something that no longer exists, which may be fixed for a moment in writing, like a trace, but has vanished" (133).

The phantasy takes place in a dystopian society located on the isle of Tierra del Fuego. It narrates a murderous Olympic sports competition under the sadistic control of faceless organizers. The players are urged to fight to their death. Everything is arbitrary and without reason. Perec places affect into the phantasy while the narrator's voice is omnipresent.

There are no individuals, only categories of athletes, spectators, organizers, men, women, and children.

The second part of *W* consists of brief paragraphs, separated by spaces, of pieces of a childhood he cannot remember and that involve losing his parents at a young age. Perec's Jewish parents came to France from Poland and their status was as refugees, while Perec was born in France. His father, Icek Judko Perec, was killed in 1940 while serving in a volunteer regiment of foreign soldiers fighting the German Army. Perec's mother, Cécile, a war widow, was subject to the racial laws of Vichy France. As a war orphan, Georges was entitled to assistance from the Red Cross and in 1941, at the age of five, Cécile was able to send him on a Red Cross convoy from German-occupied Paris to Grenoble, an unoccupied zone. After May 1942, Cécile wore the yellow star identifying her as Jewish. She lost her job at a factory, attempted to escape Paris, returned to Paris, and was arrested in January 1943, first held in the transit camp of Drancy, and, about a month later, deported to Auschwitz and murdered. Perec does not learn these facts for many years, and they are not included in the text but pieced together by his biographer, Bellos (1993). Georges spent his early childhood in the countryside and returned to Paris in the summer of 1945. He was nine years old.

A different font announces each terrible separation. The phantasy is presented in italics; Perec's descriptions of the few photographs of his mother and father are in boldface; the work of trying to remember is in Bembo typeface, old style.

Perec's (1987) cinematic technique of writing would reach its height in his marvelous built novel, *Life: A User's Manual*. That too is hard to describe, but it is a mad world of objects lost and found. There are different fonts, drawings, lists, charts, maps, letters, appendixes, indexes, notes to the reader, and studious descriptions of forty-two objects in each room of an apartment building (one of Perec's rules). There are the histories of people who once lived in the apartments and instructions for creating a jigsaw puzzle. There are the day's residues. The omnipresent narrator observes collectors and their collections and is witness to inexplicable obsessions, useless searches, and roundabout ironies. Traces of past lives are given over to their fantastic tales made from the pathos of being in agony, disappointment, and pleasure. Bellos (1993) described the technique as a language machine, arranged as a jigsaw novel. Its obsessional force is contagious. In an interview on his work, Perec (1999a) described his method: "A movement that starts with yourself and goes toward others.

It's what I call sympathy, a sort of projection, and at the same time, an appeal!" (152).

Perec wrote *Life: A User's Manual* (1987) between 1965 and 1978. The novel has ninety-nine sections, divided into six parts, and runs six hundred and fifty-five pages. Some sections are just a few pages. It is difficult to place this work in a genre of literature, and perhaps that is how it should be, since objects of life appear and disappear, characters take leave only to turn up again years later, and the omnipresent narrator's voice unfolds time in the subjunctive mood, as if everything that happened is still trying to be realized. The novel is like life: its forward momentum only comes into a story with a backward look into the past pushed into narratives.

Generations of characters, real and imagined, occupy the years between 1833 and 1975. They all lived in the same apartment building; they all climbed the staircase; they all came and went about their lives. Some were keen to hear about others. A few ran away, others were lost, and there were some world travelers. Some never left their rooms. One wrote a dictionary of forgotten words; another, an acrobat trapeze artist, refused to come down from the high wire and finally fell to his death. Their life projects extend into characters. Scattered throughout the novel are the things left behind: newspaper clippings, long lists of tools found in the basement, kitchen utensils, pictures on the walls, pictures missing from the walls, broken lifts, inventories of objects left on the stairs, quotes from famous authors, old books, and rent receipts. All appeal to the day's residues.

Some of the names of the characters in Perec's memoir *W* reappear again in *Life*. Gaspard Winckler, a jigsaw maker married to a woman who made miniature toys, is one of the characters who eventually takes his revenge on a character called Barthlebooth, who employed Winckler over the years to create jigsaw puzzles from Barthlebooth's paintings. Barthlebooth planned to spend 20 years painting and 20 years with the puzzles. He would receive the box of puzzle pieces, put them together, and then destroy the painting. He expected a total of 450 or so of these puzzles. Barthlebooth did not factor into the equation his own death.

The novel's time ran out as well: "It is the twenty-third of June nineteen seventy-five, and it will soon be eight o'clock in the evening" (1987, 563). Characters will continue their rituals and Perec's repetition of this date and time gives the feeling that the entire novel occurs on this single day.

132 | When History Returns

The letter "W" returns on the last pages of the novel. "It is the twenty-third of June nineteen seventy-five, and it will soon be eight o'clock in the evening" (563). Barthlebooth, seated at his four hundred and thirty-ninth jigsaw puzzle, has died: "The black hole of the sole piece not yet filled in has the almost perfect shape of an X. But the ironical thing, which could have been foreseen long ago, is that the piece the dead man holds between his fingers is shaped like a W" (565).

From Descriptions to Inscriptions

Perec's (1999b) most explicit essay on his analysis with Pontalis opens with his struggle to find the words that in some way would do justice to what his time in his analysis felt like to him: "Psychoanalysis isn't really like one of those advertisements for hair-restorers; there wasn't any 'before' or 'after.' There was a present of the analysis, a 'here and now,' that began, lasted, and ended. I could just as well write 'which took four years to start' or 'which ended during four years.' There was no beginning or end" (167). The analysis, Perec wrote, arrived before he walked into Pontalis's consulting room, and then he lightly commented on the rituals of coming and going, of talking and silence, and of having to lose readymade memories to write. "I shall only say," Perec (1999b) wrote of his analysis, "that it was infinitely slow; it was the movement of the analysis, but I only found that out later on" (173). Yes, there are memories to lose and, too, for Perec, there is a restored analyst: "On that day the analyst heard what I had to say to him, what for four years he had listened to without hearing, for the simple reason that I wasn't telling it to him, because I wasn't telling it to myself" (173).

I began reading Perec's panoramic novel, *Life: A User's Manual*, about three months after my mother passed away. It was my shiva novel. I needed to find life again, as old and new inheritance. And I needed to feel the passing of time. For a while, I could only do so by entering lives lived in novels and imagine their appeal to me. I wished for a readymade world, and an appetite. I imagine that, too, was Perec's grief and restoration. To associate with teeming life, he had to sort through pieces of a broken history—those that were his, those not his, and pieces from those who are no longer. Through quoting from the quirks of the day's residues and by cataloging them with his own style, Perec seemed to be putting lost things back into their place. It was a game we have all played, one of absence and presence and of sending things away and calling them back. And I now think the reader, once again, but this time with feeling, becomes affected by Perec's appeal for sympathy—"a sort of projection"—even if, in our own times, we find that transference an embarrassment.

So, what is it? Is there some truth we have to say? The desire for transference—to history, to other people, to ideas, to authors, to our teachers, to our analysts, to our mothers, to dreams, and to the potential space of culture—deepens our emotional ties with the inheritance of others. There are reservations to keep. We are requested to read and write again, but this time, with feeling. Affects as appeal, and as supplement to a history of relationality, must be given their due, even if at first the anxieties over the destruction of communication, that very particular fear of breakdown, undoes the work of freely associating with the incompleteness of inheritance. The predicaments carried on by the inklings of the day's residues belong to their transference to dreams, then to consideration of representations, then to the quest for humane learning so that the force of one's emotional life may be given over to words and to someone. Even our bits and pieces remain in appeal, suspended between those still here and those who are no longer. So, what is it? I cannot be me without you.

Notes

Chapter 4

1. Clinical writing in the psychoanalytic field and my work as psychoanalyst influences my understanding of psychical emptiness and transformation. Brazilian analyst Célia Fix Korbivcher (2014) develops the idea of "affective emptiness." In one comment on an adult patient, a woman aged 40, Korbivcher observes, "In the relationship with Ana, the analyst experiences a 'state of affective emptiness.' The contact is with an object sensorially present, but psychically absent, 'with no affective life' available to relate to others. The analyst experiences an accentuated unfamiliarity" (64).

2. For a rich discussion on depression that links the failures of the social bond with the inexpressible presented by psychical despair due the absence of a lost object, see Jacques Hassoun (1997). For a mediation on the poetics of loss, see Gohar Homayounpour (2023). For more complexity on the intensities of writing from states of depression, see Eve Kosofsky Sedgwick (1999; 2011).

3. Melanie Klein brought the term "positions" to the advent of early life to grasp the ego's vacillating relations to objects in mind with the ensuing anxieties, defenses, and phantasies that animate loving and hostile emotional situations between self and other. Hers is a theory of thinking grounded in anxiety and beholden to the breast (and the other) to reconsider, with a theory of object relations, Sigmund Freud's formulation of the pleasure and the reality principles. Thus, she specified and entwined two positions: the depressive position, whereby the self is concerned with the fate and preservation of self with other, and the paranoid-schizoid position, whereby defenses of omnipotence, fear of one's own ego, splitting, denial, and the destruction of ambivalence defend against constitutive anxiety. Essentially, these positions are phantasies made from object relations. As anxieties, they share anticipation of destruction, uncertainty toward the goodness or badness of self with other, and both are needed contrasts within the discord of mourning and melancholia. They may also serve as an allegory for depressive anxiety in teaching and learning. For this view, see Deborah P. Britzman (2016).

4. While it is beyond the scope of this chapter to trace the early psychoanalytic views on mourning and melancholia, readers may find the work of Karl Abraham (1877–1925) illuminating for our contemporary debates. Abraham, Klein's analyst and a colleague of Freud, expanded Freud's work on mourning and melancholia with a focus on the regression of libido and the processes of introjection. This led Abraham to speculate on a theory of libido in early life (Abraham 1988). In a letter to Freud, Abraham wrote, "I have assumed a basic irritation in infancy as a prototype for a later melancholia. In the last few months, Frau Dr. Klein has skillfully conducted psychoanalysis with a three-year-old-boy with good therapeutic results. This child faithfully presented the basic melancholia that I had assumed and in close combination with oral erotism. The case offers in general amazing insight into the infantile instinctual life" (Falzeder 2002, 471). For further discussion on Klein's relationship with Abraham and his influence on her work, see Britzman (2016).

5. My thinking on the uneven relation between history and phantasy leans upon Bollas (1995), "The Functions of History." Bollas asked, "Do we have to choose between the imagined and the happened? Are they opposed?" (104). His response is to turn to the psychical and social functions of history and what psychoanalysis may make from the patient's recounting of the details of "deeds done" and the "potential elaborations that surround facts" (110).

6. In Klein's (1930) view, symbolization begins with symbolic equation (220).

7. Steven Cooper (2016) overviews of the clinical limitations of psychoanalysis from the analyst's side. Like many others, Cooper explores the incompleteness of the analytic process and gives a metaphor of this work as a "melancholic errand." Of course, one is never done; there is always more to do. Yet if all goes well, both patient and analyst accept not only the complexities of ordinary unhappiness, as Freud once modestly put it. Held in mind as well is simply the capacity to tell of passing time: "One of the significant problems with bearing experience in psychoanalysis, integrating new and old experience, is that it reminds us of our impermanence. Put another away, one of the turning points in many analyses involves the patient's experience of sadness and loss accompanying new learning. Sometimes the capacity for new abilities for psychic play carries with it a sense of lost time" (31–32). Klein's (1963) last paper, "On the Sense of Loneliness," expresses well this pathos of the human feelings of incompleteness. There, the sadness of incompleteness as passing time and so as loss serves the contingencies of the pain of integration: "However much integration proceeds, it cannot do away with the feeling that certain components of the self are not available because they are split off and cannot be regained. . . . The lost parts, too, are felt to be lonely" (302). In Klein's view, the depressive position carries "a measure of resignation" emanating from the understanding not only of the other's limitations, but also, the limitations of the self: "Although loneliness can be diminished or increased by external influences, it can never be completely eliminated, because the urge

toward integration, as well as the pain experienced in the process of integration, spring from internal sources which remain powerful throughout life" (313).

On a last note, my title of this chapter, "On the Pains of Symbolization" follows from Klein's discussion of the depressive position as a good enough description of learning and as also a finely tuned presentation of the educator's "melancholic errand." For a further discussion of loneliness in conceptualizing history's return, see Britzman (1998).

Chapter 7

1. Quoted from the interview with Friedrich Danielis in Jeremy Adler (1997, 599).

2. J. Adler (1997) presents the literary challenges of his father's novels as experiments with language, image, musicality, time, and form. He has also emphasized the significant idea that H. G. Adler's novels are beholden to a modernist aesthetics where catastrophe is met with expressions of difficulty. *Panorama* was written in 1948, first published in German in 1968, then in English translation in 2011. *The Journey*, written during 1950–51, had a similar fate, published in 1962 in German but its English translation only appeared in 2008. For a fulsome biography of H. G. Adler—his life and times—see Peter Filkins (2019), *H. G. Adler: A Life in Many Worlds*.

3. The phrase "After Auschwitz" now involves more than seventy years of contentious debates within postwar European thought on the nature of history, memory, aesthetics, education, and social institutions. Much of the debate focused on the problem of social disavowal and revolved around anxieties over culture's tendency to trivialize the genocide, repeat the history of woeful disregard, deny what happened, and forget and even blame victims. Dorota Glowacka (2012) has written a powerful defense of aesthetics as she reviewed these debates.

While chapter 3 provides a close reading of Adorno's papers on education, I can only allude to the history of contentions affected by Theodor Adorno's 1949 often-quoted declaration, "To write poetry after Auschwitz is barbaric. And this corrodes even the knowledge of why it has become impossible to write poetry today" (Adorno 1983, 34). Adorno's (2003) manifesto "Education After Auschwitz" makes a similar demand: "Every debate about ideals of education is trivial and inconsequential compared to this single ideal: never again Auschwitz" (19). For a critical discussion of Adorno and Adler's debates and approaches, see J. Adler (1999). For discussions on Adorno's numerous revisions and discussions of poetry, see chapter 17 in Stefan Müller-Doohm (2005), *Adorno: A Biography*, and chapter 8, "After Auschwitz," in J. M. Bernstein's (2001) *Adorno: Disenchantment and Ethics*.

For a parallel history of the language of Jewish poets who survived and created "After Auschwitz," and see Paul Celan ([1970] 1986), *Last Poems: A Bilingual*

Edition, and Nelly Sachs (2022), *Flight and Metamorphosis: Poems: A Bilingual Edition*. For the biography of Sachs, see Aris Fioretos (2011), *Nelly Sachs: Flight and Metamorphosis: An Illustrated Biography*.

4. Hanna Segal (1918–2011) was a Polish Jew who studied medicine in Warsaw and left Europe in 1940 for exile in London, where she trained in the Kleinian tradition as a psychoanalyst. Segal was an important commentator on Kleinian symbolization and known for joining psychoanalysis to both aesthetics and political projects of social transformation. See, for example, Segal (1997). For an overview of her life and contributions, see Riccardo Steiner (2012).

5. In compulsory schools and universities, but also in the popular imaginary, for example, *The Diary of Anne Frank* is burdened with creating identification to loss and paradoxically is used as hope for the witness who did not survive. And we are left to sway between the sayings "We are all Anne Frank" and "Never Again!" I have written on the history of the *Diary*'s reception as repeating the conflicts of the *Diary*'s finding. See Britzman (1998; 2000).

6. While it is beyond the scope of this chapter to trace the deep question of psychoanalysis and aesthetics, in contemporary psychoanalysis aesthetic experiences compose the soul of psychoanalysis. See for example André Green (1979); Julia Kristeva (2000); and Giuseppe Civitarese (2013).

7. Beyond knowledge of the exile of Freud and his immediate family from Vienna to London in 1938, the social history of psychoanalysis from the vantage of how the field was affected internally and externally by Jewishness, by anti-Semitism, by racism, and by the Shoah is not well known (Frosh 2023). In this way, psychoanalysis may share the appearance of a "lost" or disclaimed history. Indeed, historiographies of psychoanalysis from the vantage of the Shoah's aftereffects on clinical technique are just becoming a topic of inquiry within psychoanalytic communities. Judith and Milton Kestenberg are the pioneers in developing new psychoanalytic approaches to the understanding of witnessing and its research methodology. See Judith S. Kestenberg and Eva Fogelman, eds. (1994), *Children During the Nazi Reign: Psychological Perspective on the Interview Process*; Judith S. Kestenberg and Ira Brenner, eds. (1996), *The Last Witness: The Child Survivor of the Holocaust*; and Laurence Kahn (2023), *What Nazism Did to Psychoanalysis*, translated by Andrew Weller.

8. For a history of psychoanalysis and the Shoah, see Eran Rolnik (2012), *Freud in Zion: Psychoanalysis and the Making of Modern Jewish Identity*; Riccardo Steiner (2000a), *"It's a New Kind of Diaspora": Explorations in the Sociopolitical and Cultural Context of Psychoanalysis*; R. Steiner (2000b), *Tradition, Change, Creativity: Repercussions of the New Diaspora on Aspects of British Psychoanalysis*; Ernst Federn (1990), *Witnessing Psychoanalysis: From Vienna Back to Vienna via Buchenwald and the USA*; Karen Brecht, Friedrich Volker, et al. (1993), *"Here Life Goes On in a Most Peculiar Way . . .": Psychoanalysis Before and After 1933*; and Rafael Moses, ed. (1993) *Persistent Shadows of the Holocaust: The Meaning*

to *Those Not Directly Affected*. On the matter of social trauma and psychoanalysis see *Psychoanalysis and Holocaust Testimony: Unwanted Memories of Social Trauma*, edited by Dori Laub and Andreas Hamburger (2017), and *Trauma, Trust, and Memory: Social Trauma and Reconciliation in Psychoanalysis, Psychotherapy, and Cultural Memory*, edited by Andreas Hamburger (2018).

While the Shoah has affected psychoanalysis, so too has it shaped the evolving concept of trauma, both benign and malignant. For a rich exploration of the ways in which the concept and event of trauma has shaped an understanding of metapsychology, fragmentation, and survival, see Raluca Soreanu, Jacob Staberg, and Jenny Willner (2023), *Ferenczi Dialogues: On Trauma and Catastrophe*. These researchers work within an interdisciplinary field that includes social science, art, literary theory, and clinical practice, and, as against the frame of current crises, ask, "What would it mean to systematically think of confusion and disorder as a process with an open outcome?" (3).

9. Hermann Broch (1886–1951) was born in Vienna. There, he wrote early experimental novels, essays, and drama, much of which focused on the "disintegration of values" (Lützeler 1999, 536) in Germany. By 1936, Broch felt literature was not adequate to political struggle and turned to writing about human rights and forced immigration. Broch immigrated to the United States in 1939. For a discussion of his life and his many disappointments in not being more known as a creative writer, see Paul Michael Lützeler (1999).

10. All letters are quoted from John White and Ronald Speirs (1999b).

11. J. Adler's (2017) "Afterword" provides an extensive commentary on the definitive history and the significance of H. G. Adler's postwar writing of *Theresienstadt, 1941–1945: The Face of a Coerced Community*. J. Adler detailed H. G. Adler's turn to sociology as a means of bearing witness as a participant observer and H. G.'s conceptualization of life that can bear objective accounts and its effects on subjectivity. With the postwar publication of *Theresienstadt, 1941–1945: The Face of a Coerced Community*, H. G. Adler demonstrated the Kafkaesque experiences of life and death in the ghetto. H. G. Adler, along with his first wife, Gertrud Klepetar, and her family, were prisoners in the ghetto Theresienstadt for two years, beginning 1942, and were then deported to Auschwitz on October 12, 1944. H. G. Adler, liberated on April 12, 1945, was the only member of his and his wife's family to survive. J. Adler's description of his father's methodology characterizes the ethos of the work: "Adler saw value judgments as an inherent part of the method. This apparent methodological incongruity needs to be understood as a reaction to the social and political order that strayed into such perfidious constructs as the notion of *unwertes Leben* (worthless life)" (810). Malinowski's anthropology and the sociological research of Simmel on mass psychology and authoritarian leaders were key influences: "When Adler sought to capture complicated and widely ramified insight across space and time that had led to the 'Final Solution,' Adler, as a historian, needed new concepts to illuminate the most troubling of

all phenomena.... To capture the hidden interplay between persons, offices, and actions in a modern totalitarian state, to apprehend a crime committed by so many people at such different locations—whether at a desk or in a concentration camp—neither a chronology nor historical scholarship proved entirely adequate to the task" (813).

H. G. Adler divided the work into three large sections: History, Sociology, and Psychology. The last section was subtitled "Psychological Face of the Coerced Community." The German text took H. G. Adler seven years to write. H. G. Adler dedicated his magnum opus "FOR GERALDINE, AS A MEMORIAL. GERALDINE, DR. GERTRUD ADLER-KLEPETAR, BORN ON DECEMBER 9, 1905, IN PRAGUE, MURDERED BY GASSING AND INCINERATED ON OCTOBER 14, 1944 IN AUSCHWITZ-BIRKENAU, ALONG WITH HER MOTHER" (2017, caps in original).

12. Georg Simmel's work and its reception shared a similar fate with Adler's early publication history. Simmel's (2010) *View of Life*, originally published in German in 1918, was considered too philosophical to be sociology and too encyclopedic in phenomenological spiritualism and universality to be taken up in current theoretical academic trends. His younger brother, Ernst Simmel (1882–1947), one of the psychoanalyst leaders of the Berlin Psychoanalytic Institute known for its capacity to exceed boundaries, went into exile in Hollywood in 1933. See Veronika Fuechtner (2011).

Chapter 8

1. A range of theories and my own emotional situations have influenced my thinking of learning as inheritance, learning as history's return, and with the psychoanalytic quest for humane learning. There is D. W. Winnicott's ([1967] 2001) discussion of the transitional space of culture through the shift from object relating (investment) to object use (playing). The shift is from the subjective object to placing the other "outside the field of subjective phenomena" (87). Then too, there is Klein (1957), who wrote of the stirrings of gratitude as the means of working through the depressive position. There are also writers and artists, discussed in this present work, whose creativity remakes what they have received. Closer to home are those *Nebenmenschen*, nearby friends, family, lovers, neighbors, and my mother's appeal to me in times of my frustration, anger, or wrongdoing, when she would say or perhaps yell of the hardest responsibility: "Be a mensch!"

2. I use the concept of affect to convey the gut immediacy of feelings that then involve the defenses of projection, introjection, splitting into good and bad, and projective identification, and idealization. Here, I bring to the reader's attention Klein's (1937) affecting phrase "the emotional situation of the baby" (306) with Wilfred Bion's (2000) insistence that whenever two people meet they

create an "emotional storm" (321). Piera Aulagnier (2015) understands emotions as "the visible part of the iceberg which is affect . . . the subjective manifestation of those movements of cathexis and decathexis that I cannot grasp because they become a source of emotion for it" (1378).

3. For an affecting view of dreams as in dialogue with the historical record and as the soft foundation for encountering political thought, see Sharon Sliwinski (2017). Sliwinski examines the intimacies of the political force of inheriting the disclosure of dreams as urgent commentary on what the political may foreclose and as an avenue for thinking differently on the history of arguments in human rights. With the idea of learning as inheritance, my approach to the dream stays with the clinical encounter of associating to the self as dream-work in attempts to transform the reception of the personal, whereby dreams become a means for conveying what experience cannot complete, namely the force of loss, a wish for continuity, and for these reasons, an impossible appeal to the (m)other. See note 4.

4. J.-B. Pontalis (1981) develops the idea that dreams lead to the mother: "to Freud the dream was a displaced maternal body" (26–27). And "My hypothesis is that every dream, as an object in the analysis, refers to the maternal body. . . . Dreaming is above all the attempt to maintain an impossible union with the mother, to preserve an undivided whole, *to move in a space prior to time*" (emphasis original, 29).

5. A culmination of these transitions from psychical experience to personal possession is found in Winnicott's ([1959] 1992) talk to psychologists, "The Fate of the Transitional Object," where he introduces a third area of living, *culture*, in correspondence to the transitional object. The first area is inner reality; the second is external reality. The third area is where we can create from culture, "glorious facts" (58). His example is going to a Beethoven concert: "I enjoy it because I say I created it, hallucinated it, and it is real and would have been there even if I had been neither conceived of nor conceived. This is mad" (58).

6. The phrasing "narrative revolt" is drawn from the work of Kristeva (2000) and signifies throughout my discussion both the internal and external destruction of meanings and the desire to refresh the capacity to speak. Of course, the intimacy of how it feels belongs to our dreams.

7. Georges Perec (1936–1982) was a Jewish French writer known for his linguistic experiments and the constraints he gave to himself in writing, sociology, literature, autobiography, plays, film scripts, opera, and social commentary. But he is difficult to place, partly made so from the historical catastrophe of the Shoah and the loss of his parents at age 5, partly so due to his phenomenology and encyclopedic knowledge of object life, and partly due to his facility in the workings of their architectonics of forms. For the most extensive biography of Perec, see David Bellos (1993), *Georges Perec: A Life in Words*. Also see an e-book format at www.randomhouse.co.uk. Bellos is also the translator for Perec's (1987) *Life: A User's Manual*.

References

Abraham, Karl. (1927) 1988. *Selected papers on Psychoanalysis*, translated by Douglas Bryan and Alix Strachey. London: Maresfield Library.

Abram, Jan. 2022. *The Surviving Object: Psychoanalytic Clinical Essays on Psychic Survival-of-the-Object*. London: Routledge.

Adler, H. G. 2008. *The Journey*. Translated by Peter Filkins. New York: Modern Library. First published in German 1962.

Adler, H. G. 2011. *Panorama: A Novel*. Translated by Peter Filkins. New York: Random House. First published in German 1988.

Adler, H. G. 2017. *Theresienstadt, 1941–1945: The Face of a Coerced Community*. Translated by Belinda Cooper. Afterward by Jeremy Adler. Cambridge: Cambridge University Press. First published in German 1955.

Adler, Jeremy. 1997. "February 8, 1942, H. G. Adler is deported to Theresienstadt and begins his life's work of writing a scholarly testimony to his experience." In *The Yale Companion to Jewish Writing and Thought in German Culture, 1096–1996*, edited by Sander L. Gilman and Jack Zipes, 599–605. New Haven, CT: Yale University Press.

Adler, Jeremy. 1999. "Good Against Evil?: H. G. Adler, T. W. Adorno and the Representation of the Holocaust." In *The German-Jewish Dilemma: From the Enlightenment to the Shoah*, edited by Edward Timms and Andrea Hammel, 255–289. Lewiston, NY: The Edwin Mellen Press.

Adler, Jeremy. 2017. "Afterword." In *Theresienstadt, 1941–1945: The Face of a Coerced Community*, by H. G. Adler. Translated by Belinda Cooper. Afterward translated by Jeremiah Riemer, 803–828. Cambridge: Cambridge University Press.

Adorno, Theodor W. 1983. "Cultural Criticism and Society." In *Prisms*. Translated by Samuel and Shierry Weber, 17–34. Cambridge, MA: MIT Press.

Adorno, Theodor W. 1998. *Critical Models: Interventions and Catchwords*. Translated by Henry W. Pickford. New York: Columbia University Press.

Adorno, Theodor W. (1959) 1998. "The Meaning of Working Through the Past." In *Critical Models*, 89–104.

Adorno, Theodor W. (1962) 1998. "Philosophy and Teachers." In *Critical Models*, 19–36.
Adorno, Theodor W. (1965) 1998. "Taboos on the Teaching Vocation." In *Critical Models*, 177–190.
Adorno, Theodor W. (1967) 1998. "Education after Auschwitz." In *Critical Models*, 191–204.
Adorno, Theodor W. (1972) 2000. *Negative Dialectics*. Translated by E. B. Ashton. New York: Continuum. First published in German 1966.
Adorno, Theodor W. (1974) 2005. *Minima Moralia: Reflections from Damaged Life*. Translated by E. F. N. Jephcott. London: Verso. First published in German 1951.
Adorno, Theodor W. 2001. *Kant's Critique of Pure Reason*. Edited by Rolf Tiedemann. Translated by Rodney Livingstone. Stanford, CA: Stanford University Press. First published in German 1995.
Adorno, Theodor W. 2003. "Education after Auschwitz." In *Can One Live after Auschwitz? A Philosophical Reader*, translated by Rolf Tiedemann, 19–33. Stanford, CA: Stanford University Press.
Adorno, Theodor W. 2010. "Guilt and Defense." Translated by Jeffrey Olick and Andrew Perrin. In *Guilt and Defense: On the Legacies of National Socialism in Postwar Germany*, edited and translated by Jeffrey Olick and Andrew Perrin, 51–185. Cambridge, MA: Harvard University Press. First published in German 1955.
Amir, Dana. 2019. *Bearing Witness to the Witness: A Psychoanalytic Perspective on Four Modes of Traumatic Testimony*. London: Routledge.
André, Jacques. 2013. "Discovering an Umbrella." In *Unrepresented States and the Construction of Meaning: Clinical and Theoretical Contributions*, edited by Howard B. Levine, Gail S. Reed, and Dominique Scarfone, 189–201. London: Routledge.
Arendt, Hannah. 1993. *Between Past and Future: Eight Exercises in Political Thought*. New York: Penguin.
Aulagnier, Piera. 2015. "Birth of a Body, Origin of a History." *International Journal of Psychoanalysis* 96 (5): 1371–1401, https://doi.org/10.1111/1745-8315.12345.
Baldwin, James. 1985. "The Devil Finds Work." In *The Price of the Ticket: Collected Nonfiction, 1948–1985*, 557–636. New York: St. Martin's/Marek. First published 1976.
Bellos, David. 1993. *Georges Perec: A Life in Words*. London: Harvill Press.
Bernstein, J. M. 2001. *Adorno: Disenchantment and Ethics*. Cambridge: Cambridge University Press.
Bion, Wilfred R. 1993. *Second Thoughts*. London: Karnac.
Bion, Wilfred R. 1994. *Learning from Experience*. Northvale, NJ: Jason Aronson.
Bion, Wilfred R. 1995. *Attention and Interpretation*. Northvale, NJ: Jason Aronson.

Bion, Wilfred R. 2000. "Making the Best of a Bad Job (1979)." In *Clinical Seminars and Other Works*, edited by Francesca Bion, 321–331. London: Karnac.

Bion, Wilfred R. 2005. *The Tavistock Seminars*. Edited by Francesca Bion. London: Karnac.

Bion, Wilfred R. 2013. *Los Angeles Seminars and Supervisions*. Edited by Joseph Aguayo and Barnet Malin. London: Routledge.

Blanchot, Maurice. 1986. *The Writing of the Disaster*. Translated by Ann Smock. Lincoln: University of Nebraska Press.

Bloom, Allan. 1979. Introduction to *Emile, or On Education* by Jean-Jacques Rousseau, translated by Allan Bloom, 3–29. New York: Basic Books.

Bohleber, Werner. 2010. *Destructiveness, Intersubjectivity, and Trauma: The Identity Crisis of Modern Psychoanalysis*. London: Karnac.

Bollas, Christopher. 1995. "The Functions of History." In *Cracking Up: The Work of Unconscious Experience*, 103–145. New York: Hill and Wang.

Bollas, Christopher. 2015. *When the Sun Bursts: The Enigma of Schizophrenia*. New Haven, CT: Yale University Press.

Bollas, Christopher. 2018. *Meaning and Melancholia: Life in an Age of Bewilderment*. London: Routledge.

Brecht, Karen, Friedrich Volker, Ludger M. Hermanns, Isidor J. Kaminer, and Dierk H. Juelich, eds. 1993. *"Here Life Goes On in a Most Peculiar Way...": Psychoanalysis Before and After 1933*. English edition prepared by Hella Ehlers. Translated by Christine Trollope. Hamburg: Kellner Verlag.

Britzman, Deborah P. 1998. *Lost Subjects, Contested Objects: Toward a Psychoanalytic Inquiry of Learning*. Albany: State University of New York Press.

Britzman, Deborah P. 2000. "If the Story Cannot End: Deferred Action, Ambivalence, and Difficult Knowledge." In *Between Hope and Despair: Pedagogy and the Remembrance of Historical Trauma*, edited by Roger Simon, Sharon Rosenberg, and Claudia Eppert, 27–58. New York: Rowman & Littlefield.

Britzman, Deborah P. 2003. *Practice Makes Practice: A Critical Study of Learning to Teach, Revised Edition*. Albany: State University of New York Press.

Britzman, Deborah P. 2009. *The Very Thought of Education: Psychoanalysis and the Impossible Professions*. Albany: State University of New York Press.

Britzman, Deborah P. 2011. *Freud and Education*. New York: Routledge.

Britzman, Deborah P. 2012. "The Adolescent Teacher: A Psychoanalytic Note on Regression in the Helping Professions." *Journal of Infant, Child, and Adolescent Psychotherapy* 11 (3) (August): 272–283.

Britzman, Deborah P. 2015. *A Psychoanalyst in the Classroom: On the Human Condition in Education*. Albany: State University of New York Press.

Britzman, Deborah P. 2016. *Melanie Klein: Early Analysis, Play, and the Question of Freedom*. London: Springer.

Canetti, Elias. 1999. *The Memoirs of Elias Canetti*. New York: Farrar, Straus and Giroux.
Canguilhem, Georges. (1966) 1991. *The Normal and the Pathological*. Translated by Carolyn Fawcett. Princeton, NJ: Zone Books.
Castoriadis, Cornelius. 1994. "Psychoanalysis and Politics." In *Speculations after Freud: Psychoanalysis, Philosophy and Culture*, edited by Sonu Shamdasani and Michael Münchow, 2–13. London: Routledge.
Celan, Paul. 1986. *Last Poems: A Bilingual Edition*. Translated by Katharine Washburn and Margret Guillemin. San Francisco: North Point Press. First published in German 1970.
Certeau, Michel de. 1988. *The Writing of History*. Translated by Tom Conley. New York: Columbia University Press.
Certeau, Michel de. 1993. *Heterologies: Discourse on the Other*. Translated by Brian Massumi. Minneapolis: University of Minnesota Press.
Civitarese, Giuseppe. 2013. *The Violence of Emotions: Bion and post-Bionian Psychoanalysis*. Translated by Ian Harvey. London: Routledge.
Civitarese, Giuseppe, and Antonino Ferro. 2020. *A Short Introduction to Psychoanalysis*. London: Routledge.
Cooper, Steven H. 2016. *The Analyst's Experience of the Depressive Position: The Melancholic Errand of Psychoanalysis*. London: Routledge.
Corbett, Ken. 2016. *A Murder Over a Girl: Justice, Gender, Junior High*. New York: Henry Holt & Company.
Derrida, Jacques. 1993. "Politics of Friendship." *American Imago* 50 (3): 53–391.
Erlich, H. Shmuel. 2024. "A Generative Paradox: The Subject Who Is the Unconscious Master in His Own House." In *The Ego and the Id: 100 Years later*, edited by Fred Busch and Natacha Delgado, 105–117. London: Routledge.
Falzeder, Ernst, ed. 2002. *The Complete Correspondence of Sigmund Freud and Karl Abraham 1907-1925, Completed Edition*. Translated by Caroline Schwarzacher. London: Karnac.
Federn, Ernst. 1990. *Witnessing Psychanalysis: From Vienna Back to Vienna via Buchenwald and the USA*. London: Karnac.
Felman, Shoshana. 1987. *Jacques Lacan and the Adventure of Insight: Psychoanalysis in Contemporary Culture*. Cambridge, MA: Harvard University Press.
Felman, Shoshana. 1992. "Education and Crisis, or the Vicissitudes of Teaching." In *Testimony: Crises of Witnessing in Literature, Psychoanalysis, and History*, by Shoshana Felman and Dori Laub, 1–56. New York: Routledge.
Felman, Shoshana, and Dori Laub. 1992. *Testimony: Crisis of Witnessing in Literature, Psychoanalysis, and History*. New York: Routledge.
Ferro, Antonino. 2017. "Attacks on Linking, or Uncontainability of Beta Elements?" In *Attacks on Linking Revisited: A New Look at Bion's Classic Work*, edited by Catalina Bronstein and Edna O'Shaughnessy, 161–178. London: Routledge.

Ferro, Antonino, and Giuseppe Civitarese. 2015. *The Analytic Field and Its Transformations*. London: Routledge.
Filkins, Peter. 2019. *H. G. Adler: A Life in Many Worlds*. New York: Oxford University Press.
Fioretos, Aris. 2011. *Nelly Sachs: Flight and Metamorphosis: An Illustrated Biography*. Translated by Tomas Tranæus. Stanford: Stanford University Press. First published in German 2010.
Fischer, Jens Malte. 2011. *Gustav Mahler*. Translated by Stewart Spencer. New Haven, CT: Yale University Press.
Forrester, John. 2016. *Thinking in Cases*. Cambridge: Polity Press.
Foucault, Michel. 1998. "Philosophy and Psychology." In *Aesthetics, Method, and Epistemology*, volume 2, edited by James D. Faubion, translated by Robert Hurley and others, 249–259. New York: The New Press.
Frank, Claudia. 2009. *Melanie Klein in Berlin: Her First Psychoanalyses of Children*. Edited with preface by Elizabeth Spillius, translated by Sophie Leighton and Sue Young. London: Routledge.
Frank, Claudia. 2022. "Thinking about Encountering Masochism/Masochistic Elements in Analytic Practice in the Kleinian Tradition Then and Now." *International Journal of Psychoanalysis* 103 (6): 1057–1072, https://doi.org/10.1080/00207578.2022.2139360.
Freire, Paulo. 1988. *Pedagogy of the Oppressed*. Translated by Myra Bergman Ramos. New York: Continuum. First published in Spanish 1968, in English 1970, in Portuguese 1972.
Freud, Sigmund. 1968. *The Standard Edition of the Complete Psychological Works of Sigmund Freud*. Edited and translated by James Strachey in collaboration with Anna Freud, assisted by Alix Strachey and Alan Tyson. 24 vols. London: Hogarth Press and Institute for Psychoanalysis. Hereafter cited as *SE*.
Freud, Sigmund. 1895. "Project for a Scientific Psychology." *SE* 1:283–398.
Freud, Sigmund. 1900a. *The Interpretation of Dreams (First Part)*. *SE* 4.
Freud, Sigmund. 1900b. *The Interpretation of Dreams (Second Part)*. *SE* 5.
Freud, Sigmund. 1905. "Three Essays on the Theory of Sexuality." *SE* 7:125–243.
Freud, Sigmund. 1913a. "On Beginning the Treatment (Further Recommendations on the Technique of Psycho-Analysis I)." *SE* 12:123–144.
Freud, Sigmund. 1913b. "The Claims of Psycho-Analysis to Scientific Interest." *SE* 13:165–190.
Freud, Sigmund. 1914a. "On Narcissism: An Introduction." *SE* 14:67–102.
Freud, Sigmund. 1914b. "Remembering, Repeating and Working Through (Further Recommendations on the Technique of Psycho-Analysis II)." *SE* 12:145–156.
Freud, Sigmund. 1914c. "Some Reflections of Schoolboy Psychology." *SE* 13:241–244.
Freud, Sigmund. 1915a. "Observations on Transference-Love (Further Recommendations on the Technique of Psycho-Analysis III)." *SE* 12:159–171.

Freud, Sigmund. 1915b. "Thoughts for the Times on War and Death." *SE* 14:275–300.
Freud, Sigmund. 1917a. "A Metapsychological Supplement to the Theory of Dreams." *SE* 14:217–236.
Freud, Sigmund. 1917b. "Mourning and Melancholia." *SE* 14:243–259.
Freud, Sigmund. 1917c. "A Difficulty in the Path of Psycho-Analysis." *SE* 17:135–144.
Freud, Sigmund. 1919. "On the Teaching of Psycho-Analysis in the Universities." *SE* 17:160–174.
Freud, Sigmund. 1923a. "The Ego and the Id." *SE* 19:12–68.
Freud, Sigmund. 1923b. "Remarks on the Theory and Practice of Dream-Interpretation." *SE* 19:109–124.
Freud, Sigmund. 1924. "The Economic Problem of Masochism." *SE* 19:159–170.
Freud, Sigmund. 1925a. "Some Additional Notes on Dream-Interpretation as a Whole." *SE* 19:125–140.
Freud, Sigmund. 1925b. "Negation." *SE* 19:235–239.
Freud, Sigmund. 1925c. "Preface to Aichhorn's *Wayward Youth*." *SE* 19:273–275.
Freud, Sigmund. 1925d. "Autobiographical Study." *SE* 20:7–74.
Freud, Sigmund. 1930. *Civilization and Its Discontents*. *SE* 21:59–148.
Freud, Sigmund. 1933. "New Introductory Lectures on Psycho-Analysis." *SE* 22:5–182.
Freud, Sigmund. 1937. "Analysis Terminable and Interminable." *SE* 23:209–253.
Freud, Sigmund. 1940a. "An Outline of Psychoanalysis." *SE* 23:144–208.
Freud, Sigmund. 1940b. "Some Elementary Lessons in Psycho-Analysis." *SE* 23:279–286.
Freud, Sigmund. 1954. *The Origins of Psycho-Analysis: Letters to Wilhelm Fliess, Drafts and Notes: 1887–1902*, edited by Marie Bonaparte, Anna Freud, and Ernst Kris, translated by Eric Mosbacher and James Strachey. New York: Basic Books.
Frosh, Stephen. 2016. "Towards a Psychosocial Psychoanalysis." *American Imago* 73 (4): 469–482, https://doi.org/10.1353/aim.2016.0025.
Frosh, Stephen. 2023. *Antisemitism and Racism: Ethical Challenges for Psychoanalysis*. New York: Bloomsbury Academic.
Fuechtner, Veronika. 2011. *Berlin Psychoanalytic: Psychoanalysis and Culture in Weimar Republic Germany and Beyond*. Berkeley: University of California Press.
Glocer Fiorini, Leticia. 2007. *Deconstructing the Feminine: Psychoanalysis, Gender, and Theories of Complexity*. London: Karnac.
Glocer Fiorini, Leticia. 2016. "Misogyny." Paper presented at the ATPPP, 44th Scientific Session, Toronto Institute for Psychoanalysis, Toronto, April 2, 2016.
Glocer Fiorini, Leticia. 2017. *Sexual Difference in Debate: Bodies, Desires, and Fictions*. London: Karnac.
Glowacka, Dorota. 2012. *Disappearing Traces: Holocaust Testimonials, Ethics, and Aesthetics*. Seattle: University of Washington Press.

References | 149

Goethe, Johann Wolfgang von. 2012. *The Sufferings of Young Werther*. Translated by Stanley Corngold. New York: W. W. Norton & Company. First published in German 1774.

Gozlan, Oren. 2015. *Transsexuality and the Art of Transitioning: A Lacanian Approach*. New York: Routledge.

Green, André. 1979. *The Tragic Effect: The Oedipus Complex in Tragedy*. Translated by Alan Sheridan. London: Cambridge University Press.

Green, André. 1982a. "*Après-coup*, the Archaic." In *The Freudian Matrix of André Green: Towards a Psychoanalysis for the Twenty-First Century*, edited by Howard B. Levine, 15–35. Translated by Dorothée Bonnigal-Katz and Andrew Weller. London: Routledge, 2023.

Green, André. 1982b. "The Double Limit." In *The Freudian Matrix of André Green*, 36–52.

Green, André. 1999. "On the Edge." In *The Work of the Negative*. Translated by Andrew Weller, 257–268. London: Free Association Books.

Green, André. 2000. "Experience and Thinking in the Analytic Practice." In *André Green at the Squiggle Foundation*, edited by Jan Abram, 1–15. London: Karnac.

Green, André. 2002. *Time in Psychoanalysis: Some Contradictory Aspects*. Translated by Andrew Weller. London: Free Association Books.

Grimbert, Philippe. 2008. *Memory*. New York: Simon & Schuster.

Grosskurth, Phyllis. 1986. *Melanie Klein: Her World and Her Work*. Cambridge, MA: Harvard University Press.

Grubrich-Simitis, Ilse. 1997. *Early Freud and Late Freud: Reading Anew Studies on Hysteria and Moses and Monotheism*. Translated by Philip Slotkin. London: Routledge.

Homayounpour, Gohar. 2012. *Doing Psychoanalysis in Tehran*. Cambridge, MA: MIT Press.

Homayounpour, Gohar. 2023. *Persian Blues, Psychoanalysis and Mourning*. London: Routledge.

Hamburger, Andreas, ed. 2018. *Trauma, Trust, and Memory: Social Trauma and Reconciliation in Psychoanalysis, Psychotherapy, and Cultural Memory*. New York: Routledge.

Hassoun, Jacques. 1997. *The Cruelty of Depression: On Melancholy*. Translated by David Jacobson. Reading, MA: Addison-Wesley.

Hohendahl, Peter Uwe. 2005. *Prismatic Thought: Theodor W. Adorno*. Lincoln: University of Nebraska Press.

Hullot-Kentor, Robert. 2006. *Things Beyond Resemblance: Collected Essays on Theodor W. Adorno*. New York: Columbia University Press.

Isaacs, Susan. 1952. "The Nature and Function of Phantasy." In *Developments in Psychoanalysis*, edited by Paula Heimann, Susan Isaacs, Melanie Klein, and Joan Riviere, 67–121. London: Karnac, 2002.

Jacobson, Edith. 1964. *The Self and the Object World*. New York: International University Press.
James, Henry. 1987. *The Spoils of Poynton*. New York: Penguin. First published 1897.
Joseph, Betty. 1996. "Transference: The Total Situation (1985)." In *Melanie Klein Today: Developments in Theory and Practice, Volume 2: Mainly Practice*, edited by Elizabeth Bott Spillius, 61–72. London: Routledge.
Kahn, Laurence. 2018. "If One Only Knew What Exists!" In *Unrepresented States and the Constructions of Meaning: Clinical and Theoretical Contributions*, edited by Howard B. Levine, Gail S. Reed, and Dominique Scarfone, 122–151. London: Routledge.
Kahn, Laurence. 2023. *What Nazism Did to Psychoanalysis*. Translated by Andrew Weller. London: Routledge.
Kant, Immanuel. 1965. *The Critique of Pure Reason*. Unabridged edition. Translated by Norman Kemp Smith. New York: St. Martin's Press.
Kant, Immanuel. 2003. *On Education*. Translated by Annette Churton. New York: Dover Publications. First published in German 1803.
Kestenberg, Judith S., and Ira Brenner, eds. 1996. *The Last Witness: The Child Survivor of the Holocaust*. Washington, DC: American Psychiatric Press.
Kestenberg, Judith S., and Eva Fogelman, eds. 1994. *Children During the Nazi Reign: Psychological Perspective on the Interview Process*. Westport, CT: Praeger.
King, Pearl, and Riccardo Steiner, eds. 1992. *The Freud-Klein Controversies, 1941–1945*. London: Routledge Press in association with the Institute of Psychoanalysis, London.
Kirshner, Lewis. 2017. *Intersubjectivity in Psychoanalysis: A Model for Theory and Practice*. London: Routledge.
Klein, Hillel. 2012a. *Survival and Trials of Revival: Psychodynamic Studies of Holocaust Survivors and Their Families in Israel and the Diaspora*, edited by Alex Holder. Boston: Academic Studies Press.
Klein, Hillel. 2012b. "Problems of Countertransference in the Psychotherapy of Holocaust Survivors and Their Children." In *Survival and Trials of Revival: Psychodynamic Studies of Holocaust Survivors and Their Families in Israel and the Diaspora*, edited by Alex Holder, 208–216. Boston: Academic Studies Press, https://doi.org/10.1515/9781618111074-015.
Klein, Melanie. 1975. *The Writings of Melanie Klein*. Edited by Roger Money-Kyrle in collaboration with Betty Joseph, Edna O'Shaughnessy, and Hanna Segal. Volume 1: *Love, Guilt and Reparation and Other Works, 1921–1945*; volume 2: *The Psycho-Analysis of Children*; volume 3: *Envy and Gratitude and Other Works, 1946–1963*; volume 4: *Narrative of a Child Analysis: The Conduct of the Psycho-Analysis of Children as Seen in the Treatment of a Ten-Year-Old Boy*. London: Hogarth Press, in association with the Institute of Psychoanalysis. Hereafter cited as *Writings*.

Klein, Melanie. 1923. "The Role of the School in the Libidinal Development of the Child." In *Love, Guilt and Reparation and Other Works, 1921–1945, Writings* 1:59–76.
Klein, Melanie. 1928. "Early Stages of the Oedipus Conflict." In *Love, Guilt and Reparation and Other Works, 1921–1945, Writings* 1:186–198.
Klein, Melanie. 1930. "The Importance of Symbol Formation in the Development of the Ego." In *Love, Guilt and Reparation, Writings* 1:219–232.
Klein, Melanie. 1932. *The Psycho-Analysis of Children, Writings* 2.
Klein, Melanie. 1935. "A Contribution to the Psychogenesis of Manic-Depressive States." In *Love, Guilt and Reparation, Writings* 1:262–289.
Klein, Melanie. 1937. "Love, Guilt and Reparation." In *Love, Guilt and Reparation, Writings* 1:306–343.
Klein, Melanie. 1940. "Mourning and Its Relation to Manic-Depressive States." In *Love, Guilt and Reparation, Writings* 1:344–369.
Klein, Melanie. 1946. "Notes on Some Schizoid Mechanisms." In *Envy and Gratitude and Other Works, 1946–1963, Writings* 3:1–24.
Klein, Melanie. 1952. "The Origins of Transference." In *Envy and Gratitude, Writings* 3:48–56.
Klein, Melanie. 1957. "Envy and Gratitude." In *Envy and Gratitude, Writings* 3:176–235.
Klein, Melanie. 1959. "Our Adult World and Its Roots in Infancy." In *Envy and Gratitude, Writings* 3:247–263.
Klein, Melanie. 1961. *Narrative of a Child Analysis: The Conduct of the Psycho-Analysis of Children as Seen in the Treatment of a Ten-Year-Old Boy, Writings* 4.
Klein, Melanie. 1963. "On the Sense of Loneliness." In *Envy and Gratitude, Writings* 3:300–313.
Kohut, Heinz. 1982. "Introspection, Empathy, and the Semi-Circle of Mental Health." *International Journal of Psychoanalysis* 63: 395–407, pep-web.org.
Kohut, Thomas. 2020. *Empathy and the Historical Understanding of the Human Past*. London: Routledge.
Korbivcher, Célia Fix. 2014. *Autistic Transformations: Bion's Theory and Autistic Phenomena*. Translated by Milena Basaria. London: Karnac.
Kristeva, Julia. 1990. "The Adolescent Novel." In *Abjection, Melancholia and Love: The Work of Julia Kristeva*, edited by John Fletcher and Andrew Benjamin, 8–23. London: Routledge.
Kristeva, Julia. 1991. *Strangers to Ourselves*. Translated by Leon Roudiez. New York: Columbia University Press.
Kristeva, Julia. 1995. *New Maladies of the Soul*. Translated by Ross Guberman. New York: Columbia University Press.
Kristeva, Julia. 2000. *The Sense and Non-Sense of Revolt: The Powers and Limits of Psychoanalysis, Volume 1*. Translated by Jeanine Herman. New York: Columbia University Press.

Kristeva, Julia. 2001. *Melanie Klein*. Translated by Ross Guberman. New York: Columbia University Press.

Kristeva, Julia. 2010. *Hatred and Forgiveness*. Translated by Jeanine Herman. New York: Columbia University Press.

Lacan, Jacques. 2006. "The Freudian Thing, or the Meaning of the Return to Freud in Psychoanalysis." In *Écrits: The First Complete Edition in English*. Translated by Bruce Fink, 334–363. New York, Norton. First published in French 2006.

Laplanche, Jean. 1999a. *Essays on Otherness*. Translated by John Fletcher. London: Routledge.

Laplanche, Jean. 1999b. *The Unconscious and the Id*. Translated by Luke Thurston with Lindsay Watson. London: Rebus Press.

Laplanche, Jean. 2017. *Après-coup*. Translated by Jonathan House and Luke Thurston. New York: The Unconscious in Translation.

Laub, Dori, and Andreas Hamburger, eds. 2017. *Psychoanalysis and Holocaust Testimony: Unwanted Memories of Social Trauma*. New York: Routledge.

Leader, Darian. 2000. *Freud's Footnotes*. London: Farber and Farber.

Leader, Darian. 2011. *What is Madness?* London: Hamish Hamilton.

Levine, Howard B. 2013. "The Colourless Canvas: Representation, Therapeutic Action, and the Creation of Mind." In *Unrepresented States and the Construction of Meaning: Clinical and Theoretical Contributions*, edited by Howard B. Levine, Gail S. Reed, and Dominique Scarfone, 42–71. London: Routledge.

Levine, Howard B. 2022. *Affect, Representation and Language: Between the Silence and the Cry*. London: Routledge.

Levine, Howard B. 2023. "Introduction: Why Green?" In *The Freudian Matrix of André Green: Towards a Psychoanalysis for the Twenty-First Century*, edited by Howard B. Levine, 1–14. Translated by Dorothée Bonnigal-Katz and Andrew Weller. London: Routledge.

Lützeler, Paul Michael. 1999. "1937 Hermann Broch writes a narrative entitled *The Return of Virgil*, thus beginning an eight-year project that culminates in the novel *The Death of Virgil*." In *Yale Companion to Jewish Writing and Thought in German Culture, 1096–1996*, edited by Sander L. Gilman and Jack Zipes, 537–543. New Haven, CT: Yale University Press.

Mahalel, Anat Tzur. 2022. "Georges Perec's Zeit-Raum: Creating a Space of Remembrance." *Journal of the American Psychoanalytic Association* 70 (5): 875–901, https://doi.org/10.1177/00030651221123605.

Major, René and Chantal Talagrand. 2018. *Freud: The Unconscious and World Affairs*. Translated by Agnes Jacob. London: Routledge.

McDougall, Joyce. 1992. *Plea for a Measure of Abnormality*. London: Free Association Press.

McDougall, Joyce. 2005. *Donald Winnicott the Man: Reflections and Recollections*. London: Karnac Books on behalf of The Winnicott Clinic of Psychotherapy.

Meltzer, Donald. 1998. "Richard Week-by-Week (A Critique of the 'Narrative of Child Analysis' and a Review of Melanie Klein's Work)." In *The Kleinian Development*, 144–269. London: Karnac.
Meltzer, Donald, and Meg Harris Williams. 1988. *The Apprehension of Beauty: The Role of Aesthetic Conflict in Development, Art, and Violence*. Scotland: The Clunie Press for the Roland Harris Library.
Milner, Marion. 1996. "The Child's Capacity for Doubt." In *The Suppressed Madness of Sane Men: Forty-four Years of Exploring Psychoanalysis*, 12–15. London: Routledge, in association with the Institute of Psychoanalysis. First published 1942.
Moses, Rafael, ed. 1993. *Persistent Shadows of the Holocaust: The Meaning to Those Not Directly Affected*. Madison, CT: International Universities Press.
Müller-Doohm, Stefan. 2005. *Adorno: A Biography*. Translated by Rodney Livingstone. Malden, MA: Polity Press.
M'Uzan, Michel Émile de. 2019. *Permanent Disquiet: Psychoanalysis and the Transitional Subject*. New York: Routledge.
Neubauer, John. 1992. *The Fin-de-Siècle Culture of Adolescence*. New Haven, CT: Yale University Press.
Ogden, Thomas. 2016. "Destruction Reconceived: On Winnicott's 'The Use of the Object and Relating through Identifications.'" *International Journal of Psychoanalysis* 97 (5): 1243–1262, https://doi.org/10.1111/1745-8315.12554.
Olick, Jeffrey K., and Andrew J. Perrin, eds. and trans. 2010. "Guilt and Defense: Theodor Adorno and the Legacies of National Socialism in German Society." In *Guilt and Defense: On the Legacies of National Socialism in Postwar Germany*, 3–42. Cambridge, MA: Harvard University Press.
Orange, Donna M. 2020. *Psychoanalysis, History, and Radical Ethics: Learning to Hear*. New York: Routledge.
O'Shaughnessy, Edna. 2015. "Words and Working Through." In *Inquiries in Psychoanalysis: Collected Papers of Edna O'Shaughnessy*, edited by Richard Rusbridger, 69–83. London: Routledge.
Pandolfo, Stefania. 2018. *Knot of the Soul: Madness, Psychoanalysis, Islam*. Chicago: University of Chicago Press.
Parker, Ian. 2019. *Psychoanalysis, Clinic, and Context: Subjectivity, History, and Autobiography*. London: Routledge.
Peck, Raoul, director. 2016. *I Am Not Your Negro*. Written by James Baldwin and Raoul Peck. Velvet Films, 93 min.
Perec, Georges. 1987. *Life: A User's Manual*. Translated by David Bellos. New Hampshire: Godine.
Perec, Georges. 1988. *W or The Memory of Childhood*. Translated by David Bellos. Boston: Godine.

Perec, Georges. 1999a. "The Work of Memory: Interview with Franck Venaille." In *Species of Spaces and Other Pieces*, edited and translated by John Sturrock, 127–153. New York: Penguin.

Perec, Georges. 1999b. "The Scene of a Stratagem." In *Species of Spaces and Other Pieces*, edited and translated by John Sturrock, 165–173. New York: Penguin.

Pitt, Alice and Deborah P. Britzman. 2015. "Speculations on Difficult Knowledge in Teaching and Learning: An Experiment in Psychoanalytic Research." In *Doing Educational Research: A Handbook, Second Edition*, edited by Kenneth Tobin and Shirley R. Steinberg, 395–420. Rotterdam: Sense Publishers.

Pollock, Friedrich, Theodor Adorno, and Colleagues. 2011. *Group Experiment and Other Writings: The Frankfurt School on Public Opinion in Postwar Germany*. Edited, translated, and introduced by Andrew J. Perrin and Jeffrey K. Olick. Cambridge, MA: Harvard University Press.

Pontalis, J.-B. 1981. "Between the Dream as Object and the Dream-text." In *Frontiers in Psychoanalysis: Between the Dream and Psychic Pain*, translated by Catherine Cullen and Philip Cullen, 23–48. New York: International Universities Press.

Ricoeur, Paul. 2004. *Memory, History, Forgetting*. Translated by Kathleen Blamey and David Pellauer. Chicago: University of Chicago Press.

Rolnik, Eran. 2012. *Freud in Zion: Psychoanalysis and the Making of Modern Jewish Identity*. Translated by Haim Watzman. London: Karnac.

Roper, Michael. 2016. "From the Shell-Shocked Soldier to the Nervous Child: Psychoanalysis in the Aftermath of the First World War." *Psychoanalysis and History* 18 (1): 39–69, https://doi.org/10.3366/pah.2016.0177.

Rose, Jacqueline. 1993. *Why War? Psychoanalysis, Politics, and the Return to Melanie Klein*. Oxford: Blackwell.

Rose, Jacqueline. 2014. *Women in Dark Times*. London: Bloomsbury Press.

Rose, Jacqueline. 2018. *Mothers: An Essay on Love and Cruelty*. New York: Farrar, Straus and Giroux.

Sachs, Nelly. 2022. *Flight and Metamorphosis: Poems: A Bilingual Edition*. Translated by Joshua Weiner with Linda B. Parshall. New York: Farrar, Straus and Giroux. First published in German 1959.

Salah, Patrisha. 2018. "Remarks on 'Trans Literatures as Psychoanalysis.'" Book Launch for *Current Critical Debates in the Field of Transsexual Studies: In Transition*, edited by Oren Gozlan. Massey College, University of Toronto, May 7, 2018.

Scarfone, Dominique. 2015. *The Unpast: The Actual Unconscious*. New York: The Unconscious in Translation.

Scarfone, Dominique. 2016. "The Time Before Us (The Unpast in W. S. Merwin, W. Benjamin, and V. Woolf)." *Psychoanalytic Dialogues* 26 (5): 513–520, https://doi.org/10.1080/10481885.2016.1214462.

Scarfone, Dominique. 2018a. "Free Association, Surprise, Trauma, and Transference." *Psychoanalytic Inquiry* 38 (6): 468–477, https://doi.org/10.1080/07351690.2018.1480232.
Scarfone, Dominique. 2018b. "From Traces to Signs: Presenting and Representing." In *Unrepresented States and the Constructions of Meaning: Clinical and Theoretical Contributions*, edited by Howard B. Levine, Gail S. Reed, and Dominique Scarfone, 75–94. London: Routledge.
Schmidt, James, ed. 1996. *What is Enlightenment? Eighteenth-Century Answers and Twentieth-Century Questions*. Berkeley: University of California Press.
Schwartz, Henry P. 2016a. "On the Analyst's Identification with the Patient: The Case of J.-B. Pontalis and G. Perec." *Psychoanalytic Quarterly* 85 (1): 125–154, https://doi.org/10.1002/psaq.12061.
Schwartz, Henry P. 2016b. "The Oneiric Autobiography of Georges Perec." *Psychoanalytic Quarterly* 85 (1): 155–178, https://doi.org/10.1002/psaq.12062.
Sedgwick, Eve Kosofsky. 1999. *A Dialogue on Love*. Boston: Beacon Press.
Sedgwick, Eve Kosofsky. 2011. *The Weather in Proust*. Edited by Jonathan Goldberg. Durham, NC: Duke University Press.
Segal, Hanna. 1952. "A Psychoanalytic Approach to Aesthetics." In *Psychoanalysis and Art: Kleinian Perspectives*, edited by Sandra Gosso, 42–61. London: Karnac, 2004.
Segal, Hanna. 1997. *Psychoanalysis, Literature and War: Papers, 1972–1995*, edited by John Steiner. London: Routledge.
Shapira, Michal. 2013. *The War Inside: Psychoanalysis, Total War, and the Making of the Democratic Self in Postwar Britain*. Cambridge: Cambridge University Press.
Siegal, Nina. 2017. "Anne Frank Who? Museums Combat Ignorance about the Holocaust." *New York Times*, March 21, 2017.
Simmel, Georg. 2010. *The View of Life: Four Metaphysical Essays with Journal Aphorisms*. Translated by John A. Y. Andrews and Donald N. Levine. Chicago: University of Chicago Press. First published in German 1918.
Sliwinski, Sharon. 2017. *Dreaming in Dark Times: Six Exercises in Political Thought*. Minneapolis: University of Minnesota Press.
Smith, Zadie. 2023. "The Instrumentalist." *New York Review of Books* 70 (1) (January 19), 12–15.
Soreanu, Raluca. 2018. *Working-Through Collective Wounds: Trauma, Denial, Recognition in the Brazilian Uprising*. London: Palgrave Macmillan.
Soreanu, Raluca, Jakob Staberg, and Jenny Willner. 2023. *Ferenczi Dialogues: On Trauma and Catastrophe*. Belgium: Leuven University Press.
Steinberg, Michael. 2022. *The Afterlife of Moses: Exile, Democracy, Renewal*. Stanford, CA: Stanford University Press.
Steiner, John, ed. 2017. *Lectures on Technique by Melanie Klein*. London: Routledge.

Steiner, Riccardo. 2000a. *"It's a New Kind of Diaspora"*: Explorations in the Socio-political and Cultural Context of Psychoanalysis. London: Karnac.

Steiner, Riccardo. 2000b. *Tradition, Change, Creativity: Repercussions of the New Diaspora on Aspects of British Psychoanalysis.* London: Karnac.

Steiner, Riccardo. 2012. "Hanna Segal 1918–2011, Obituary." *International Journal of Psychoanalysis* 93 (2): 457–469, https://doi.org/10.1111/j.1745-8315.2011.00537.x.

Stonebridge, Lyndsey. 2015. "Statelessness and the Poetry of the Borderline: André Green, W. H. Auden and Yousif M. Qasmiyeh." *Textual Practice* 29 (7): 1331–1354, https://doi.org/10.1080/0950236X.2015.1095454.

Strachey, Alix. 1941. "A Note on the Use of the Word 'Internal.'" *International Journal of Psychoanalysis* 22:37–43.

Swartz, Sally. 2019. *Ruthless Winnicott: The Role of Ruthlessness in Psychoanalysis and Political Protest.* London: Routledge.

Taylor, Barbara. 2014. *The Last Asylum: A Memoir of Madness in Our Times.* London: Hamish Hamilton.

Togashi, Koichi. 2020. *The Psychoanalytic Zero: A Decolonizing Study of Therapeutic Dialogues.* London: Routledge.

Van Haute, Philippe, and Tomas Geyskens. 2004. *Confusion of Tongues: The Primacy of Sexuality in Freud, Ferenczi, and Laplanche.* New York: Other Press.

Verhaeghe, Paul. 2004. *On Being Normal and Other Disorders: A Manual for Clinical Psychodiagnostics.* Translated by Sigi Jottkandt. New York: Other Press.

Wake, Naoko. 2011. *Private Practices: Harry Stack Sullivan, the Science of Homosexuality, and American Liberalism.* New Brunswick, NJ: Rutgers University Press.

Walsh, Julie. 2020. "Confusing Cases: Forrester, Stoller, Agnes, Woman." *History of the Human Sciences* 33 (3–4): 15–32.

White, John, and Ronald Speirs, eds. 1999a. "An Introduction and Notes." In "Hermann Broch and H. G. Adler: The Correspondence of Two Writers in Exile." In *Comparative Criticism: Myths and Mythologies*, edited by E. S. Shaffer, 21:131–144. Cambridge: Cambridge University Press.

White, John, and Ronald Speirs, eds. 1999b. "Hermann Broch and H. G. Adler: The Correspondence of Two Writers in Exile." In *Comparative Criticism: Myths and Mythologies*, edited by E. S. Shaffer, 21:145–200. Translated by Ronald Speirs.

Winnicott, Clare. 1992. "D. W. W.: A Reflection." In *Psychoanalytic Explorations*, edited by Clare Winnicott, Ray Shepherd, and Madeleine Davis, 1–18. Cambridge, MA: Harvard University Press.

Winnicott, D. W. 1988. *Human Nature.* Bristol, PA: Brunner/Mazel.

Winnicott, D. W. 1990. *Home Is Where We Start From: Essays by a Psychoanalyst*, edited and compiled by Clare Winnicott, Ray Shepherd, and Madeleine Davis. New York: W. W. Norton.

Winnicott, D. W. (1968) 1990. "*Sum*, I Am." In *Home Is Where We Start From*, 55–64.
Winnicott, D. W. (1960) 1990. "Aggression, Guilt and Reparation." In *Home Is Where We Start From*, 80–89.
Winnicott, D. W. 1992. *Psycho-Analytic Explorations*, edited by Clare Winnicott, Ray Shepherd, and Madeleine Davis. Cambridge, MA: Harvard University Press.
Winnicott, D. W. (1959) 1992. "The Fate of the Transitional Object." In *Psycho-Analytic Explorations*, 53–58.
Winnicott, D. W. (1963?) 1992. "Fear of Breakdown." In *Psycho-Analytic Explorations*, 87–95.
Winnicott, D. W. 1996. *The Maturational Processes and the Facilitating Environment: Studies in the Theory of Emotional Development*. Madison, CT: International Universities Press.
Winnicott, D. W. (1958) 1996. "The Capacity to be Alone." In *The Maturational Processes and the Facilitating Environment*, 29–36.
Winnicott, D. W. (1962) 1996. "The Aims of Psycho-Analytical Treatment." In *The Maturational Processes*, 166–178.
Winnicott, D. W. 2001. *Playing and Reality*. London: Routledge.
Winnicott, D. W. (1967) 2001. "The Location of Cultural Experience." In *Playing and Reality*, 95–103. New York: Routledge.
Young-Bruehl, Elisabeth. 1996. *The Anatomy of Prejudices*. Cambridge, MA: Harvard University Press.
Young-Bruehl, Elisabeth. 2012. *Childism: Confronting Prejudices against Children*. New Haven, CT: Yale University Press.
Zeavin, Hannah. 2021. *The Distance Cure: A History of Teletherapy*. Cambridge, MA: MIT Press.

Index

Abraham, Karl, 136n4
Adler, H. G., 97–98; and Georg Simmel, 113, 140n12; and Hermann Broch, 109–11, 139n9; *The Journey*, 98, 108–109, 115–116; and literary approach, 99–100, 111–112, 113–114, 139–140n11; *Panorama*, 98, 114–115; *Theresienstadt 1941–1945: The Face of a Coerced Community*, 110, 139–140n11
Adler, Jeremy, 97, 137n1, 137n2
Adorno, Theodor, 38–39; "After Auschwitz," 44, 44, 46, 137n3; and cold mentality, 30, 32–33, 39–40; and Kant, 17–18; and 'melancholic science,' 39; and postwar German education, 29–30, 35, 37–38, 40, 43–44; and regressed group experience, 37–38; on teachers, 35, 43–44
aesthetics, 97, 99, 100; and aesthetic conflict, 11, 73, 101, 102, 107–108; after Auschwitz, 46–47, 98–99, 137–138n3; and study of, 46, 73
affect, 56, 73, 87, 98, 100–101, 133, 135n1, 140–141n2; and middle range of agency, xiii–xiv
Amir, Dana, 128
André, Jacques, 26

anthropological situation, 22, 27
anxiety, 16, 18, 31–32, 59, 83; and aggression, 92–93; and interpretations of 83, 85–86, 87, 88; and loss, 21, 32, 51, 53–54; and separation, 51, 68, 79; as situation, 51–52, 55–56, 59, 83; and symbolization, 51–52, 57
Arendt, Hannah, 6, 65
Aufklärung (Enlightenment), 5–6
Aulagnier, Piera, 140–141n2

Baldwin, James, 123–124
Bellos, David, 128
Bildung (upbringing), 5, 7–8; and *Bildungsroman* (adolescent novel), 7
binding, 24, 80, 99, 103, 108
Bion, Wilfred, xxiv–xxv, xxviii–xxix, 15; and emotional storms, 140–141n2; and knowledge (K), 19–20, 73; and thinking, 17, 71–72
Bohleber, Werner, 102
Bollas, Christopher, 56, 136n5

Canetti, Elias, 113–114
Canguilhem, Georges, 3–4
care, 22, 32–33, 57
case studies, 80–82; and readers, xxiii–xxiv

159

Castoriadis, Cornelius, 32
Certeau, Michel de, ix, 16, 73
Civitarese, Giuseppe, xxii
communication, xvi; and comprised messages, 22; and uncertainty, xxii, 12, 20–22; as unconscious, 89, 125. *See also* transference
concern, xiii, 24, 46, 58–59, 68
Cooper, Steven, 1, 136n7
Corbett, Ken, 69–70

decolonization, 4, 25
denial, 40, 83, 99
depression, 46, 49–50, 78, 100
depressive position, 32–33, 45, 53–54, 60–61, 68, 79, 136–137n7
Derrida, Jacques, 80
dialogue, 92, 103; and inner and outer, 58–60
Diary of Anne Frank, The, 42–43, 138n5
difficult knowledge, xiii; and history of, xiii–xiv, 34, 111; and lexicon, 44–45, 100
doubts, 86–87
dreams, ix–x, 121–122, 128, 141n3, 141n4; Clare's dream of Winnicott, 126–27 and day's residues, 120–121; and dream-work, ix–xi, 120–121

education, 1, 3, 30, 35, 61; after Auschwitz, 29, 34–35, 38, 44, 46, 101, 137n3; and human rights, 36–37; and narcissism, 9; as psychical, 9–11; and the psychoanalytic field, 2, 5, 7–9, 12; as repetition, 36–40; as situation, 13, 27, 61; and transference, 11, 27, 34
ego, 18, 22; and ego defenses, 31, 38, 40, 51, 53, 64, 98, 106, 135n3; and emotional situation of baby, 140n2

emotional situation, 21, 27
empathy, 14–15, 24–25, 39, 114
emptiness, 25, 30–31, 49, 125, 135n1
enlightenment, 5–7
Erlich, H. Shmuel, 52
ethics, 16, 17, 24–25, 27; and ethical turn, 15–16, 24–26
experience, xiii, xxiii, xxiv, 19–20, 22, 125; as frustration, 10, 17, 71, 73

failure, 14–15, 36, 45, 66, 69–70, 94, 101, 107
Felman, Shoshana, 99
Ferro, Antonio, xxii, 20
Filkins, Peter, 100, 110
Fisher, Jens Malte, 94–95
Forrester, John, xxiii–xiv
Foucault, Michel, 6
free association, x, xvi, xvii, 8, 16, 103
Freire, Paulo, 50–52; on concern, 58–59; and historical reality, 54, 56; on humanization, 58–59, 60; on oppression, 60
Freud, Sigmund ix: on consciousness, 27, 71, 120; and dreams, ix; and dream-work, ix–xi, 120–21; and drives, 10–12, 21; and education, 2–3, 7–8, 10, 16; and free association, xvii, 53, 103; and imagoes, 19; and impossible professions, 1; and mourning and melancholia, 35–36, 52–53; and narcissism, x, 2; on negation, 67; on remembering, repeating, and working through, 40, 45; the unconscious, 120; on war, 12, 35–36; and Wilhelm Fliess, xv–xvi; as writer, ix, xv–xvii
friendship, 79–81, 96
Frosh, Stephen, 123
frustration, xiii, 10, 17, 20, 27, 71

Glocer Fiorini, Leticia, 63–64, 74
Gozlan, Oren, 74
Green, André, xiv–xv, xxii, 14, 58, 80, 99
Grimbert, Philippe, 41–42
Grosskurth, Phillis, 94–95; and adult "Richard," 93–96
Grubrich-Simitis, Ilse, xv, xvii–xviii
guilt, 7, 21, 40, 90–91, 98, 105–106

history, xi–xii, xxv; fear of, xix–xx; and phantasy, 136n5; and prehistory, xix, xx, 11, 51, 52, 54, 67, 110; and trauma, 101–102
Holocaust, 34–35; and 'Holocaust syndrome,' 105; and 'Human Trembling,' 105. *See also* Shoah
Hullot-Kentor, Robert, 44–45

identification, 19, 51–52, 53, 55, 80, 101, 124, 128; and projective identifications, 55–56, 65
infancy, 22, 26–27, 50–51, 53–54, 55, 67, 71, 107, 121–122
infantile sexuality, xix–xx
internal reality, xviii, 36, 53, 54, 59–60; and external reality, 19, 32, 54. *See also* object relations
Isaacs, Susan, 57

James, Henry, 73
Joseph, Betty, 23

Kahn, Laurence, 17
Kant, Immanuel, 6, 16–17; and the Kantian Block, 18
Klein, Hillel, 33–34, 104–107
Klein, Melanie, 50–52, 77–79; on aggression, 92–93; on anxiety, 55–56; and case of "Richard," 83–84; on countertransference, 77, 82; and emotional situations, xix–xx, 18–19, 32, 53, 140–141n2; and Erna, 68; on interpretation, 79, 85, 88–89; on loneliness, 95, 136–137n7; and loss of the breast, 51, 53; on mourning, 53–54; and objects, 55; and object relations, 31–32, 55, 79; and paranoid-schizoid and depressive positions, 23, 32, 51–52, 54–55, 57, 68, 100, 135n3; and play technique, 56, 89–90; and psychic polarities, 95–96; and reparation and gratitude, 18–19; on symbolic equation, 56; on transference, 19; and transference situation, 22–23; on weaning, 53, 56, 58, 60, 71; as writer, 80–82, 85, 93
Kohut, Heinz, 15, 24
Kohut, Thomas, 24–25
Korbivcher, Célia Fix, 135n1
Kristeva, Julia, 57–58, 70, 73, 92

Lacan, Jacques, 15
Laplanche, Jean, 16, 22, 27
Leader, Darian, 4
learning: as appeals, 125; and earliest, 121–122; and emptiness, 125, 136n7; and field theory of, xxii; as inheritance, 122, 125, 140n1, 141n3; and psychical difficulties, xiv–xv; as situations, 13–14, 17; and transference, 11; and transformations in, 122–123; and working through, 34–35
literature, 111–113, 131, 139n9

Mahalel, Anat Tzur, 128
Mahler, Gustav, 94; and Fifth Symphony, 94–95
maternal care, xii, 17; and containment, 17; and good enough mother, xiii

McDougall, Joyce, 15
Meltzer, Donald, 83, 107; and Meg Harris Williams, 107
memory, 53, 66, 103; as belonging, 103–104; and binding, 102–104; and history, xii, 8, 16, 39, 97–101, 123; and 'memories in feelings,' xix, 121; and mourning, 40, 52, 61
Milner, Marion, 86
misogyny, 64–66; and gender violence, 69–70
mothers, xii–xiii, 17, 65, 67, 107, 141n4

Nacherziehung (after-education), 5, 7–8
Nachträglichkeit (deferred action), xii–xii, 66, 79
narratives, 92, 93, 122; and revolt, 141n6
Nebenmensch (fellow human being), xii–xiii, xiv, 4, 46
negation, x, 52, 67–68, 71, 74, 123

object relations, 19, 31–33, 55, 79, 96, 135n3
objects, xii, 31, 55, 57, 59; and good and bad, 55–56, 91
oppression, 49–50, 60
Orange, Donna, 17, 24–25
other, the, 122. See also *Nebenmensch*
otherness, 13–15, 16, 26

paranoid-schizoid position, 23, 60, 68, 90
Peck, Raoul, 123–124
pedagogy: and depressive position, 60; and interpsychic conflicts, 34, 100; kinds of, 9–10, 41–42, 45–46, 55; as object relations, 31–32, 35; and paradoxes, 32–33, 100. See also warm pedagogy

Perec, Georges, 130, 141n7; on analysis with Pontalis, 132; *Life: A User's Manual*, 131–132; *W or The Memory of Childhood*, 129–130; and writing method, 130–131
phantasies, xix, xx, 31, 51, 57, 71
Pontalis, J.-B., 120, 121, 141n4
psychical reality, xiv–xv, 5, 59; as apparatus, 21; as emotional world, 19, 54; and emotional situations, 18–21. See also dreams; phantasies
psychoanalytic principles, x, 74, 92, 89

reading, 55–56, 72–73
reality: dimensions of, xxiv, 16–17; and 'unreal reality,' 18, 51
regression, 36–37, 44–45, 90, 136n4
resistance, 8, 21, 53, 74
reverie, xvii, 17, 71–72, 120
Ricoeur, Paul, xi–xii
Rose, Jacqueline, 65, 68–69; on feminism, 69

Scarfone, Dominique, xxi, 16, 22
Schwartz, Henry P., 128
Sedgwick, Eve Kosofsky, xiii–xiv, 100
Segal, Hanna, 56, 99, 138n4
sexuality, xix–xx, 2, 6–7, 22, 72
Shoah: and historical memory, 98, 100–102; and psychoanalysis, 102–103, 138n7, 138–139n8; and survivors, 103–104, 105–106; and writing, 112–113
Simmel, Georg, 113
situations, 13–14
Sliwinski, Sharon, 141n3
Soreanu, Raluca, xiii, 139n8
Stonebridge, Lyndsey, 67
Strachey, Alix, 59–60
Swartz, Sally, 25
symbolic equation, xix–xx, 42, 56, 65, 136n6

symbolization, 50, 53, 57, 59, 72

Taylor, Barbara, 4
teachers, 33, 37, 43–44; and teacher game, 19–20
Theresienstadt (Ghetto), 98, 104. *See also* H. G. Adler
Togashi, Koichi: and decolonization, 24; and ethical situation, 24–25; and psychoanalytic zero, 14, 25–26
transference, xxiii, 1, 11, 16, 19, 23, 133; and counter-transference, 25, 34, 58, 105–106; and education, 1–2, 5, 8, 11; and reading, xxiii; and situations, 13, 22–23; and writing, 120
trauma, xii; and countertransference, 105–106; as encounter, 34, 102, 138–139n8; and randomness, 24, 26; and social conflict, 45; and time, xii, 100, 102, 136n7; and witnessing, 105

uncertainty, 14, 26, 107–108

unconscious, the, xxi, xxvii, 5, 21, 120; and impressions, 22–23, 49, 63, 71, 119, 123; and reality, xviii
uneven development, 18–19

Verhaeghe, Paul, 3

Walsh, Julie, xxii
warm pedagogy, xi, xiii, 31, 45–47, 60
Winnicott, Clare, 126
Winnicott, D. W., xiii, xvi; and culture, 66, 125, 140n1; on death, 127; "Fear of Breakdown," 125; and good enough, xiv, 15; on psychical transitions, 141n5
working through, 34, 40–42, 52–53
writing, xxiii–xxvi, 99, 100, 111, 119–120, 124–125, 130, 135n1; and infancy, 119–120

Young-Bruehl, Elisabeth, 38, 74–75

Zeavin, Hannah, xv–xvi